THE LOG OF CHRISTOPHER COLUMBUS

Indians fleeing from Columbus. (Giuliano Dati, Isole Trovate Nuovamente Per El Re di Spagna, *Firenze, 1495)*

THE
LOG
OF
CHRISTOPHER COLUMBUS

TRANSLATED BY ROBERT H. FUSON

INTERNATIONAL MARINE PUBLISHING
Camden, Maine

Four hardcover printings.
First paperback printing 1992.
10 9 8 7 6 5 4 3 2

TAB BOOKS offers software for sale. For information and a catalog, please contact TAB Software Department, Blue Ridge Summit, PA 17294-0850.

Library of Congress Cataloging-in-Publication Data

Columbus, Christopher.
  The log of Christopher Columbus.

  Translation based on Las Casas' abstract of the Log with additions from his Historia and Fernando Columbus's Historie [of the Columbus family].
              Bibliography: p.
  1. Columbus, Christopher—Diaries. 2. America—Discovery and exploration—Spanish. 3. Explorers—America—Diaries. 4. Explorers—Spain—Diaries.
  I. Fuson, Robert Henderson.   II. Title.
  E118.C725 1987   970.01'5   87-16918
  ISBN 0-87742-316-4

Typeset by Graphic Composition, Inc., Athens, Georgia.
Printed by the Hamilton Printing Company,
Rensselaer, New York.
Jacket and interior design by Richard C. Bartlett.
Photo research by Pembroke Herbert/Picture Research Consultants.
Production management by Molly Mulhern.
Cover printed by New England Book Components,
Hingham, Massachusetts.

Text Illustration Credits

Illustrations on pages 38, 39, 59, 65, 74, 77, 95, 99, 100, 111, 114, 117, 126, 152, 156–57, 160, 176, and 189 were drawn by Richard Schlecht. Maps on pages 14, 56, 75, 94, 128, 164, 178, 203, 204–07, and 232 were drawn by the author. Sources for all other illustrations and maps are given in the art captions.

CONTENTS

EPILOGUE

For Amelia

who has shared every mile
of this fascinating journey

ACKNOWLEDGMENTS

Many people have contributed to the pages that follow, in a variety of ways and throughout the writing process. To all of them I extend my sincerest thanks and deepest appreciation.

At the outset, I would like to acknowledge the help and support of my colleagues in The Society for the History of Discoveries. This organization has been the catalyst for most of the serious Columbian scholarship undertaken during the last six years. Since 1981 the Society has consistently devoted a portion of each annual meeting to Columbus and his times. In 1983 it dedicated an entire issue of its journal, *Terrae Incognitae,* to the subject, and in 1985 it made this issue available to the general public under the title of *In the Wake of Columbus: Islands and Controversy.* At no time during the development of

the book did a single member of the Society ignore a call for help. Thank you, all of you.

Appreciation goes to the Phileas Society, and to its president Mr. Frederick G. Ruffner and executive director Dr. Robert W. Tolf. Not only has Phileas sponsored two Columbus convocations since 1985, but graciously invited me to participate in an excursion to the Turks and Caicos Islands in 1985 in search of the first landfall.

In 1986 I had the pleasure to serve the National Geographic Society as a consultant in their search for the landfall. Many of the NGS family have been generous with their time and support, and senior associate editor Joseph Judge has shared his thoughts with me for five years. Largely because of our long-running debate concerning the first landfall, I was compelled to read and reread the Log. To a large degree this prompted me to create the modernized and readable version found here.

I cannot thank Luis Marden enough for his friendship, encouragement, and honest criticism. It is not easy to get a colleague to take apart something you have labored over for many months, but Luis did just that. He kept a close weather-eye on my usage of medieval Spanish maritime terminology, and any errors that have crept in are mine, written when he was looking the other way! For many years Luis was chief of the foreign editorial staff for *National Geographic;* he also discovered the wreck of the *Bounty.* Twice he has sailed Columbus' route across the Atlantic, and his nautical savvy helped me untangle many difficult passages in the Log. He has honored me by writing the Foreword.

The personnel in the *National Geographic's* news service extended many courtesies to me. I wish to thank Paul Sampson (director of the news service), and his associates, Barbara S. Moffett, Joy Aschenbach, and Mercer Cross. The latter even braved a blizzard one day to do me a favor.

Dr. Kathleen Deagan (chair, Department of Anthropology, Florida State Museum, University of Florida) provided extensive material on the ongoing archaeological work at En Bas Saline, Haiti, the probable site of La Navidad. Additional information and maps came from Maurice Williams (Research Archaeologist of the Museum). This material is the basis for most of the references to the first Spanish settlement discussed in the book. Their help is warmly appreciated.

Other archaeological assistance came from Dr. and Mrs.

Charles Hoffman (Department of Anthropology, Arizona State University). I appreciate their help in providing me with a grasp of the fundamentals of Bahamian archaeology. Dr. Irving Rouse (Professor of Anthropology, Yale University) helped me sort out the linguistic pattern of the pre-Columbian Bahamas and West Indies. This was greatly appreciated.

Dr. Benjamin Keen (Professor Emeritus, Rutgers University) merits a very special word of thanks. He gave permission to use unlimited material from his book *The Life of the Admiral Christopher Columbus by his son Ferdinand,* as it pertained to the first voyage. This translation from the 15th century Italian edition has become the standard English version. Without Professor Keen's generous help it would not have been possible to augment the abstracted *Diario* of Las Casas with the additional original material from Fernando.

Two men who have lent me their time and expertise over a number of years are Joseph B. Dobkin (head, Special Collections, University of South Florida Library) and Paul E. Camp (Assistant Librarian, USF Library). They have facilitated my research among the rare books, documents, and maps, and have granted permission to photograph materials from the collection. Many of the reproductions of early woodcuts and 19th century line drawings were made possible through the courtesy of the USF Special Collections Library.

Another librarian came to my rescue on numerous occasions. Dr. John A. Wolter (Head, Geography and Map Division, Library of Congress) never turned down a request from me, no matter how trivial it may have seemed to him. His help in locating manuscript maps, providing liasion with European libraries and museums, and pointing me toward information I needed contributed greatly to this book.

Modern maps and charts have been supplied to me by Harry Kline, former editor of the *Yachtsman's Guide*. As a sailor *extraordinaire,* Mr. Kline has long been interested in Columbus' first voyage and has been most supportive of my research.

Over the years no two Columbus scholars have been more helpful than Dr. Oliver C. Dunn (Professor Emeritus, Purdue University) and James E. Kelley, Jr. (computer specialist and management consultant). Hundreds of pages of correspondence have passed among us during the last few years. We have read each other's work, criticized one another, and attended most of the same conferences. Jim Kelley made a critical reading of this text when it was in the early manuscript stage, and Oliver Dunn has sometimes answered a single question of mine with a five-page critique. I cannot thank either of them sufficiently for their interest and help.

I would like to thank Ruth G. Durlacher-Wolper for her friendship, contagious energy, bountiful correspondence, and wonderful hospitality. She opened her home to me on the island now called San Salvador (Watlings, until 1926), as she has done for so many Columbus seekers in the past, and proved that research can be a pleasurable experience. Mrs. Wolper is a painter of established reputation, a Columbus scholar in her own right, and someone to whom I owe a great debt.

Special thanks are also due to artist Richard Schlecht for his stunning set of original line drawings, so richly evocative of the flavor of Columbus' Voyage of discovery.

My sincerest appreciation goes to my editor, Cynthia Bourgeault, whose enthusiasm for this project exceeded all bounds. Her skill brought the final book together from dozens of manuscript parts and hundreds of illustrations, maps, and photographs. To Cynthia I give a standing ovation.

I would also like to thank The Society for the History of Discoveries and Wayne State University Press for the use of a portion of my article appearing in *Terrae Incognitae* (vol. 15, pp. 51–58) and in its trade reprint, *In the Wake of Columbus*. This material appears in the Prologue, concerning the history of the various transcriptions and translations of the Log.

And to many others whose paths I crossed and who remain nameless, thank you all.

FOREWORD

By Luis Marden

Some achievements of the human mind and spirit are so sublime they seem inevitable. They fall with the finality of fate into the pages of history and the memory of every school child. Even when we strip away the accretion of legend that sheathes the hard crystal of fact we remain filled with wonder.

Such is the discovery of America by Christopher Columbus. The first footfall of Columbus on the shore of the New World echoed like a thunderclap down the centuries, and its reverberations have not yet died away.

The supreme sailor was born circa 1451, by his own testimony in Genoa, one of the four maritime republics of Italy (the other three were Venice, Pisa, and Amalfi), and he never forgot his native city. "Though my body may be here," he wrote from Spain, "my heart is always there." In a letter to Ferdinand and Isabella written in 1501 he said, "I went to sea at an early age, and there I have continued to this day; the same art inclines those who follow it to wish to know the secrets of this world. . . . I have sailed everywhere that is navigable. . . . Our Lord found this my desire very proper. . . . [He] . . . opened my understanding with his hand, so that I became capable of sailing from here to the Indies," and He set fire to my will to carry this out, and with this fire I came to your Highnesses.

It is this above all else that we must remember about Columbus: he was a professional seaman, a master mariner supremely skilled at his trade. As his son Fernando wrote: "From this testimony we may understand how experienced the Admiral was in things of the sea, and the many lands and places to which he went before he undertook the enterprise of discovery."

Only experienced seamen can comprehend fully what Columbus did and how he did it, and their guidance is indispensable to the historian. In particular, the mariner's viewpoint sheds light on two important (and often misconstrued) points about this, the most momentous sea voyage in history: one, the state of geographical knowledge at the time, and two, Columbus's training and ability as a seaman.

No literate person in 1492 thought the world was flat; the Greeks had proved the sphericity of the earth long before Christ. In fact, in that same year of 1492 Martin Behaim in Germany produced a terrestrial globe, still extant (see page 23). The question under debate was the *size* of the globe. In the third century B.C., the Greek astronomer Eratosthenes, using only his brain and a shadow-casting column, came astonishingly close to the true circumference, but 500 years later the geographer Ptolemy described an earth one fourth smaller than the true dimension. It is this Ptolemaic earth that is represented on the Behaim globe. If we superimpose Columbus's first westward passage on that globe, the Admiral at the end of 33 days and a bit comes ashore squarely amidships of Cipango—Japan. Columbus made his landfall where he expected to find it, when he expected to find it. It was only that the Americas lay in the way.

Second point: For nearly nine years Columbus sailed out of Portugal, at that time the world center of bluewater navigation and of the nascent science of navigation by the sun and stars, yet he used none of that rudimentary celestial knowledge to find his way on the first crossing. Columbus's First Voyage is a classic example of the art of deduced or dead reckoning, the method of keeping account of a ships's way used since ancient times and still followed today by some yachtsmen. In dead reckoning the mariner keeps careful account of his direction by compass, speed through the water, direction and strength of winds, and perhaps leeway, the downwind skid caused by wind pressure on the hull and rigging. By plotting the direction and distance traveled by his ship, the sailor marks down what he believes is his daily position. The difficulty is that once out of sight of land, no mariner without modern aids can know what currents affect his vessel, whether they push him on his way, hinder him, or cause him to crab to the left or the right.

Absolutely nothing that floats, a corked bottle or a 50,000-ton ship, can escape the effect of current. Anyone who has tried to row a boat across a flowing stream to an opposite point on the far bank knows this.

On the First Voyage current and leeway were of no interest to Columbus because he was not heading for a precisely known point. He was sailing generally west, except when forced to deviate by contrary winds or the complaints and advice of shipmates. As an experienced mariner, he would do his best to take current and leeway into account when sailing from one known port to another. In a broad search for unknown lands current and leeway did not enter into his reckoning. On the other hand, these are indispensable elements for any investigator seeking to retrace the Admiral's crossing. If we plot Columbus's daily runs on a modern chart, noting heading and distance but making no allowance for current or leeway, we arrive at an unreal destination. Such a plotted line moves purposefully westward on a motionless chart, but an actual ship moves on a liquid medium in constant motion that bears anything floating in it in the direction and at the speed the currents flow.

For most of the crossing Columbus's ships carried the wind—the northeast trade that begins near Madeira—over the helmsman's right shoulder. Along much of the track the currents also flow from there so that as the vessels advanced they were carried inexorably to the south.

Today we may plot the current's strength and direction, as well as the prevailing winds for leeway, from a pilot chart. When these factors are added or subtracted, we obtain a much more realistic track, one traced by real ships and flesh-and-blood sailors, not paper ones. A plotting of Columbus's daily runs with allowance for current and leeway, forward from the Canaries to the first landfall or backward along the courses of the subsequent inter-island wanderings, brings one to Samaná Cay, a small island some 65 miles to the southeast of Watling-San Salvador, the island widely accepted as the Admiral's landing place.

Winds and currents of the world, products of the earth's rotation and of the upwelling and sinking of warm and cold water masses, cannot have changed much in only 500 years, a blink of geophysical time. As we do not know, nor will ever know, what were the precise winds and currents of those 33 days in 1492 (we do have a study of the probable magnetic variation), we cannot say that we have established beyond all peradventure the exact point of the first landfall. But we do know that a currentless track is unreal. We can only hope to find the *most probable position,* in modern navigator's parlance,

at the end of the most extraordinary voyage in the history of man.

Landsmen sometimes do not comprehend the nature of a ship's log. It is a record kept for the vessel's aid and safety, a running notebook of the daily progress of the ship. The dead-reckoning navigator keeps scrupulous account of his heading, speed, sea state, winds, leeway, and any other factor that may affect the way of his ship in the sea. He is painstaking and assiduous because that is all he has, his compass and the evidence of his senses, duly placed on record. On that record depend the safety of the ship and the lives of the crew. The navigator is alone in a 360-degree circle of sameness. Nothing tells him where he is but the needle of the compass that, Columbus said, "always seeks the truth."

Scholars who study the Columbus log should remember that it was written not for posterity, nor to prove a point, but to record sailing events as they happened. The Admiral later wrote a preamble before sending the original log, now lost, to his sovereigns, but we must assume that it was, like other logs, a true account of what happened day by day.

A sailor reading Columbus's log today will understand every entry; the sea is unchanging, and the rig of a modern sailing vessel, while more efficient, has not changed much from the caravels of the Discoverer. So it is not surprising—to a sailor—to find that (except for racing yachts and the clipper ships) a vessel propelled by sail, anywhere from something over 30 feet to fair-sized windships, will make on the average the same daily run—about 100 miles a day. I have sailed twice from east to west across the Atlantic in my own ketch, bracketing the waters traversed by Columbus. I made one passage from the Canaries to Antigua in the Lesser Antilles, 2,800 miles, in 28 days. My second crossing from the Canaries to the Little Bahama Bank and Florida totaled 3,700 miles in 36 days. Five hundred years earlier, when Columbus raised his first island in the New World, he had sailed some 3,200 miles in slightly over 33 days.

Both my passages were made in the winter trades, halcyon days of sailing within a circle of blue sea and sky, with lamb's wool clouds passing overhead to show the way. With wind and current on the starboard quarter, a vessel running down the trades rolls heavily, lifting to the swell coming from the northwest where the heavy weather builds, happily a long way from this southern track first traced by the Admiral of Castile.

Columbus's southern route was used by sailing vessels heading for the West Indies for more than 400 years, and it is still sailed by yachtsmen wishing to make a longer but safer and more comfortable passage with no bashing beats to windward to the Caribbean and the Americas. In the 18th and 19th centuries, when a bridge of ships spanned the southern half of the North Atlantic, Columbus's route was called "the ladies' run," and the thumbnail direction for sailing from Britain to the West Indies was: "south till the butter melts, then west."

Columbus, who believed he had been chosen by God to spread the Catholic faith in the lands he would discover, must have had the hand of providence on his shoulder. He sailed in the hurricane season, right into the track of the killer cyclones but he experienced only ". . . the most temperate breezes . . . [and] great was the pleasure of the mornings, lacking only the singing of the nightingales." Happy the sailor who lacks gales as well as nightingales, and for whom the winds are "very gentle, as in April in Seville."

So it went, day after pleasant day, "downhill" sailing except for six days when contrary winds forced Columbus to make a bight to the northward, then return to his westward course. One day succeeded another, "the airs always gentle," with circling sea fowl and flying fish flashing across the forefoot of the flagship, and always on the horizon the piled fleecy clouds that sometimes assumed the shape of wished for land.

Every autumn a fleet of yachts gathers in the Canaries to begin the passage to the West Indies or Bahamas. Let one of these sailors, departing toward the end of October to be free of the hurricane menace and yet reasonably close to Columbus's own time, take aboard a copy of Columbus's log and, leaving modern navigation for safety to someone who will keep it to himself, follow meticulously Columbus's daily headings and, so far as possible, his daily runs. At the end of the passage his first sighted island will cast one more beam of light on the dark puzzle of that first landfall in the New World.

The late Professor E. G. R. Taylor eloquently described those ancient mariners who, at the dawn of the haven-finding art, bereft of observing instruments or tables, kept zealous watch on ship, wind, sea, and sky.

"For every master and pilot prided himself on knowing exactly how much way his ship was making. He knew the ship, he considered the wind, he watched the sails, he watched the water. In fact it was a matter which just could not be explained to the landsman. A good sailor knows his ship, and that is all."

Christopher Columbus knew his ship but that was not all. He knew his men and he knew himself and above all he knew his burning faith in that vision that drew him across unknown seas to a new land of hope and promise for all mankind.

The Sea of Darkness. (Winsor, 1886, from Olaus Magnus, 1555)

PROLOGUE

CHAPTER ONE

THE LOG

The *Log of Christopher Columbus* is a daily record of the Voyage of Discovery to the New World and the return trip to Spain. It is derived from the personal account written by Columbus between August 3, 1492, and March 15, 1493. The Log carefully documents an undertaking that has no historic parallel; one that altered the course of history immediately and directly. It is, in essence, a singular, documentary link between the Middle Ages and the Renaissance.

With little fanfare, and unknown even to the participants, the destruction of the Medieval World began on that August morning when Columbus and his fleet of *Niña, Pinta,* and *Santa María* set sail from the Spanish port of Palos. Destination: the East Indies (Asia), with a planned stopover at the Canary Islands. These volcanic islands, lying some 800 miles southwest of Spain, off the southern coast of Morocco, were not completely in Spanish hands at that time. Though the conquest by Spain began in 1404, resistance was not stifled until 1496. For this reason, Columbus set his course for Gomera, an island firmly under Spanish authority.

In a clumsy ship such as the *Santa María,* the run from Spain to the Canary Islands took almost a week. But it was a week on familiar waters for Columbus and many of his crew. Despite some high seas, periods of calm, and trouble with the *Pinta's* rudder, Columbus had sufficient leisure time to contemplate his enterprise. It was during this period, perhaps on the afternoon of August 3, that the Admiral wrote an "introduction" to his Log:

I decided to write down everything that I might do and see and experience on this voyage, from day to day, and very carefully.

The monastery of Santa Maria de la Rábida, near Palos, Spain. In 1484 Columbus came here with young Diego and was befriended by Fr. Juan Pérez de Marchena. (Photo: Patronato Provincial de Turismo de Huelva)

True to his pledge, during good times and bad, and with only two minor exceptions, Columbus kept a daily account of the voyage, the *Diario de a bordo* (*The Onboard Log*). Without doubt this was the most accurate and complete ship's log ever produced up to its time. For that matter, no daily maritime record was to equal it for many years hence.

When Columbus returned to Spain, on Friday, March 15, 1493, he learned that the Court was in Barcelona. We know that his famous letter to Luis de Santangel announcing the discovery (see illustration) contained a letter to the Sover-

eigns. Columbus apparently waited for its transmittal to Barcelona, and in due course he was summoned to that city, arriving sometime in mid-April.

It was at that time that Columbus presented the original Log to Queen Isabela. With very little delay, she commanded a scribe to prepare an exact copy for the Admiral. Just prior to his departure for the second voyage (September 25, 1493), the copy was delivered to him at the port of Cádiz. Today this version of the Log is known as the Barcelona copy.

The holograph original has not been seen since the death of Queen Isabela in 1504, and it is only presumed to have been in her possession up until that time. There is the remote possibility that it may be discovered someday, somewhere. The Barcelona copy, however, did survive for awhile, at least until 1554.

Upon the death of Columbus, in 1506, the Barcelona copy, various charts, books, manuscripts, and personal papers passed to Diego, Columbus' eldest son. In 1526, when Diego died, the inheritance passed to Diego's son (Columbus' grandson), Luis.

At this time Luis was a minor, under the guardianship of his mother, María Álvarez de Toledo. He was not to gain absolute control of the family papers for 23 years. It is probable that even María did not possess all the Columbus materials until after the death of Fernando (Ferdinand), in 1539. Fernando, an illegitimate child and Diego's half-brother, was the family's archivist and its only real scholar.

Fernando had an obsession with books, and in his home on the banks of the Guadalquivir River in Sevilla he assembled

La Carta de Colón, written to Luis de Santangel, announcing the Discovery, 15 February 1493; postscript dated 4 March 1493. (First Spanish edition, ca. April 1493, in New York Public Library)

The house and garden of Fernando, and the monastery of Las Cuevas, Sevilla. (Winsor, 1892) one of the finest private libraries on the continent of Europe. Estimated to contain over 15,000 items, the library welcomed scholars from all over Europe. It is almost a certainty that Diego entrusted most of the important family books and papers to Fernando. If this were the case, María would not have had complete control until Fernando's death in 1539.

For all practical purposes, Fernando's library (which probably contained the Barcelona copy of the Log) was sealed for five years after his death due to legal complications. In 1544, María removed everything from Fernando's home and placed the bulk of it in the Dominican monastery of San Pablo in Sevilla.

María herself was to live for only five years more. Upon her death in 1549, any papers still in her possession passed to Luis, and he acquired unrestricted access to Fernando's collection that was being held in trust in Sevilla. Luis, certainly the dimmest star in the Columbus constellation, was now free to run amok through the reassembled collection of Columbus memorabilia. This was one of the greatest tragedies that could have befallen future scholars.

Luis Columbus was a ne'er-do-well who was, as the emminent Columbus scholar Henry Vignaud once stated, "devoid of morality." He placed his immediate financial interest above everything else, though women ran a close second. In later years he was imprisoned for having three wives (at the same time!) and managed to acquire a fourth by bribing his jailers for overnight passes. His only fondness for books or family papers was the price they might fetch in the marketplace, thereby providing the means to support his debauchery.

Family of Columbus.

The Barcelona copy of the *Diario de a bordo* was in Luis' possession in 1554, the year in which he was granted authorization to publish it. Inasmuch as it was never published, it is reasonable to assume that he sold it to a higher bidder. It is known that he sold Fernando's manuscript of the Admiral's biography to a Genoese physician, who took it to Venice for publication.

It is always possible that Luis lost the Barcelona copy, but not very likely. He probably sold it to some member of the nobility who placed the manuscript in a private library, where it still lies hidden or whence it was destined eventually to disappear. It is unlikely that the copied Log ever passed to the cathedral of Sevilla, which acquired Fernando's library from the San Pablo monastery in 1552. Even if it had, its survival would have been doubtful, for the library was mishandled and dwindled to a fraction of its original size within a few years.[1]

Fortunately for history, however, before Columbus' Log dropped entirely out of sight, it passed through the hands of Fray Bartolomé de Las Casas, a Dominican friar and close personal friend of the Columbus family. Las Casas had been enraptured with the Admiral since the triumphant return from the first voyage, which he had witnessed in Sevilla when only 18 years of age. Las Casas' father and uncle accompanied Columbus on the second voyage, and in 1502 Las Casas himself made the voyage to Española, with the new governor, Ovando.[2] Once there, he immediately began to collect materials for what would prove to be his monumental work, his *Historia de las indias*. Begun in 1527, the *Historia* would become a lifetime labor of love; Las Casas was still editing, rewriting,

Portrait of Bartolemé de Las Casas. (Winsor, 1886)

and polishing it as late as 1563, three years before his death at the age of 92.

Somewhere during the course of this life's work, Las Casas obtained access to the Barcelona copy.[3] He never reveals how he managed to acquire the document, but it could have come from any number of sources.

Some scholars cling to the notion that Las Casas found the Barcelona copy among the remains of Fernando's library sometime between 1544 and 1552 while Las Casas was residing

Las Casas' signature on his manuscript of La Historia de las indias, *1559. (Winsor, 1886)*

in the San Pablo monastery, which at that time still housed the collection. Clearly, however, this date is much too late, for internal evidence in the *Historia* clearly demonstrates that the section derived from the Log was written in Española after 1527 and before 1539.[4] It is known positively that Diego gave certain materials to Las Casas when they both resided in Santo Domingo. Fernando may have sent the copied Log to his brother in Española, who, in turn, loaned it to Las Casas; or Las Casas might have gotten the manuscript directly from Fernando during trips to Spain in 1515 or 1517. There is even the outside possibility that the Barcelona copy was recopied specifically for Las Casas. If so, that leaves us with a third missing version. But this is highly unlikely. Regardless of how Las Casas came upon the Log, it is fortunate that he did.

From the scribe's copy (Barcelona copy) of the *Diario de a bordo*, Las Casas prepared a handwritten abstract, which he called *El libro de la primera navegación* (The Book of the First Navigation), generally known today as the *Diario de Colón* (Journal of Columbus), or simply the *Diario* (Journal). Most of the critical portion involving the first landfall and the voyage through the Bahamas is quoted directly and written in the first person (or, as Las Casas said, "in the formal words of the Admiral.").

As for the accuracy of the material, we could say that it is all we have. One can only assume that the copy from which Las Casas worked was reasonably correct. Columbus himself had held it long enough to make any necessary amendments, if any were required. Further, Las Casas was a man of saintly honesty; a slave to exactness. His firsthand knowledge of the general geographical area described, his personal acquaintance with many of the participants in the venture, and his possession of other supporting evidence provided him with several means of verification. Other than the fact that Las Casas omitted selected portions of the Barcelona copy (virtually none that pertained to navigation) and edited others, the abstract must be accepted as an excellent synopsis of the copied original.

There is some question as to whether or not Las Casas ever intended to use the abstract he made for any purpose other than as a reference for the history he was writing. It is almost as if he borrowed the Barcelona copy for a short time and excerpted as much as he could before having to return it. The manuscript is now in the *Biblioteca Nacional* in Madrid. Of all the documents relating to the first voyage, this is the one of greatest importance. It is the closest thing we have to the onboard log of the *Santa María,* and 95 percent of the Log presented here is derived from it.

But there are some details in Las Casas' *Historia de las indias* that are not to be found in the abstract. These may come from additional notes taken after the abstract was made, or even from memory. These bits and pieces are an important second source of information as one attempts to reconstruct the missing original; in point of fact, they should be treated as part of the Log itself, inasmuch as they are derived from the same source. Unlike the abstracted *Diario,* Las Casas' *Historia* has never been translated into English.

A third and last source of material from the Log comes to us by way of Fernando Columbus. In writing the biography of his father (usually called the *Historie*), Fernando had access to the Barcelona copy, as well as to all the personal papers of

Las Casas' abstract of a page from Columbus' log, corresponding to pages 89–90 in this book. (Sanz, 1962; original in Biblioteca Nacional, Madrid)

his father. It is unfortunate that the Spanish original of Fernando's work is lost and our source is a very poor 1571 Italian translation of the Spanish. Though Benjamin Keen has made an excellent English translation of this 1571 edition, there is no way to ascertain the quality of the Spanish original. There are many blatant errors that may be dismissed. But what does one do with logical statements that conflict with either the Las Casas abstract or the *Historia,* or both? The general rule is to stick with Las Casas when in doubt. He is of proven integrity. There may be an instance or two when Fernando's *Historie* is correct, but the law of probability is on the side of Las Casas.

In those cases where there is no conflict of fact, but only of elaboration, then Fernando may be taken at his word. Also, where Fernando is the only source and his statements are reasonable, they should be given a qualified admission.

The Log, then, has passed down through history in three parts, all derived from a copy of the holograph original. One of these parts, Las Casas' *Historia de las indias* has never been translated into English. Another, Fernando's *Historie,* exists in an excellent English translation of a poor Italian translation of a missing Spanish manuscript. The abstract made by Las Casas has been transcribed (into printed Spanish) and translated (into English and many other languages) on numerous occasions. It is to this document that we must turn our attention.

TRANSCRIPTIONS OF THE LOG

The abstract made by Las Casas is written in Spanish, on both sides of 76 large, folio pages. It contains many abbreviations, cancelled words and phrases, and notes that are both interlinear and marginal. On five occasions Las Casas makes reference to the Castilian Spanish of Columbus, reminding readers that, after all, Spanish was not the mother tongue of the Admiral. At other times Las Casas complains of the scribe's handwriting.

Generally speaking, the manuscript is not difficult to read if one is familiar with the script of 16th century Spain. Nevertheless, there are some words that are simply unreadable and there are some blanks. There are also some mistakes, which may have their source in Las Casas, the copyist, or even Columbus himself.

There have been seven transcriptions of the handwritten abstract of Las Casas into printed Spanish, the first made by Martín Fernández de Navarrete in 1825. Thirty-five years earlier, in 1790, Navarrete had come upon the Las Casas original lying dormant and forgotten in the library of the Duke of the Infantado; his discovery and painstakingly studious transcription laid the cornerstone for modern Columbus scholarship.

Between 1892 and 1896, in commemoration of the fourth centennial of the Discovery, the Italian government published a massive 14-volume set (the *Raccolta,* edited by Cesare de Lollis), which included not only the transcribed Log, but most of the other documents pertinent to the first voyage. Another transcription, prepared by Julio Guillén y Tato, appeared in 1943.

In 1962 Carlos Sanz published a truly innovative transcription that included a facsimile of the original document, providing the opportunity to make a line-by-line comparison of the printed and manuscript versions. Joaquin Arce and M. Gil

North coast of Expañola. Once thought to have been drawn by Columbus himself, the map is undoubtedly a later forgery. Not only is Columbus' first colony, La Navidad, *incorrectly spelled* Nativida, *but the island itself is labeled* La Española, *a form that never occurs in the log itself.*

Esteve published yet another example of the Log in 1971, with no accompanying facsimile.

In 1976 Manuel Alvar produced a monumental two-volume work on the Log, *Diario del Descubrimiento,* which not only included the facsimile, but for the first time offered the written and printed versions in a paired format, together with an explanation of cancelled and inserted words, and considerable supplementary materials. This was the first definitive transcription. Unfortunately, this was a limited edition, printed in the Canary Islands, and now out of print.

In 1987 American scholars Oliver C. Dunn and James E. Kelley, Jr., published what will in all likelihood become the definitive transcription accompanied by an English translation. Using computer technology to build on the foundation laid by Alvar, Dunn and Kelley have devised a system of diacritical markings and symbols that enable them to recreate the entire manuscript in printed form. Every strike-out, misspelling, marginal or interlinear note, abbreviation, punctuation mark, and insertion is reproduced. The folio and line numbers conform to the original, and many questionable items are explained in the notes. Furthermore, there is a concordance that provides alphabetical access to every significant word in the text. Not since Fernández de Navarrete's discovery of the Las Casas manuscript in 1790 has there been such a singularly important contribution to the inventory of Columbus materials.

TRANSLATIONS OF THE LOG

The Log has been translated in whole or in part into almost every literary language on earth. The entire document has been translated into English six times. The first three (by Samuel Kettell in 1827, Clements R. Markham in 1893, and John B. Thacher in 1903) were based on the 1825 transcription by Fernández de Navarrette. The 1930 translation by Cecil Jane (which was revised by L. A. Vigneras in 1960) was the first English translation based on the *Raccolta*. In 1963 Samuel E. Morison published a new translation based on the same Italian transcription. Dunn and Kelley's work also includes a new translation, keyed directly to the transcription, and based directly on the Las Casas manuscript. This is the only direct English translation of the entire Spanish manuscript, as opposed to the others that depend on an intermediary Spanish transcription done by someone else.[5]

Inasmuch as no translation is any better than the transcription used, it bears noting that in all transcriptions prior to Alvar's, and that of Dunn and Kelley, there are transcriptive errors, some of immense proportions, such as mistranscribed directions. The lack, until now, of a trustworthy English rendition of the Las Casas manuscript has plagued those who have attempted to reconstruct the voyage and determine the first landfall. Not only have students of the problem been using different translations; they have been using incorrect ones as well.

The portion of the Log that covers only the period from first landfall at San Salvador to landfall in Cuba has been translated countless times. There are, however, only two good renditions, that of H. L. Thomas (1882), based on Navarrete, and that of Eugene Lyon (1986), based on his own transcription of the Las Casas manuscript. It is by no means coincidental that both these excellent partial translations have been used to support the theory that the first island Columbus visited in the New World was Samana Cay. The work done by Gustavus V. Fox, the first champion of the Samana Cay landfall, rests on the Thomas translation (see Epilogue); that of the National Geographic Society, vindicating Fox's theory, rests on the foundation provided by Lyon. There appears to be an obvious explanation for this, which at the same time sheds light on another flagrant source of error in many of the other translations.

Neither Thomas nor Lyon had any preconceptions themselves as to Columbus' first landfall. Their sole purpose was to translate as accurately as possible. In contrast, an examination of those translations made to support various landfall theories reveals that words are often translated with a particular objective in sight. For example, if Columbus said *isleta* ("little island," "islet"), but the translator thought that Columbus was at a much larger island, he might render the English word as "island" rather than "islet." Or vice versa. Even directions have been changed in some translations, distances altered, and weather conditions invented. To make things fit a small island (that Columbus said was large), Morison invented a new unit of measurement, the "land league," unknown by anyone in the 15th century.

One translation moves a period by two words. The resulting sentence displaces a cape by 45 nautical miles. Another translation confuses sunrise and sunset; yet another has Columbus anchor at one point and, when he hauls up anchor, he is in another harbor some distance away. Even simple words such as "gulf" and "cape" are abused. Granted, it is always difficult to convey the precise meaning of something from one language to another, for nuances and subtleties may be different even with cognate words. But many translations make no attempt at being diplomatic; they are often contrived to "make things fit."

THE TRANSLATION AT HAND

The account of the First Voyage presented in the following pages is unique, though no less accurate than the other good translations. It has, however, been edited and modernized. It is edited in the sense that some of the missing elements have been reassembled from the *Historia* of Las Casas and the *Historie* of Fernando to form a more complete narrative. Nothing is removed from the Las Casas abstract of the Log except certain redundancies. The first person is restored where Las Casas and Fernando switch to third person, and any obvious clerical errors (especially where they pertain to distance and direction) have been noted and cleared up.

Where necessary, sentences have been reordered to provide the original chronology of events. Like all of us who have kept diaries (or attempted to!), Columbus sometimes fell behind in his entries. On a few occasions the press of duties made it impossible to record things as they happened. Sometimes he combined two days under one date, or one day's events under two dates. Often his explanations of completed actions are confusing, especially to readers who think that the entire Log was written in the present tense, on a moment-to-moment basis. As with most diaries, the Log was composed during leisure times, sometimes late in the day to record all the happenings since sunset the day before, or even the day before that. The result is occasional redundancy, with the same occurrence described in two or three different entries, though in slightly different words.

This version of the Log is modernized in several ways. Where possible, archaic language is avoided. The translation flows as freely as the subject permits. Spanish miles and leagues are converted to nautical miles, approximately three nautical miles equal to one Spanish league. The National Geographic Society accepts 4,284 feet for the Columbian mile, or 17,134 feet to the league (2.82 nautical miles). Kelley places a lower value of 4,060 feet for the mile, or 16,240 feet for the league (2.67 nautical miles). Morison uses *both* 4,842 and 4,855 feet to the mile, but consistently says a league is 3.18 nautical miles. Three nautical miles to the league, or a trifle less, seems a good approximation.

The last example of modernization is the matching of Columbus' locations with those on today's nautical charts. Although the debate will never end during my lifetime (and I have already been a part of it for more than 30 years) I am now prepared to support the landfall theory of Gustavus V. Fox, first advanced in 1882 and verified by the National Geographic Society in 1986. Columbus discovered America at Samana Cay in the Commonwealth of the Bahamas. Although as many as nine different landfall theories have been proposed during the past 200 years, Samana Cay is revealed when one accepts the precision and integrity not only of Columbus, but also of Las Casas. For a detailed summary of the landfall controversy, see Epilogue.

Nothing in the Log suggests anything less than a completely truthful account of the voyage, from beginning to end. Even when later events furnished Columbus with the information to make a correction or clarification in his Log, he never did so. Columbus appears to have been a man willing to stand by his original words and actions, and Las Casas reported these faithfully. They were, indeed, remarkable men.

All the basic elements of a ship's log are contained herein: speed, distances, bearings, tides, currents, depths, port conditions, types of sail used, damage reports, maintenance performed, sea and weather conditions, and other miscellaneous data. It also contains much ethnographic information, some geography, and a smattering of botany. For the careful reader there are a few glimpses into the psyche of the Admiral, as we shall see in the next chapter.

1. Today this collection, still housed in the great cathedral in Sevilla, is known as the *Biblioteca Colombina*. Here one may view some of the original books of Columbus, many of them with marginal notes written in the Admiral's own hand.

2. Las Casas stayed on in Española and participated in the conquest of Cuba in 1514. It was during this campaign that he began to champion the cause of the Indians. He was consecrated Bishop of Chiapas in 1544 and is known as "The Apostle of the Indians." He made two trips to Spain in 1515 and 1517, returned for a longer sojourn between 1539 and 1544, and was back in Spain permanently by 1547. In 1551 he resigned as Bishop and concentrated on his writing and pleading for the Indians until his death in Madrid in 1566.

3. Although some scholars have claimed that Las Casas may have had temporary possession of the *original*, Las Casas himself denies this, saying that he used a scribe's copy when writing his monumental *Historia de las indias*.

4. Las Casas consistently uses terms such as "*these* Indies" and "*this* Española" in the *Historia*, strongly implying that his frame of reference during this period of composition is Española, not Spain; furthermore, positive references to dated discoveries establish the period of composition.

5. It should be cautioned, however, that while Dunn and Kelley's *transcription* is flawless; their translation is not a diplomatic one, which produces some problems. The reader cannot be assured, when reading the English, that he or she is receiving the same information found in the transcribed material that parallels it on the facing page. For a work of this magnitude, the translation is a little too free.

CHAPTER TWO

COLUMBUS, THE MAN

To paraphrase Winston Churchill, Columbus is a riddle wrapped in a mystery inside an enigma. At almost every turn of the maze there is an obstruction.

When was Columbus born? We are not sure. The year 1451 is usually given, sometime between August 25 and October 31. But some have placed it as early as 1435 and others as late as 1460. Columbus made conflicting statements concerning the date, and Fernando did not know.

Nor do we know for certain where he was born. Genoa has the edge, for Columbus said he was born there, but this is one case where his honesty may be open to question, as will be seen shortly. Substantial arguments have also been made for a birthplace on the island of Chios, now Greek but formerly a Genoese colony, where Columbus is even today a common surname. Other places mentioned as a possible birthplace include such logical choices as Majorca (in the Catalán-speaking Spanish Balearic Islands), Galicia (a Spanish province where a dialect of Portuguese is spoken), and various other places in Spain.

We do know that Columbus arrived in Portugal in 1476 (as young as 16 or as old as 41). There is reasonable evidence that he swam ashore after his ship was sunk in a well-documented naval battle off Cape St. Vincent. But we do not know which side he was on (a Franco-Portuguese fleet versus a Genoese fleet), nor do we know in what capacity he served. We are not even sure that Columbus was on one of the ships in the skirmish; he may have used the occasion as a fortuitous way to explain his presence in Lisbon.

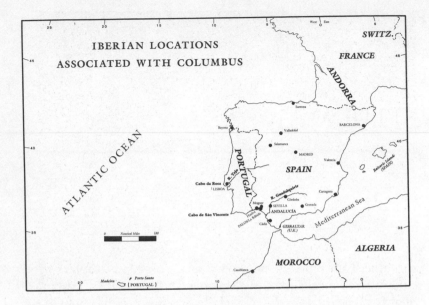

IBERIAN LOCATIONS
ASSOCIATED WITH COLUMBUS

Whatever the circumstances of his arrival in Portugal, Columbus married Doña Felipa Perestrello e Moniz in 1479, and Diego was born the next year in the Madeira Islands. Doña Felipa died sometime between 1481 and 1485, whereupon Columbus returned to Lisbon and then moved to Spain, settling in Córdoba in 1485. Here he took a lover, Beatriz Enríquez de Arana, who was to bear his second son, Fernando, in 1488. The events from that time on are reasonably clear, with one exception: although his death in Valladolid on May 20, 1506, is one of the few points that has unanimous agreement, it is not known where he is buried. He lies in one of three places: Sevilla, Santo Domingo, or Havana. Or in none of these. And

there are at least eight containers of various sizes, ranging from urns to vials and lockets—scattered from Italy to New York—said to hold the ashes of the Admiral!

This veil of mystery surrounding Columbus' personal background is not simply an accident of history; it is in large part Columbus' own doing. Fernando tells us in his *Historie* that his father elected to leave everything pertaining to his birthplace and family in obscurity. Even this, however, would appear to be an understatement. There is ample evidence that Columbus altered his identity, keeping many facts from his own sons. His brother Bartolomé was obviously in on the cover-up, but even Bartolomé's life has been obscured. Morison, in *Admiral of the Ocean Sea,* believes Bartolomé to be slightly younger than Columbus, by a year or two. But some make him the older brother, already established in his chart shop in Lisbon when Christopher arrived there in 1476. Frederick Pohl, in *The New Columbus,* argues that Bartolomé was Christopher's *uncle,* who taught his younger nephew most of what there was to learn about maps and geography. Fernando's account of his father says it was the reverse: Christopher was the teacher.

But why all the secrecy? There are only a few logical reasons, all of them familiar to us in the 20th century. First, there may have been a *political* reason. Columbus may at one time have served a country at war with Spain, or a kingdom that would later be swallowed up by Spain. Even if he were originally of Spanish birth, the fact would avail him little if he had been on the wrong side in a political controversy. In a way, the argument becomes even more compelling if he *had* been a

Repository, Municipal Hall, Genoa, thought to contain the ashes of Columbus. (Thacher)

Silver caravel carrying the Castillo Locket with ashes of the Admiral. Photographed in Boston, ca. 1880. (Thacher)

Spaniard by birth, for this would absolutely require a new identity; it would also explain his preference for the Spanish language;[1] if Catalán or Gallego, it would explain his reported accent.

Second, there may have been a *religious* reason. There is abundant circumstantial evidence that Columbus was of a Jewish background, at least on one side of the family. Salvador de Madariaga and Simon Wiesenthal have provided more than enough documentation to convince any objective person. This does not mean that Columbus was anything less than a devout Christian; on that point the Log itself gives eloquent testimony. But a convert, or the descendant of a convert, did not boast of Jewish ancestry in 15th century Spain. This was something kept within a very tight circle of friends, and often only within the family.

Third, there may have been a *hereditary* reason. Was Columbus really the son of poor woolweavers? How did he acquire his considerable education? How could a commoner, and a foreign one at that, marry into the Portuguese nobility? How was Columbus able to move among royalty as a peer? Was the Admiral of higher birth than many suppose? Frederick Pohl thinks so. Others, as well, hint at a blood link to a royal line.

However this may be, Columbus does seem to have had a "regal" look about him. Fernando describes the Admiral as "a well-built man of more than average stature, the face long, the cheeks somewhat high, his body neither fat nor lean. He had an aquiline nose and light-colored eyes; his complexion, too, was light and tending to bright red. In youth his hair was blonde, but when he reached the age of 30, it all turned

The Jovian Portrait, the earliest known representation of Columbus. Engraved in 1575 by Tobias Stimmer from an original, ca. 1550, in the collection of Paulus Jovius. (Thacher)

white." Blue eyes are reported by several contemporaries. There is universal agreement that he had an exceptionally keen sense of smell. Columbus makes several references to fragrances while on the first voyage, and it is known that he could distinguish different kinds of perfumes. There is ample proof that he had excellent eyesight and perfect hearing. From all indications, the Admiral was in perfect physical condition in 1492. Fernando describes him as moderate in drink, food, and dress, and claims that he never swore. His strongest oath was said to have been "By Saint Ferdinand!" When he was very angry with someone, he might say "God take you!"

COLUMBUS, AS REVEALED BY THE LOG

It has already been said that the Log provides a link between the Middle Ages and the Renaissance. It is not surprising, then, that the man who wrote this remarkable and incredible document stood astride both these historical periods. Columbus had one foot in the medieval world and one in the modern.

Paolo Emilio Taviani, Europe's leading Columbian scholar, has pointed out that Columbus' theoretical approach to phi-

The Thevet Portrait. Andre Thevet, 1584. (Thacher)

The De Bry Portrait. Engraving, 1595. (Winsor)

CRISTO: COLOMBO

Portrait of Columbus. (Giraudon/Art Resource)

losophy, theology, and certain scientific concepts places him firmly in the Middle Ages. But his overwhelming scientific curiosity, his bent for investigation, his interest in the natural world, and his ability to accept facts hitherto unknown make him a man of the Renaissance. Linguistically, too, Columbus was far ahead of his time. In a detailed linguistic analysis of the Log, another scholar, Virgil Milani, documents more than 100 words that were not known in any other example of Spanish literature before the *late* 16th or early 17th centuries. A Renaissance vocabulary in the late Middle Ages!

Milani uses internal evidence from the Log to build a strong case for a Genoese ethnic origin of the Admiral. He demonstrates convincingly that spelling mistakes and introduced words derive from Genoese, not from Portuguese, as many claim. This is not to say, however, that Columbus was born in Genoa, but merely into a Genoese-speaking family. He *may* have come from Genoa or its vicinity, or a Genoese colony, such as Chios, or from some other place to which his Genoese-speaking parents migrated. Inasmuch as every close acquaintance of Columbus, including members of his own family, testified that Castilian Spanish was not his primary language, but one which he wrote somewhat incorrectly and spoke with an accent, it is reasonable to assume that he was not native to Castilian Spain.

Accepting for the moment that the first language of Columbus was Genoese, where then did he learn fluent, though accented, Spanish? He probably learned it in Portugal, where he resided for a number of years and where Spanish was spoken in all the upper-class circles in which Columbus moved. Also, it is to be remembered that the Log was written after Columbus had lived in Spain for seven years, and his syntax and grammar would have improved markedly.

In addition to shedding light on the puzzling question of Columbus' birthplace, the Log also reveals a bit about his age—that is, if the Admiral were being candid. On Friday, December 21, 1492, Columbus wrote: "I have followed the sea for 23 years, without leaving it for any appreciable time." Later, in another entry, he claimed to have first gone to sea at age 14. That would place his age at the time of the Discovery somewhere between 37 and 44, depending on whether the seven years in Spain (between 1485 and 1492) were included or not in the 23 years at sea.[2]

The Log provides a solid foundation upon which we may reconstruct the religious framework that guided the Admiral. That he was a devout Christian there can be no doubt. His devotion and faith are no better demonstrated than on February 14, 1493, when he vowed to fulfill two different pilgrimages if delivered from the terrible storm surrounding his ship. While saying that his faith should relieve him of fear, he admitted weakness and anxiety, two very human emotions.

Although Columbus seems to have believed that God intervened directly on several occasions by providing signs (such as a rough sea, with no wind, on September 23), or by showing them land (as on March 4), he never prayed for miracles. It was as though "what is to be, will be." When he made direct references to the scriptures, they were to Old Testament ones.

Running throughout the Log are ample proofs that Columbus was not a superstitious person. For example, he preferred

The Durlacher Portrait, 1965. (Courtesy Ruth Durlacher-Wolper)

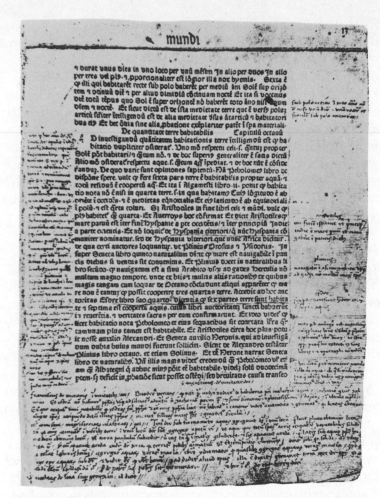

*Letter from Columbus to treasurer Alonso de Morales, 22 October 1501.
(Thacher)*

Columbus' notes on Imago Mundi. *(Original in Biblioteca Colombina,
Sevilla)*

*Letter written by Columbus in Santo Domingo,
16 November 1498, referring to the first voyage.
(Thacher; original in Casa de Alba, Madrid)*

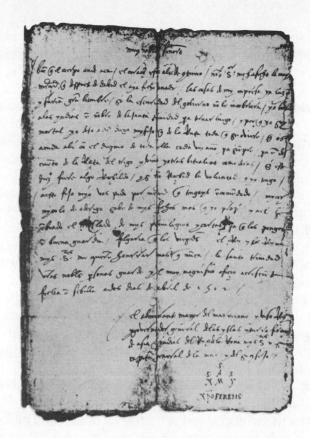

*Letter written by Columbus to the Bank of Saint
George, Genoa, 2 April 1502. (Revelli; original in
Palazzo del Commune, Genova)*

not to sail from a port on Sundays, but said that this was because of piety, not superstition. He did not believe in the monstrosities that were supposed to inhabit the unknown regions of the world, and for a long time he would not even accept the reports of Carib cannabilism that came to his attention. There is no evidence that he expected to find sea monsters or fall off the earth, or any other such foolishness. At all times he was willing to accept the unexpected and offer a rational explanation for its occurrence.

Columbus found no conflict between religion and science. Even though many of his scientific principles were derived from medieval concepts, he was perfectly willing to discard those that proved faulty and to offer new interpretations of his own. The declination of the compass, noted on the transatlantic crossing, was taken in stride and very reasonably accounted for. The eruption of the volcano at Tenerife was explained to the crew in order to allay their fears. And when the crew became frightened at the thickness of the seaweed in the Sargasso Sea, Columbus commented that fear conjures up imaginary terrors.

A number of scientific concepts that he possessed upon departure and had confirmed by the voyage were probably unknown to the majority—if not all—of the crew. The belt of easterly winds blowing steadily in the latitude of the Canary Islands was one of these concepts. Columbus' earlier residency in the Madeira Islands and voyages with the Portuguese along the west coast of Africa had provided this knowledge. His understanding of this wind system, the Trades, is what determined the Canary Island departure point for the second leg of the outward journey. Furthermore, it is what led him to rerig the *Niña* in the Canaries, to provide maximum sail to catch these winds.

Columbus also knew that he could return with the westerlies, winds he had experienced in at least one voyage to England and perhaps one to Iceland. His homeward route is a clear indication that he knew exactly the latitude to seek in order to fetch these winds. But to keep this information from the crew was a real balancing act. Had the crew understood the Atlantic circulation, they might have turned back prematurely. He had to convince his sailors to continue westward, while at the same time offering them some hope of return. It almost caused a mutiny.

Other things he had to learn in the Bahamas, and his grasp of new conditions is quite remarkable. Early on he discovered the concept of land and sea breezes in the islands, the wind reversal that occurs with the differential heating and cooling of land and water. This allowed for port departures during darkness, before the winds reversed in the heat of the day.

One of the most amazing feats of "instant learning" concerns the coral reefs and shallows of the Bahamas. To those familiar with the region, it is hardly short of miraculous that Columbus, with no charts, lighthouses, landmarks, or local knowledge, managed to avoid a major accident at the outset. Even the grounding of the *Santa María* came about because an officer failed to follow instructions, not because Columbus did not understand the environment. (During my last trip to Samana Cay, where Columbus probably made his first landfall, I counted three modern boats on the reef and one old freighter. Presumably the captains of these vessels had charts and radios.)

For those who might wonder why Columbus thought he was in Asia (and went to his grave so believing), it should be pointed out that this was a valid geographical concept for his era. A number of voyages of rather short duration had been made to North America before Columbus; all of these were to "Asia" as far as anyone was concerned. The Viking discoveries had been incorporated into papal territories and mapped as part of Asia, with a bishop assigned to Greenland. English fishermen were working the Newfoundland banks before 1492, and at least two scholars believe that Columbus himself had visited these regions with the Portuguese in the 1470s (see Epilogue).

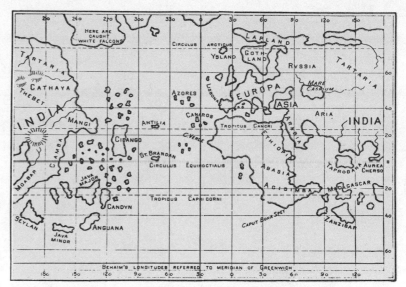

Martin Behaim's Globe in Mercator projection. (Fiske, 1902)

It was not until about 1510 that *some* Europeans began to suggest that a new continent had been found—though indeed, a number of European cartographers continued to append the American discoveries to the Asiatic coast as late as the middle or late 16th century. John Cabot's whole proposition to the English in 1494 seems to have been based on the premise that Columbus simply did not go far enough; that he (Cabot) would take the shorter northern route to the Asian mainland and then sail south to the Cathay of Marco Polo, behind the offshore islands discovered by Columbus. It was a sound geographical argument in the late 1490s.

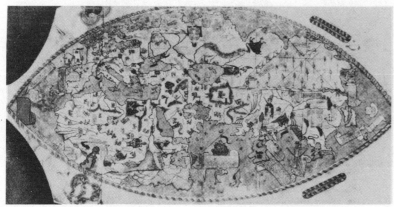

Genoese World Map, 1457. (© George Kish)

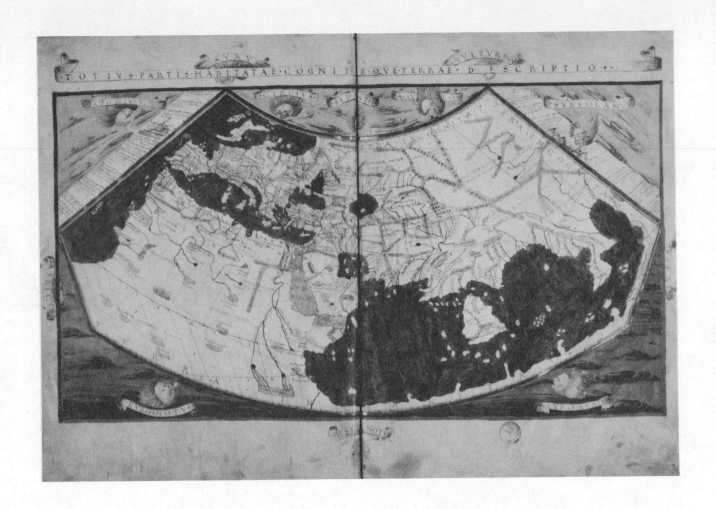

Ptolemy World Map, 1472. (Biblioteca Apostolica, Vaticana)

One of Columbus' most important geographical conceptions, perhaps the foundation of his whole enterprise, was in fact erroneous. Columbus believed the length of a degree to be 56.66 miles, and many notes to this effect may be found in marginal notes written in the Admiral's own books. For Columbus, the earth had a circumference of approximately 20,400 miles, an underestimate of about 25 percent. According to his degree calculations, Europe and "Asia" should be separated by only about 1,100 leagues (figuring four Spanish miles to the league). The Log records 1,111 leagues from the Canary Islands to landfall, and this surely proved to the Admiral that his calculations were correct. Had Columbus known the correct value of a degree (approximately 69 statute miles at the Equator), he might never have embarked on such a long voyage over open ocean. His belief that the earth was much smaller than most his contemporaries thought was one of the most fortunate mistakes in history.

Before we rush to condemn Columbus for this incredible inaccuracy, it should be pointed out that the approximate determination of a degree of longitude at the Equator was not made until 1669–1670. Even Sir Isaac Newton, writing at about the same time that the longitudinal degree was reasonably approximated, underestimated the earth's circumference by one-seventh.

Columbus most certainly read and reread every book available to him on the subject of cosmography, geography, history, travel, and natural history. Especially important to him were such classical works as Strabo's *Geographia,* Ptolemy's *Geographia,* Pliny's *Natural History,* Sir John Mandeville's *Travels,* Pierre d'Ailly's *Imago Mundi,* and Marco Polo's *Travels*. Many of the books in his personal library have survived.

In addition, there were a number of maritime charts at his disposal, not only those of Genoese, Venetian, and Catalán origin, but the readily accessible Portuguese charts of the 15th century. These were of particular significance, for Portuguese voyages along the west coast of Africa, to the Azores, and as far away as Iceland, Greenland, and possibly Newfoundland (all before 1492) were creating a revolution in cartography.

As early as 1424, the Portuguese had commenced to map islands in the western Atlantic Ocean, including one called "Antilia." The continuous mapping of "mythical" islands to the west, and the gradual refinement of positions and shapes, suggests that some evidence of their real existence was trickling back to European cartographers.

To this hesitant probing toward the unknown west by the seafaring peoples of western Europe must be added the earlier reports—and speculations—of those Europeans who lived in the easternmost regions of Europe and sought the ends of the known world toward the rising sun. By 1472 there was a Latin edition of *Bibliothecae historicae,* written by the Sicilian-born Greek, Diodorus, in the first century B.C. In it he described a very great island in the western Atlantic, many days' sail from Africa, which had been discovered by the Phoenicians. Sir John Mandeville, in a work well known to Columbus, told of a journey made to India and beyond (i.e., to the east of India), where there were more than 5,000 islands. Marco Polo was even more specific: there were no less than 7,440 islands, and Japan was 1,500 miles off the coast of China.

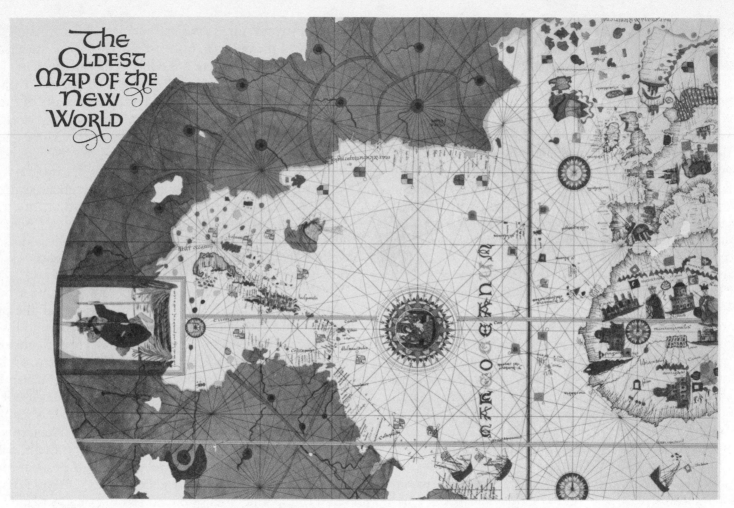

The Oldest Map of the New World

Juan de la Cosa's Map of the New World, 1500. (Courtesy New York, Public Library; original in Museo Naval, Madrid)

THE LOG OF CHRISTOPHER COLUMBUS

New World detail from Juan de la Cosa's Map.

Japan, called then *Zipangu* or *Cipango,* was mapped accordingly in the late 15th century, and was probably illustrated in this way on the map that Columbus carried on the first voyage. This map, which Columbus shared with Martín Alonso Pinzón, captain of the *Pinta,* and which he mentions under the Log entry for September 25, obviously reflected the current state of knowledge. It was logical and reasonable to launch a search for "nearby Cipango" within a few days of discovering the outer islands of the Bahamas. And China lay just beyond!

With regard to Columbus' nautical chart, there is a still-prevalent belief that it was furnished to him in about 1481 by the Florentine physician Paolo del Pozzo Toscanelli. Toscanelli is said to have written a letter in 1474 to Fernan Martins, a canon in Lisbon, urging King Alfonso V of Portugal to pioneer the Atlantic route to Asia. Upon learning of this correspondence, Columbus reputedly wrote to Toscanelli, who sent him a copy of the original letter, along with a chart (see Epilogue). Fernando, in the *Historie,* provides a second letter from Toscanelli to the Admiral.

I am inclined to agree with Henry Vignaud, however, that this entire correspondence was forged after the deaths of all parties concerned, in order to squelch a rumor that Columbus originally picked up on the idea of an Atlantic crossing from a dying Portuguese sailor who had already accomplished the feat. The letters were to provide a scientific justification for the undertaking, thus preserving the good name of the Discoverer.

The rumor of the shipwrecked sailor, (whom Columbus

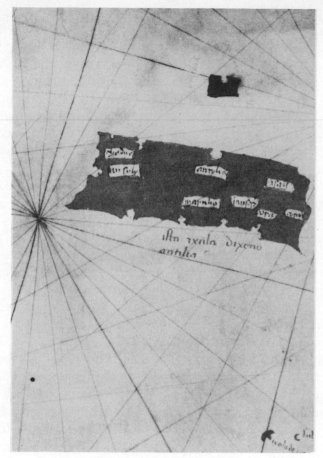

"Antilia" on Pizzigano Chart of 1424. (Used with permission of the Associates of the James Ford Bell Library, University of Minnesota)

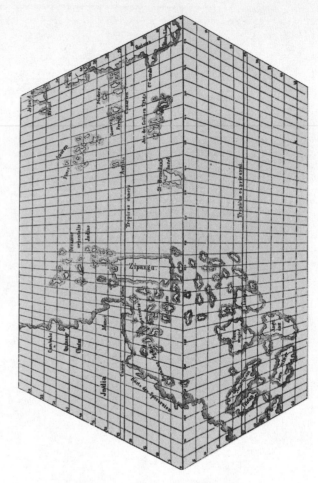

Toscanelli Chart. (Reconstructed by Winsor, 1886, based on letters in Fernando's Historie)

met while living on Madeira) is of no consequence. There is no need to postulate a secret, visionary source of information; sufficient information was already available to anyone willing to risk the voyage. The best evidence that the Toscanelli correspondence was a fake rests with the fact that the information in the letters is ridiculously out-of-date. No informed scholar in Florence would have written such a letter in 1474; only someone in Spain who was not current with the sophisticated learning of the Florentines could have been responsible. Vignaud thinks that Bartolomé was the culprit, but Fernando was also capable of the ruse. Columbus' main contributions to the enterprise were his erroneous belief that the world was smaller than contemporary scholars (correctly) thought, and his incredible tenacity. Had he not been so obsessed, had he really listened to the experts, he might have learned the true value of the earth's circumference and never attempted to cross 10,000 miles of open ocean. No wonder so many of his contemporaries thought Columbus to have been mad. But not one could fault his sailing ability.

Columbus always rates the highest accolades from scholars when it comes to his seamanship. He was, without question, the finest sailor of his time. Perhaps he was the greatest dead-reckoning sailor who ever lived. His navigation to the Azores on the return voyage, through one of the most terrible storms the residents of those islands could recall, is sufficient proof of his ability.

He also had an uncanny sense of speed and distance. Granted that these were measured by the crude methods of turning a glass of sand to establish half-hour time intervals, or by using a rhythmic chant (or pulse beat) to time the passage of a bit of flotsam from bow to stern, he often equaled modern calculations. The entire voyage had no more than nine percent error for the total distance and possibly came within 100 nautical miles of the correct distance of about 3,100 nautical miles, depending on how one figures the Columbian league (2.67 nautical miles, 2.82 nautical miles, or 3.18 nautical miles; see page 11).

Within the islands the distances rival modern standards of precision. It is this incredible precision that weighs in favor of Samana Cay, over Watling Island or any other, as the first landfall site. Only by starting at Samana Cay do the inter-island distances recorded by Columbus conform with reality. It is one fact that opponents of Samana Cay cannot refute.

In every way the Log offers testimony to the seamanship of Columbus. Virtually every student of Columbus accepts the opinion of Las Casas that "Christopher Columbus surpassed all of his contemporaries in the art of navigation."

The Log also shows us another side of Columbus. He was the first ethnographer in the New World. His commentary on the Taino people (or Island Arawak), who at first were called Lucayan (and the Bahamas, the Lucayos), is of indispensible value to the modern anthropologist. Though deficient in some respects (Columbus failed to discern their religious culture), his remarks afford the only good overview of these island people before they vanished from the earth. The most advanced concept he offered was that of a cultural region, unified

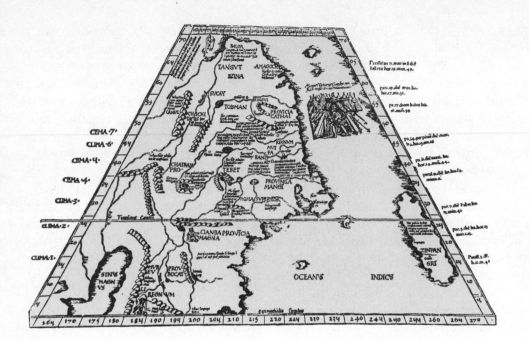

Ptolemy Map of East Asia, redrawn in 1522. (Nordenskiold, 1899)

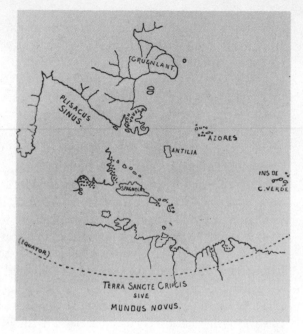

Johann Ruysch's Map of the New World, 1508. (Winsor, 1886)

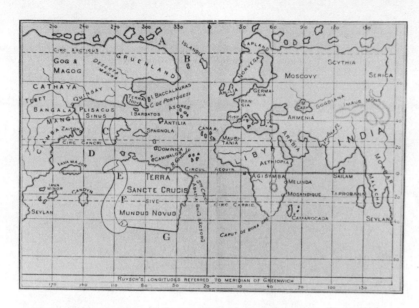

Johann Ruysch's Map of the New World, 1508. Note "Antilia." (Fiske, 1902)

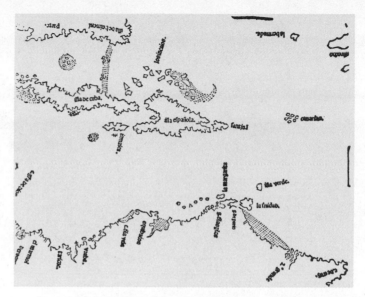

Peter Martyr's Map of the New World, 1511. (Winsor)

by language and customs. As he approached the eastern part of what is now the Dominican Republic, he became increasingly aware of the Caribs, of whom he had heard reports. And as the language began to shift, he attributed this to distance from the cultural hearth. Also, when encountering the rather warlike and unattractive Ciguayo people, the Admiral said, "If they are not Caribs they must be of lands fronting them." Here is a distinct recognition of a cultural transition zone.

The cultural unity of the Taino greatly impressed Columbus; he commented on this harmony over and over. We cannot fault him for viewing these simple people as ripe for Christianity. For a devout person, as Columbus was, such missionary zeal was a way of assuring entry into Heaven and of bringing about spiritual equality on earth. Those who see Columbus as the founder of slavery in the New World are grossly in error. This thought occurred to Morison (and many

Castiglioni World Map, 1525. (© George Kish)

others), who misinterpreted a statement made by Columbus on the first day in America, when he said, "They (the Indians) ought to be good servants." In fact, Columbus offered this observation in explanation of an earlier comment he had made, theorizing that people from the mainland came to the islands to capture these Indians as slaves because they were so docile and obliging.

All through the Log, Columbus expresses nothing but love and admiration for the Indians. His affection for the young chief in Haiti, and vice versa, is one of the most touching stories of love, trust, and understanding between men of different races and cultures to come out of this period in history. His

instructions to the men he left behind at *La Navidad*, on January 2, clearly illustrate his sincere fondness and respect for the Indians.

There is no contradiction between Columbus' warm feelings for the natives and his desire to secure Spanish authority over them. After all, Europeans were subjects of this ruler or that—and a subject is one who is subjected. Furthermore, to bring Christianity was a noble thing. The fact that today we can point out countless abuses has nothing to do with 15th century morality.

John Boyd Thacher, the great Columbian scholar at the turn of this century, believed that Columbus' ultimate design

Contemporary descendants of Columbus' Caribbean Indians. (Photos: John H. Vann)

was expressed in the Log entry of December 26: the conquest of Jerusalem and the restoration of the Holy Land to the Church. This could only be financed by discovering new lands and gathering enough gold, silver, and precious stones. Slavery was not part of the ultimate design.

Columbus also displayed an affection for his crew, despite the fact that many tried to undermine his enterprise. He was a tolerant captain who did everything in his power to maintain their morale. He allayed their fears in various ways; he cheered them on; he protected them. And he certainly was willing to fight for them, as he proved on the return trip, when half the crew of the *Niña* was interned by the Portuguese authorities in the Azores. He threatened to "blow up the whole island," killing every Portuguese citizen on it unless his men were returned. They were. He also stood his ground in the middle of Lisbon harbor, against Portuguese authority once again, and infinitely poor odds.

Some scholars have been so eager to concoct mysteries around Columbus (I can't imagine why; there seem to be enough of them already!) that even simple and reasonable actions have been clouded. A case in point is the so-called secret log. Usually this is construed as some sort of private record, in which Columbus hid the truth about the voyage from his men, showing them only a phony journal with doctored figures. There was only one Log, the one reproduced here. There were two sets of figures for distance made good, at least for part of the outward voyage, 23 of the 33 days. The lower figures reported to the crew, Columbus thought, would be psychologically more acceptable on a long voyage. But if he were

going to keep a "secret" journal, he would not have written it in Spanish.

In summary, the Log tells us much about Columbus the sailor, the scientist, and the captain. As captain/sailor he was unsurpassed. As a scientist, he lacked much, especially in botany (dismal!), ornithology (only fair), and ichthyology (poor). In other sciences he was better: astronomy (good), meteorology (better-than-average), navigation (A-plus), ethnology (good), geography (excellent).

Paolo Taviani, not only Europe's leading authority on Columbus, but one of modern Italy's leading politicians, finds Columbus deficient in only one main aspect: political acumen. Taviani believes that Columbus lacked two essential qualities that must be possessed by any good politician: (1) he could not make firm, long-term decisions, and (2) he did not possess that magic ability to appoint the right man to the right job at the right time. Nevertheless, after sifting and sorting all the good things and bad, and the countless contradictions swirling about the man, Taviani sums up the Admiral in one short sentence: "The man was a genius."

Others have called him a swindler, charlatan, pirate, thief, fanatic, hypocrite, liar, and dreamer. I prefer to think of the Discoverer as stern, compassionate, literate, courageous, cautious, loyal to his God and his Sovereigns, dedicated almost beyond reason, and certainly the best navigator of his time.

Here, then, is *The Log of Christopher Columbus*. It is an account of an epic journey; one of triumph and tragedy, happiness and sorrow, benevolence and greed—everything that makes for a story of high adventure on the high seas.

1. Of the 40 surviving letters and documents that carry authenticated signatures of Columbus, all are written in Castilian Spanish. Even letters to Italian friends and to the Bank of Saint George, in Genoa, were written in Spanish. His marginal notes in the books he possessed were almost always in Spanish, although two of the books, printed in Latin, have marginal notes in that language. All the notes written on the pages of an Italian edition of Pliny's *Natural History* were in Spanish, with one exception in poor Italian. One other short note in Italian glosses a blank space in the *Libro de las profecias*.

2. During the Fourth Voyage in 1503, Columbus said that he was 28 when he entered Spanish service, which was in the year 1485. This would place his age at 35 in 1492. If one accepts the Cristoforo Colombo named in a deposition filed in Genoa on August 13, 1479, as the same Cristóbal Colón who discovered America, we find that he was 27 years old (or "thereabouts") in that year. This makes him 41 at the time of the first voyage, the age most scholars accept.

Columbus standing with globe, 1621. (The Bettmann Archive)

THE LOG OF CHRISTOPHER COLUMBUS

CHAPTER THREE

THE SHIPS AND THEIR NAVIGATION

The three ships of the Columbus fleet were obtained in the tiny seaport town of Palos de la Frontera. Apparently the town and/or its citizens had committed some acts that were detrimental to the Crown. As a punishment, the town had to provide two caravels whenever commanded to do so, for a period of up to 12 months. Furthermore, the town was ordered to pay all the costs of equipping the vessels. On April 30, 1492, the Crown called in its marker, and the Royal Council ordered the two caravels placed under the command of Columbus. The Council also authorized the payment of four months' wages to those who signed aboard and a decree granting amnesty to any criminal who volunteered to ship out on the voyage. Only four did (see Crew Lists, in the Epilogue).

It has been suggested by some scholars that Columbus chose Palos because of its proximity to the monastery of La Rábida (only a mile away), where two of his earliest supporters, Fr. Marchena and Fr. Pérez resided. This was an interesting coincidence, but the real reason was the debt owed the Crown; in other words, the voyage cost the government very little.

Palos, as all coastal ports, offered a plentiful supply of good seaman. Most of the crew hailed from the immediate area— Palos, Huelva, and Moguer. The "northerners" on the voyage were mostly crewmembers of Juan de la Cosa's ship, *La Gallega*. Columbus, in effect, chartered de la Cosa's vessel, changed its name to *Santa María,* retained most of its complement of sailors, and made her the flagship.

The caravels supplied by Palos were the *Pinta* and the *Santa Clara*. The latter, named for the patron saint of Moguer, was

Profiles of Santa María *(left) and* Pinta.

more affectionately known as the *Niña,* the feminine form of its owner's surname, *Niño.*

Considering the significance of the Voyage of Discovery, very little has come down to us concerning these vessels. All were to be gone, if not forgotten, within eight years of the date the fleet departed for America.

The *Santa María* was a three-masted, square rigged *nao,* or ship. She was obviously a run-of-the-mill cargo vessel; slow, clumsy, and, according to the later statements of Columbus, not very well suited for exploration. She carried a crew of about 40 men. José María Martínez-Hidalgo, former director of the Maritime Museum in Barcelona, believes that the *Santa*

The *Pinta* was second in size among the three vessels, but just barely. She was a three-masted, square-rigged caravel, approximately 70 feet in length, with a beam of about 22 feet, and a draft of just over 7 feet. Under normal conditions she carried a ship's company of about 26 men. During the First Voyage, *Pinta* (because her captain, Martín Alonso Pinzón, deserted Columbus) discovered the island of Babeque, the present-day Great Inagua. She missed the Azores on the return trip, but somehow found her way to Bayona, in northwestern Spain, and returned to Palos just after Columbus did—in fact, on the same day. *Pinta* was to make several more trips across the Atlantic, her last voyage in 1499–1500. Under

María displaced 202 tons, with a length of 77.4 feet, a beam of 26 feet, and a draft of 6.9 feet.

The *Santa María* was lost on Christmas Eve, 1492, when she ran aground off the north coast of what is now Haiti. Though one of her anchors may have been found, searchers have never been able to pinpoint the wreckage.

Niña *with lateen rig (above), and after conversion at Gomera.*

First page of the Book of Privileges, as compiled by Columbus himself—one of four authenticated copies. (Revelli; original in Biblioteca Colombina, Sevilla)

the command of Vincente Yáñez Pinzón, she served as the flagship for the discovery of the Amazon River. In July 1500, *Pinta* was caught in a hurricane and went down in the vicinity of the Turks and Caicos Islands. At the present time an active search by marine archaeologists is underway in hopes of locating this historic caravel.

The *Niña* (nee *Santa Clara*) was about the same size as the *Pinta,* according to the recent research of Eugene Lyon. She carried some 58–60 tons of cargo, was 67 feet long, had a beam of 21 feet, and a draft of just under 7 feet. An earlier computation by Martínez-Hidalgo, with whom Lyon consulted, made *Niña* out to be 70 feet in length, 23 feet in beam, and 5.8 feet in draft. The more recent, and slightly reduced, figures cited by Lyon are based on a detailed study of cargo and fittings. Though the smallest of the three vessels, *Niña* carried four masts. Originally lateen-rigged, she was square-rigged by Columbus during his stopover in the Canary Islands on the First Voyage. While researching the *Libro de armadas* in the *Archivo Generale de Indias* in Sevilla, Lyon discovered, much to his surprise, that *Niña* carried 10 breech-loading swivel guns, called *bombardas*.

Niña was quite obviously the favorite of Columbus, perhaps because she served him so well during the terrible Atlantic storms he confronted on the return voyage. She was to make at least four more voyages to the New World after the 1492–1493 voyage. She was part of the fleet on Columbus' Second and Third Voyages, and on at least two other occasions she carried cargo to Española. *Niña* disappeared from the pages of history after she was sold in 1499. Her complement was

Niña, *as depicted by Richard Schlecht. (Courtesy National Geographic Society)*

THE SHIPS AND THEIR NAVIGATION

about 24 men, but on the Third Voyage in 1498, she might have carried as many as 40 colonists to America.

All three vessels carried one small sailing boat apiece (called a *batel*). All used hinged rudders and all had pumps.

NAVIGATION

Two basic methods of navigation were available to Columbus and his pilots: dead-reckoning, by means of the compass, and celestial. The former was generally preferred by Mediterranean mariners; the latter, by Northern Europeans.

For 14th and 15th century navigators, the well-known portolan charts (see earlier illustrations) were a mainstay of dead-reckoning. The compass bearings were plotted on these charts as straight lines, known as loxodromes, or rhumbs. Through trial and error, over the course of many years, magnetic variation and (probably) the effects of currents were partially incorporated into these loxodromes. In other words, a pilot needed only to follow the bearing of the loxodrome (usually the 32 points of the compass were provided, on a compass rose), and he would arrive at his destination.

Mediterranean mariners were apparently not very concerned with exact latitude. At the end of the 16th century, Venice was still positioned too far to the north on the charts by three degrees; Genoa by two degrees. Moreover, a five- to six-degree easterly variation in the Mediterranean still went virtually unnoticed! Italians, Spaniards, and Portuguese seem to have followed the loxodrome on their chart, and once the high coast appeared (and it was always high), they made a visual correction.

Northern Europeans, particularly the Flemish, were not so casual. They not only wrote about these irregularities but published charts with *two* sets of loxodromes; one for Italian compasses and one for Flemish compasses. The Flemish compass lines gave the correct variation.

Two important points emerge from this. First, Columbus and all his pilots were dead-reckoning, loxodromic sailors. Absolute celestial fixes were not especially important to them, as can be seen from the data in the Log. A fix on the North Star was a rare event during the Voyage, and at least once it was taken to confirm that the star moved rather than the needle. The trust in the compass was almost slavish. On another occasion, when Columbus found his celestial fix to be at variance with his computations and common sense, he decided his quadrant was broken and stowed it for the remainder of the voyage!

Second, if Columbus made a chart—and he undoubtedly did—he would have placed all his American discoveries too far to the north. As a matter of fact, *all* the early 16th century Mediterranean charts, beginning with Juan de la Cosa's, place Cuba *north* of the Tropic of Cancer. Because of this tendency of dead-reckoning Spanish pilots to locate land masses too far north, we must discount any theory that places the Bahamian landfall due west of Hierro, Canary Islands, even though Columbus himself stated that San Salvador was on an east-west line from that island.

Columbus had at least one celestial instrument, possibly two. He refers to his quadrant, which he did not think was working properly and used only four or five times during the

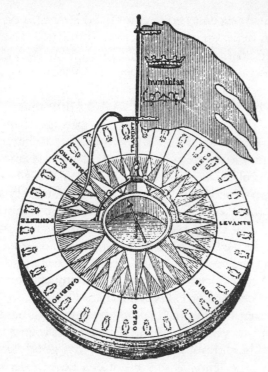

A 16th century compass. (Winsor, 1886)

A 15th century astrolabe. Suspended pendulum fashion, it measured the angle between the vertical and the line of sight to the celestial body. An "improved," lightweight version of the astrolabe, known as the quadrant, was carried by Columbus on the first voyage, although he seems to have put little faith in it. (Courtesy National Maritime Museum, Greenwich, England)

voyage. This crude forerunner of the sextant was next-to-impossible to use at sea. Since it had no optics whatsoever, and since its plumb bob had to hang perpendicular to the surface, one can only imagine the comedy routine that would result if there were even a slight chop. To complicate matters still further, the early quadrant had not one, but *five* scales: sine, cosine, tangent, and cotangent, in addition to the standard equal-interval degree scale. Kelley suggests, and I tend to agree, that a mistaken reading of the arc tangent scale gave the exotic latitudes reported by Columbus in Cuba and Haiti.

Astrolabe of Regiomontanus (Winsor, 1886)

It is possible, though not very probable, that Columbus could have combined dead-reckoning and celestial navigation. By *assuming* that sunrise was east and sunset was west, he *could* have followed the sun to America. Inasmuch as he departed the Canaries a few days before the autumnal equinox, he would have been north of west for about a week, dead-on west at equinox, and south of west thereafter. Such a plot would bring the fleet to a position between the Caicos Islands and Mayaguana. This method would have required that he always refer to sunrise as east (90 degrees) and sunset, west (270 degrees). Magnetic variation, at least, would not have affected this arrangement.

Dead-reckoning requires a means of measuring speed. In Columbus' era, when the chronometer was still an invention of the future, this was accomplished by dropping a piece of wood into the water and timing the passage from bow to stern, probably by reciting a rhyme or chant. Longer time intervals were measured with a sand glass (see ahead). The glasses Columbus carried were turned every half hour. Probably the ship's speed was logged and plotted on a board every half hour, then totaled at the end of each four-hour watch. Summaries were made every 12 hours, and it is from these that Columbus derived his speed and distance-made-good calculations during the voyage. Compass bearings were also recorded at the same time speed was entered, and any change in course would have been recorded whenever it occurred.

In summary, Columbus followed his compass, paid scant or no attention to variation, made virtually no use of his quadrant (which he did not trust), and placed a good deal of faith in his own experience at sea. He was a keen observer of the sky and could literally "smell" a storm brewing. He understood changes in the color of water and in clouds overlying land masses. He also knew something of bird migrations and habits. And he quickly readjusted his position on the return voyage when he noted that the sargassum weed did not agree with his plotted course, for he had logged the weed's location on the outward leg.

TIMEKEEPING

In 1492 Spain used the same system of timekeeping that we employ today, with one exception. The Christian world followed the Julian Calendar, which became more-or-less operational in 4 AD. The length of the Julian year had been set at 365.25 days when, in fact, the correct value was 365.242199 days. Because of this each year was 11 minutes 14 seconds too long.

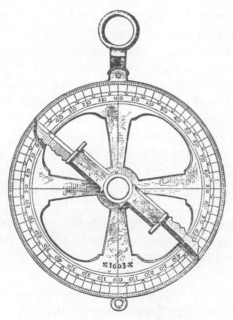

Camplain astrolabe of 1503 (Winsor, 1886)

By 1492 the astronomical year (tropical year) was 9 days out of phase with the calendar, and moving religious festivals were becoming chaotic. The Gregorian Calendar, adopted by the Catholic world in 1582, corrected this anomaly. All Columbian dates, therefore, such as Discovery Day, 12 October, must have nine days added to bring them in line with our current calendar. The English-speaking world did not change until 1752, by which time an 11-day error had accumulated. As a matter of fact, Columbus Day is the only celebrated historical event that has not been corrected from the Old Style dates of the Julian calendar. It should be 21 October.

Months and days were the same in 1492 as now, with the same names. The week had seven days and the day 24 hours. Columbus did not use *ante meridian* (AM) and *post meridian* (PM), but rather, morning, afternoon, and night. And he used two 12-hour periods, with the new day beginning at midnight. Throughout the Log, however, his dated entries usually began at sunrise; events of the early morning hours (midnight to sunrise) were included under the preceding day. This results in some confusion, especially when he was so busy that he continued the Log with no indication at all of the day change (such as on 11–12 October).

Hours at sea were determined either astronomically or by the sand glass. Sunrise and sunset are positive references that need no verification, and tables were available for their times of occurrence. Most people at sea can determine noon (local time) to within ± 30 minutes. Here, then, was another time check.

Columbus, his pilots, and many of the crew understood the sun's path through the sky. The sun's position, with reference to the mast, bow, stern, etc., would provide reasonable approximations of hourly passages.

At night the stars provided excellent time signals. All stars and constellations move 15 degrees each hour, from rise to dawn (as does the sun), and set position at dawn is always the angle of the rise point plus 270 degrees. A star that rises at 45 degrees in the east sets at 315 degrees in the west. Columbus was probably able to identify a new rising star for every hour.

All navigators of this period used the Regiment of the North for keeping track of elapsed time. The North Star was imagined to be centered on the body of a man, with the outermost stars of the Little Dipper (*Ursa Minor*) slowly revolving counterclockwise, like the backward-moving hand of some gigantic clock. These two stars, the "Guards" (Kochab and Pherhad; *Beta Ursae Minoris* and *Gamma Ursae Minoris*), move 15 degrees every hour. One must know the daily positions of the guard stars, but given that information, timetelling is relatively simple. The man's figure is used to aid one's memory. If the guards move from head to foot, they have moved 180 degrees (180 ÷ 15 = 12), or 12 hours. Imaginary lines are drawn through the man, each representing three hours, or 45 degrees. If the stars move three lines, nine hours have passed. Columbus refers to this timekeeping method in the Log entry for 30 September 1492.

Columbus also used the ampolleta, or sand glass. It was turned every half-hour, and probably a bell was rung at this time (hence, 8 bells in a four-hour watch). On 13 December he measured the length of the daylight period, saying it was 20 glasses long, and then added, "Unless some error was made because the glass was not turned quickly enough or because some of the sand did not run through." That experiment was done on the winter solstice (Julian 13 December + 9 days = 22 December), the shortest day of the year. If twilight is excluded, the daylight period is 10 hours 55 minutes on that date (20 degrees N), but splitting the morning and evening twilight periods (i.e., adding half of the twilight time to his daylight period) makes his reading tolerably close. His reading on 5 December was considerably off, by at least an hour, but his readings on 19 December and 21 January were reasonable.

The watch was changed every four hours, beginning with the first quarter watch at 7:00 PM. Log events are sometimes related to the watch being stood. Canonical times are also used, by name: Prime, Terce, Sext, Nones, Vespers, Compline. These equate with 6 AM, 9 AM, 12 noon, 3 PM, 6 PM, and 9 PM, but times were not strictly kept. Vespers, for instance, might be as early as 4 PM or as late as 8 PM, depending on the workload.

Small units of time, such as seconds, were used only for measuring speed through the water. This was done by floating a chip from bow to stern and measuring its progress with rhymes, chants, or pulse beats.

WEIGHTS AND MEASUREMENTS

There are many references to measurements in the Log, including weight, length (both distance and depth), angular

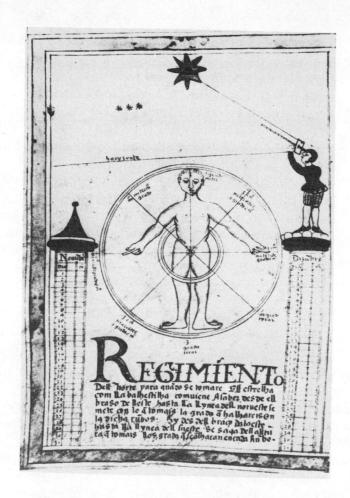

Regiment of the North Star. Anon., ca. 1550–6. (National Maritime Museum, Greenwich, England)

Two 16th century sand glasses, used on shipboard for timing the watch and measuring the length of day. (Courtesy National Maritime Museum, Greenwich, England)

measurement, and time (already discussed). Most of the units are well known, having been established by law and scrupiously enforced. Castilian laws (*leyes*) were published in 1538 and 1581, relating specifically to weights and measurements.

WEIGHT

Three different units are mentioned in the Log.

> *quintal* = 101.425 lbs. (avoir.)
> *arroba* = 25.356 lbs. (avoir.)
> *tonel* ("ton") = 1,267.81 lbs. (avoir.)

This latter term (*tonel*) has confused some scholars. It is not the true ton (*tonelada*), but the weight of 1.66 wine casks, containing 45.15 *arrobas* of wine, plus the weight of the casks. In other words, a *bota* or *pipa* (wine cask) holds 27.5 *arrobas* of wine (83.45 US gals.). One such cask, filled with wine or water, weighs 760.686 lbs. (avoir.). There was also a *tonel macho* (male *tonel*) in 1492, equal to two casks, but there is no evidence that Columbus used this unit.

Obviously, the *tonel* could be a liquid measure (and was at the time), but Columbus used the unit only as an expression of weight. Some have estimated the size of the casks and come up with a cubic (volume) measure, but it has no relevence to the Log. Displacement tonnage is not a factor, either.

LENGTH

Eight linear units are used by Columbus in the Log, some a little difficult to ascertain with any degree of precision.

> *palmo* (span) = 8.22 inches
> *paso* (pace) = 4.75 feet (approx.). Columbus defined the *paso* as "1,000 *pasos* equals 0.25 league." Inasmuch as there is still no complete agreement on the length of the

league, the *paso* could range from 4.06 feet to 4.86 feet. On one occasion Columbus used the term *passada*, apparently as a synonym for *paso*.

> *remo de barca* (boat oar) = 8 feet (approximately)
> *tiro de lombarda* (lombard-shot) = 900 feet (300 yards)
> *tiro de ballesta* (crossbow-shot) = 1,000 feet
> *milla* (mile) = between 4,060 and 4,856 feet. The best documentary evidence points to 4,284 feet.
> *legua* (league) = between 2.67 and 3.2 nautical miles. For Columbus, each league equaled 4 of his miles. For simplification in this book, one league equals 3 nautical miles, approximately. Unless otherwise noted, the word "miles" in this translation always refers to nautical miles.
> *braza* (fathom) = 5.5 feet. The maximum soundings taken by Columbus seem to have been of 40 *brazas*, or 220 feet.

One other implied unit may be found in the Log: the distance-to-the-horizon. From the crow's nest of the *Santa María*, the horizon was at 10 nautical miles; from the sterncastle, approximately seven nautical miles. With clouds, smoke, and haze as indicators, Columbus could probably perceive a low island from a distance of up to 20 miles. A convenient rule-of-thumb for obtaining distance-to-the-horizon is: the square root of the height of the observer (above sea level), *added* to the square root of the above sea-level height of the sighted object, and *multiplied* by 1.3 for nautical miles (1.5 for statute miles).

THE LOG OF CHRISTOPHER COLUMBUS

PART ONE

THE OUTWARD VOYAGE
3 August to 10 October 1492

In the Name of Our Lord Jesus Christ

ost Christian, exalted, excellent, and powerful princes, King and Queen of the Spains and of the islands of the sea, our Sovereigns: It was in this year of 1492 that Your Highnesses concluded the war with the Moors who reigned in Europe. On the second day of January, in the great city of Granada, I saw the royal banners of Your Highnesses placed by force of arms on the towers of the Alhambra, which is the fortress of the city. And I saw the Moorish king come to the city gates and kiss the royal hands of Your Highnesses, and those of the Prince, my Lord. Afterwards, in that same month, based on the information that I had given Your Highnesses about the land of India and about a Prince who is called the Great Khan, which in our language

means "King of Kings," Your Highnesses decided to send me, Christopher Columbus,[1] to the regions of India, to see the Princes there and the peoples and the lands, and to learn of their disposition, and of everything, and the measures which could be taken for their conversion to our Holy Faith.

I informed Your Highnesses how this Great Khan and his predecessors had sent to Rome many times to beg for men learned in our Holy Faith so that his people might be instructed therein, and that the Holy Father had never furnished them, and therefore, many peoples believing in idolatries and receiving among themselves sects of perdition were lost.

Your Highnesses, as Catholic Christians and Princes devoted to the Holy Christian faith and to the spreading of it, and as

Los principes muy eccellentes de castilla y de aragon.

enemies of the Muslim sect and of all idolatries and heresies, ordered that I should go to the east, but not by land as is customary. I was to go by way of the west, whence until today we do not know with certainty that anyone has gone.

Therefore, after having banished all the Jews[2] from all your Kingdoms and realms, during this same month of January Your Highnesses ordered me to go with a sufficient fleet to the said regions of India. For that purpose I was granted great favors and ennobled; from then henceforward I might entitle myself *Don* and be High Admiral of the Ocean Sea and Viceroy and perpetual Governor of all the islands and continental land that I might discover and acquire, as well as any other future discoveries in the Ocean Sea. Further, my eldest son shall succeed to the same position, and so on from generation to generation for ever after.

I left Granada on Saturday, the 12th day of the month of May in the same year of 1492 and went to the town of Palos, which is a seaport. There I fitted out three vessels, very suited to such an undertaking. I left the said port well supplied with a large quantity of provisions and with many seamen on the third day of the month of August in the said year, on a Friday, half an hour before sunrise. I set my course for the Canary Islands of Your Highnesses, which are in the Ocean Sea, from there to

Columbus at the court of Ferdinand and Isabela. (Giraudon/Art Resource)

embark on a voyage that will last until I arrive in the Indies and deliver the letter of Your Highnesses to those Princes, and do all that Your Highnesses have commanded me to do.

To this end I decided to write down everything I might do and see and experience on this voyage, from day to day, and very carefully. Also, Sovereign Princes, besides describing each night what takes place during the day, and during the day the sailings of the night, I propose to make a new chart for navigation, on which I will set down all the sea and lands of the Ocean Sea, in their correct locations and with their correct bearings. Further, I shall compile a book and shall map everything by latitude and longitude. And above all, it is fitting that I forget about sleeping and devote much attention to navigation in order to accomplish this. And these things will be a great task.

----

1. The transcription reads, *"pensarō de embiarme a mi xpōual Colon."* ("You thought of sending me, Cristóval Colón"). Inasmuch as Columbus never signed his name in this conventional form, some believe that the entire Prologue was written by Las Casas. It is more reasonable to assume that Las Casas inserted the name when he made his abstract.

2. The General Edict on the expulsion of the Jews from Spain was actually issued on March 31, 1492. This complicated situation, which evolved over the course of many years, is carefully analyzed by Simon Wiesenthal in *The Secret Mission of Christopher Columbus.*

A 16th century mariner navigating with a cross-staff. The cross-staff is an ancient instrument for measuring the altitude of stars and sun, probably Near Eastern in origin. The main staff is calibrated, and a shorter staff, perpendicular to it, is moved along it until the horizon line and celestial lines meet at the base. The angle of the celestial body is then read from the scale. (Culver Pictures)

A 15th century ship, with lines suggestive of the Santa Maria. *First illustrated Latin edition of the* Carta de Colón, *Basel, 1493. (Courtesy Rare Book Division, New York Public Library, Astor, Lenox, and Tilden Foundations)*

Friday, 3 August 1492

We set sail on this third day of August, 1492, at 8 o'clock[1] in the morning, from the bar of Saltes. The wind is strong and variable, and we had gone 45 miles to the south by sunset. After dark I altered course for the Canary Islands, to the SW and south by west.

---
1. In the Prologue, Columbus states that he departed Palos "half an hour before sunrise." Apparently, he had to await high tide to clear the bar of Saltes, at the mouth of the Odiel-Tinto rivers.

Saturday, 4 August 1492

We went SW by south.

Sunday, 5 August 1492

I held the same course to the SW by south and made more than 120 miles.

Monday, 6 August 1492

The rudder of the *Pinta*, in which Martín Alonso Pinzón was traveling, slipped from its socket. I believe this was deliberately caused by Gómez Rascón[1] and the owner of the caravel, Cristóbal Quintero. Neither of these men wanted to make this voyage, and even before we departed Palos they had attempted to delay or prevent the enterprise. All the time they were complaining and concocting excuses for not sailing.

Columbus departing Spain and the sovereigns. Honorius Philoponus, Nova typis transacta
Navigatio, *Venezia, 1621. (Courtesy Rare Book Division, New York Public Library, Astor,
Lenox, and Tilden Foundations)*

PART ONE THE OUTWARD VOYAGE *3 August to 10 October 1492*

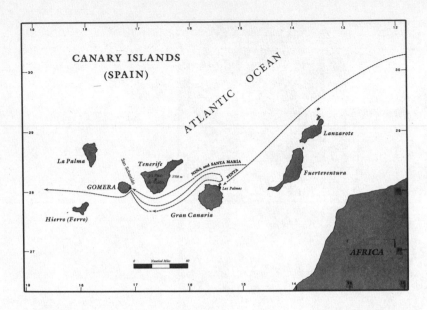

Tuesday, 7 August 1492

Today the wind blew very hard, and the ropes holding the *Pinta*'s rudder broke. We were again delayed while makeshift repairs were made. Martín Alonso wanted to go directly to the island of Lanzarote, but I ordered him to proceed to Grand Canary. We made 75 miles today between day and night.

Wednesday, 8 August 1492

The pilots of the three ships disagreed as to where we were this morning, but I came closest to the truth. I decided to go to Grand Canary and leave the *Pinta* there, for she was badly disabled and leaking. I wanted to obtain another ship there if possible, but was unable to fetch Grand Canary this day.

Thursday, 9 August 1492

(The Log entry for this day includes events up to 6 September 1492. Additional material from the Log for these days is taken from Fernando's Historie. Some data are interpolations by the author.)

The *Pinta* was able to reach Grand Canary this morning, where I ordered Martín Alonso to remain until the caravel could be repaired properly or replaced. I took the *Santa María* and, with the *Niña*, set out for Gomera. I told Martín Alonso that if I could find another ship at Gomera, I would return with it. If I cannot find another vessel, I will come back in a few days and assist with the repairs.

I cannot reach Gomera today because of contrary winds and long periods of calm.

The heavy sea prevented me from helping without danger to myself, but I was able to come alongside the *Pinta* and hearten the crew. I was relieved to learn what a resourceful captain I had in Martín Alonso Pinzón, who is an experienced and ingenious man. He has been able to temporarily repair the rudder with some ropes in order that we might proceed. Despite the trouble with the *Pinta* we were able to make 87 miles last night and today.

----

1. Gómez Rascón was an able seaman from Palos, who some scholars once thought was half-owner of the *Pinta*. This was because of a poor translation of the Las Casas abstract.

Friday, 10 August 1492
I am unable to reach Gomera because of calms.

Saturday, 11 August 1492
I have been becalmed for two days and am still unable to reach Gomera, though I can see it in the distance.

Sunday, 12 August 1492
Today—Praise be to God!—I arrived at Gomera and sent a boat ashore.

Monday, 13 August 1492
The boat returned from Gomera this morning with the bad news that no ship is available on the island, but that the island's mistress, Doña Beatriz[1] de Peraza y Bobadilla, is expected to return momentarily from Grand Canary with a 40-ton ship. This vessel, owned by a man from Sevilla named Grajeda, would be perfect for my needs.

----

1. Doña Beatriz was the young widow of Hernando Peraza, governor of Gomera. Upon his death at the hands of rebelling natives, she became governor.

Tuesday, 14 August 1492
There has been no ship from Grand Canary, and I am compelled to lie at anchor, biding my time.

Wednesday, 15 August 1492
Today a brig departed Gomera for Grand Canary, and I seized the opportunity to send a man to assist Martín Alonso with the repair of the *Pinta*'s rudder. I wrote Martín a note, saying that I would have gone myself if the *Santa María* were not such a bad sailer. I also informed Martín of our location and told him that we were waiting anxiously for his arrival.

Thursday, 16 August 1492
I passed yet another day at anchor, still with no sign of Doña Beatriz.

Friday, 17 August 1492
Two weeks have passed since our departure from Palos, and the crew has become restive. I am beginning to fear for the safety of Doña Beatriz. I am also wondering why Martín is taking so long.

Saturday, 18 August 1492
I went ashore today to determine if some other ship might be available to me, but none of the few craft at Gomera is capable of a voyage of any length over the open sea. I must accept those things that I cannot control.

Sunday, 19 August 1492
A special mass was said today for the safe return of Martín Alonso and Doña Beatriz. My enterprise is in God's hands.

Monday, 20 August 1492
I have determined to wait three more days for word from Martín on Grand Canary. If I have heard nothing by then, I shall sail there with the *Santa María* and *Niña*.

Tuesday, 21 August 1492
I still have had no message from Grand Canary.

Wednesday, 22 August 1492
We remain at anchor, awaiting word from Grand Canary.

Thursday, 23 August 1492
If no ship arrives by sundown, I shall depart tomorrow with my two ships for Grand Canary. It is essential that we sail west soon. The crew is uneasy, for tomorrow will make three weeks since departing Palos.

Friday, 24 August 1492
At break of day I weighed anchors, and the *Niña*, and I in the *Santa María*, departed Gomera for Grand Canary. By midday we overtook the brig that had sailed from Gomera on the 15th. It had been delayed by contrary winds and had made no headway for more than a week. I took my man aboard who was carrying the message to Martín, and by Divine Providence the wind shifted and we made some progress.

I passed this night near Tenerife, where the great volcano on that island erupted in a fiery display. Many members of the crew were astonished and frightened, for they had never seen such an occurrence. I calmed them by telling about Mount Etna in Sicily and other volcanoes that I have observed, and I explained to them the cause of this great fire.

Saturday, 25 August 1492
I reached Grand Canary this morning at the hour of nine and had no difficulty locating Martín and the *Pinta*. He had not repaired the rudder, a fact that disturbs me somewhat. I am still of the opinion that Gómez Rascón and the *Pinta*'s owner, Cristóbal Quintero, are reluctant to make this journey and have done everything possible to delay or even prevent it.

I learned that Doña Beatriz had sailed for Gomera on Monday the 20th, and I cannot explain why her ship did not reach Gomera before we departed that island. God must have planned it that way. If I had been able to obtain her ship, there would have been still another delay in preparing it for the long voyage and in transferring supplies from the *Pinta* to it.

I have determined that the most efficient action is to make a new rudder for the *Pinta*. Also, I have determined that the *Niña* should be square-rigged as the other ships and have ordered the lateen sails altered. This will enable the *Niña* to follow the other ships more closely and safely in the belt of the easterlies. These winds blow steadily from the east or NE every day of the year, and a square-rigged ship has every advantage in these latitudes. We will return from the Indies with the westerly winds, which I have observed firsthand in the winter along the coast of Portugal and Galicia. When I sailed to England with the Portuguese some years ago, I learned that the westerlies blow year-round in the higher latitudes and are as dependable as the easterlies, but in the opposite direction.

"I passed this night near Tenerife, where the great volcano on that island erupted in a fiery display."

PART ONE THE OUTWARD VOYAGE *3 August to 10 October 1492*

« 59 »

Sunday, 26 August 1492

Martín Alonso and his men have no good excuse for making such little progress with the *Pinta*. I am aware that there are few facilities on Grand Canary, but sometimes one must make do with what is at hand. I placed Maestro Diego, boatswain on the *Santa María,* in charge of constructing a new rudder. He is a good man who quickly assembled the most experienced carpenters in the fleet and set about his task with great enthusiasm. I was pleased to find that Juan Pérez Viscaino had recaulked the *Pinta,* and the leaks were completely sealed.

Monday, 27 August 1492

The work proceeds well; I should be able to sail in three or four days. I assigned another group to rerig the *Niña.* Vincente Yáñez Pinzón, captain of the *Niña,* questioned this decision, but I was able to convince him that it was more efficient for sailing westward in the belt of the easterlies.

Tuesday, 28 August 1492

All repairs move apace.

Wednesday, 29 August 1492

The rigging of the *Niña* was completed this afternoon. Once Vincente accepted my decision, he threw himself into the project totally and surprised me with his determination and skill.

Thursday, 30 August 1492

The rudder is almost finished. Praise God!

Friday, 31 August 1492

All repairs to the *Pinta*'s rudder were completed by midday. In the afternoon I ordered the anchors hoisted, and the fleet sailed for Gomera, where I had left a detachment of men to gather fresh supplies for the voyage. Our unexpected delay has forced us to consume many of the provisions placed on board in Palos.

Saturday, 1 September 1492

The weather is good, and a fresh breeze is behind us. Also, the current is helping. We should make Gomera early tomorrow.

Sunday, 2 September 1492

I arrived this morning in Gomera without incident. There are many fine Spaniards on this island, including Doña Beatriz de Pedraza y Bobadilla, the mistress of the island. These Spaniards swear under oath that every year they see land to the west, where the sun sets. I remember that when I was in Portugal, in 1484, a man came from the island of Madeira to ask the King for a caravel to go to the land that he had seen in the west. Also, people in the Azores say that they see land to the west every year. All these people see this land to the west under the same conditions and report it to be about the same size.

Monday, 3 September 1492

When I went to Grand Canary to help Martín Alonso with his rudder, I left a dozen men on Gomera under the command of

Pedro Gutiérrez. As an officer of the royal household, he is most experienced in obtaining supplies and is well qualified in the areas of food acquisition and storage.

Gutiérrez has already acquired all the wood and water necessary for the voyage, which I estimate will last 21 days. However, to be on the safe side, in case of contrary winds or currents, I ordered Gutiérrez to prepare for a voyage of 28 days. I anticipate no problem in replenishing our supplies when we reach the Indies.

Some of our provisions have already been assembled, such as salt, wine, molasses, and honey, but others are being prepared and will not be ready for loading until tomorrow and Wednesday.

Tuesday, 4 September 1492

Today we loaded and stored dried meat and salted fish and some fruits. The fruit will have to be consumed early, for it will spoil if the voyage is of three weeks' duration. We will load the biscuits tomorrow. Their preparation has been slow, for Gomera does not have the facilities found in Spain and Portugal. The Portuguese have wonderful facilities for provisioning ships, but they have had many years' experience. Everything considered, I have no complaints about the assistance I have received from the people of Gomera.

Wednesday, 5 September 1492

The ships have been loaded, and all is ready for the voyage. Tonight I shall order a special service of thanksgiving; at sunrise I will lift anchors to begin the journey westward.

Thursday, 6 September 1492

Shortly before noon I sailed from the harbor at Gomera and set my course to the west. I am somewhat disturbed by word I received this morning from the captain of a caravel that came to Gomera from the island of Hierro.[1] He reported that a Portuguese squadron of three caravels is in the vicinity of Hierro, apparently with orders to prevent me from departing the Canaries. There could be some truth in this, for King John[2] must be angry that I went over to Castile. I sailed all day and night with very little wind; by morning I find myself between Gomera and Tenerife.

----

1. *Hierro* ("iron") is the Spanish name, but the Portuguese *Ferro* is more often used on charts today. Columbus always used *Hierro*.

2. King John II of Portugal (João II). Spain and Portugal were at peace, but the Portuguese would have been concerned with a Spanish expedition to their West African claims. This may have been the reason why there was a Portuguese squadron in the area.

Friday, 7 September 1492

I have been becalmed all this day and night, until 3 o'clock in the morning.

Saturday, 8 September 1492

At 3 o'clock this morning the NE wind began to blow, and I set my course to the west. The *Santa María* took in so much water forward that my progress was impeded, and I only made 27 miles last night and today.

Sunday, 9 September 1492

(Most of this entry [except for course, speed and distance notations] has been interpolated from Fernando's Historie.*)*

This day we completely lost sight of land, and many men sighed and wept for fear they would not see it again for a long time. I comforted them with great promises of lands and riches. To sustain their hope and dispel their fears of a long voyage, I decided to reckon fewer leagues than we actually made. I did this that they might not think themselves so great a distance from Spain as they really were. For myself I will keep a confidential accurate reckoning.

Tonight I made 90 miles at a speed of 7½ knots. The helmsmen steered badly, letting the ship get off course to the west by north and even to the WNW. I reprimanded them several times for this.

Monday, 10 September 1492

Today I made 180 miles at a speed of 7½ knots. I recorded only 144 miles in order not to alarm the sailors if the voyage is lengthy.

Tuesday, 11 September 1492

I held to my westward course and made 60 miles or more. I saw a large piece of a ship's mast from a vessel of at least 120 tons. I tried to haul it aboard but was not able to. Tonight I made another 60 miles, but recorded only 48 miles.

Wednesday, 12 September 1492

I continued to the west and made, by day and night, 99 miles, again reckoning less.

Thursday, 13 September 1492

I sailed 99 miles, but recorded 10 less, holding my course to the west by day and by night. The currents are contrary. At sunset the needles of our compasses declined to the NW, and in the morning they declined to the NE.

Friday, 14 September 1492

I sailed day and night to the west for 60 miles. I logged somewhat less. The men of the *Niña* saw a tern and a ringtail,[1] two birds that are never seen over 75 miles from land.

----

1. *Rabo de junco* in the Log.

Saturday, 15 September 1492

I sailed to the west day and night for 81 miles, or more. Early this morning I saw a marvelous meteorite fall into the sea 12 or 15 miles away to the SW. This was taken by some people to be a bad omen, but I calmed them by telling of the numerous occasions that I have witnessed such events. I have to confess that this is the closest that a falling star has ever come to my ship.

Sunday, 16 September 1492

I sailed day and night to the west and must have gone about 117 miles, but I logged only 108. There were a few storm clouds today, and it drizzled. The weather is like April in Andalucía, with mild breezes, and the mornings are a delight. The only thing lacking is the call of the nightingales. We have begun to see large patches of yellowish-green weed, which seems to have been torn away from some island or reef. I know that the weed has not come from the mainland because I make the mainland to be farther on.

Monday, 17 September 1492

I held my course to the west and made, day and night, 150 miles or more, but I only logged 141 miles. I have a favorable current. I saw a great deal of weed[1] today—weed from rocks that lie to the west. I take this to mean that we are near land. The weed resembles stargrass, except that it has long stalks and shoots and is loaded with fruit like the mastic tree. Some of this weed looks like river grass, and the crew found a live crab in a patch of it. This is a sure sign of land, for crabs are not found even 240 miles from shore.

The sea is less salty by half[2] than it is in the Canaries, and the breezes are more gentle. Everyone is cheerful, and the *Pinta*, the fastest sailing vessel, went ahead as fast as it could in order to sight land. We saw a lot of porpoises, and the men of the *Niña* killed one with a harpoon. All the indications of land come from the west, where I trust Almighty God, in whose hands are all victories, will soon deliver us to land. This morning I also saw another ringtail—a white bird with a long plumed tail—a bird that is not accustomed to sleeping on the sea.

Last night the pilots took a reading on the North Star and found that the compasses declined to the NW a full point. This caused some apprehension at the moment, but I ordered the north to be fixed again just before sunrise, and the needles were found to be true. This is because the North Star moves, not the compasses.[3]

----

1. Columbus was entering the Sargasso Sea; any weed of the genus *Sargassum* is called "sargasso weed" or simply "sargassum."

2. There is no basis for this comment.

3. This is correct, because in 1492 *Polaris* prescribed a circle around the north celestial pole, with a radius of 3 degrees 27 minutes. Today the radius is 00 degrees 78 minutes and will be closest to the north celestial pole in 2100 AD.

Tuesday, 18 September 1492

I sailed day and night more than 165 miles, but I recorded only 144 miles. The sea has been as smooth as the river at Sevilla. Martín Alonso Pinzón, who had sailed ahead yesterday in the *Pinta,* a very fast sailer, lay-to for me to come up. He told me that he saw a great flight of birds moving westward. He hoped to sight land last night; that is why he was going so fast. He is a fine captain and very resourceful, but his independence disturbs me somewhat. I trust that this tendency to strike out on his own does not continue, for we can ill afford to become separated this far from home.

He tells me that at sundown he saw land about 45 miles to the north, covered by darkness and clouds. A number of the crew urged me to change course for the north from the west and search for this land, but my calculations do not indicate that land is in that direction, and I am not going to waste time with it. I have sailed for 11 days under a full sail, running ever before the wind, but tonight the wind freshened to the point that I ordered the topsails taken in.

Wednesday, 19 September 1492

The wind of last night has left us, and today we are almost becalmed. I sailed only 75 miles between day and night, and I logged 66. At 10 o'clock this morning a tern flew over the ship, followed by others in the afternoon. These birds do not go more than 60 miles from land. I ordered soundings to be taken but could not find bottom with 20 fathoms of line.[1] The currents are setting to the SW, and it has started to rain without wind, which is a sure sign of land.

Martín Alonso Pinzón continues to urge me to look for land to the north, which he says he saw. According to my charts there are islands in that direction, and also to the south, and I am sailing between them. It is my desire to go directly to the Indies and not get sidetracked with islands that I shall see on the return passage, God willing. The weather is good.

I ordered our pilots to calculate our position. Juan Niño of the *Niña* reckoned that we are 1,320 miles west of the Canaries; Cristóbal García Salmiento of the *Pinta* calculated 1,260 miles. My pilot, Sancho Ruíz, figured 1,200 miles.

----
1. The "20 fathoms of line" is from Fernando, who actually said "200 fathoms." Twenty is more realistic.

Thursday, 20 September 1492

Today I changed course for the first time since departing Gomera because the wind was variable and sometimes calm. I first sailed west by north and then WNW, making 21 or 24 miles. About 10 o'clock in the morning two terns flew over the ship, and a little while later another one came. The men caught a bird like a tern, except it was black, with a white tuft on its head, and it had webbed feet. Very early this morning three little birds flew over the ship, singing as they went, and flew away as the sun rose. This was a comforting thought, for

"I have sailed for 11 days, running ever before the wind."

unlike the large water birds, these little birds could not have come from far off. The sailors caught a little fish, and we saw much weed of the kind I have already mentioned, even more than before, stretching to the north as far as you can see. In a way this weed comforted the men, since they have concluded that it must come from some nearby land. But at the same time, it caused some of them great apprehension because in some places it was so thick that it actually held back the ships. Since fear evokes imaginary terrors, the men thought that the weed might become so thick and matted that there might happen to them what is supposed to have happened to St. Amador, when he was trapped in a frozen sea that held his ship fast. For these reasons we kept as clear as possible from those mats of weed. Later in the day I saw another tern that came from the WNW and flew to the SE. This is a sure sign that land lies to the NNW because these birds sleep ashore and go to sea in the morning in search of food, and they do not fly 60 miles.

Friday, 21 September 1492

Today was mostly calm, but there was a little wind later in the afternoon. By night and by day I made about 39 miles, some of them on course and some not. At sunrise we saw so much weed that the sea seemed to be a solid mat, coming from the west. The sea is as smooth as a river and the air the best in the world. This afternoon I saw another ringtail and a tern. I also saw a whale, which is another sign of land, for whales always stay near the coast.

Saturday, 22 September 1492

I sailed to the WNW more or less, steering first one way and then the other. I made about 90 miles and saw very little weed during the morning hours. I did see some petrels and another bird. For three days now I have been deviating from my set course to the west, but this is of no great concern, for the winds are contrary and have been blowing mostly from the SW and even from the west. Also, these contrary winds are very helpful because the crew is agitated, thinking that no winds blow in these parts that will return them to Spain. Later in the afternoon the weed was very thick.

Sunday, 23 September 1492

I sailed NW and sometimes NW by north, and sometimes on my original westerly course, making about 66 miles. I saw a dove, a tern, another small river bird, and some white birds. There is a lot of weed and I have seen more crabs in it. The crew is still grumbling about the wind. When I get a wind from the SW or west it is inconstant, and that, along with a flat sea, has led the men to believe that we will never get home. I told them that we are near land and that is what is keeping the sea smooth. Later, when the sea made up considerably without wind, they were astonished. I saw this as a sign from God, and it was very helpful to me. Such a sign has not appeared since Moses led the Jews out of Egypt, and they dared not lay violent hands on him because of the miracle that God had wrought. As with Moses when he led his people out of captivity, my people were humbled by this act of the Almighty. Soon thereafter a wind arose from the WNW, and the sea grew rougher. The crew was relieved. The men tried to catch some fish but could not get any to bite at the hooks. Eventually they harpooned several.

Monday, 24 September 1492

I returned to my westerly course and made about 43½ miles, logging only 36. A tern came to the ship, and I saw many petrels.

I am having serious trouble with the crew, despite the signs of land that we have and those given to us by Almighty God. In fact, the more God shows the men manifest signs that we are near land, the more their impatience and inconstancy increases, and the more indignant they become against me. All day long and all night long those who are awake and able to get together never cease to talk to each other in circles, complaining that they will never be able to return home. They have said that it is insanity and suicidal on their part to risk their lives following the madness of a foreigner. They have said that not only am I willing to risk my life just to become a great Lord, but that I have deceived them to further my ambition. They have also said that because my proposition has been contradicted by so many wise and lettered men who considered it vain and foolish, they may be excused for whatever might be done in the matter. Some feel that they have already arrived where men have never dared to sail and that they are not obliged to go to the end of the world, especially if they are delayed anymore and will not have sufficient provisions to return. I am told by a few trusted men (and these are few in number!) that if I persist in going onward, the best course of action will be to throw me into the sea some night. They will then affirm that I fell overboard while taking the position of the North Star with my quadrant.[1] Since I am a foreigner, little or no account will be asked of the matter, but rather, there will be a great many who will swear that God had given me my just desserts on account of my rashness. I know that the men are taking these complaints to the Pinzóns and that the Pinzóns have sided with them.

Inasmuch as most of these people are from Palos and the surrounding area, they stick together, and I know that Martín Alonso cannot be trusted. He is a skilled mariner, but he wants the rewards and honors of this enterprise for himself. He is always running ahead of the fleet, seeking to be the first to sight land. But I am fully aware that I must use him, for his support is too great among the men. I am also confident that if I lose command, the fleet will never reach the Indies and will probably never get back to Spain. With God's help I shall persevere.

----

1. An "improved," lightweight mariner's astrolabe. For a more extensive discussion of navigation in Columbus' time, see Prologue.

Tuesday, 25 September 1492

It was very calm this morning, but later the wind blew. I maintained a course to the west until sunset. I talked with Martín Alonso, captain of the *Pinta,* about a chart I had sent to him three days ago. On it I had drawn certain islands and he agreed that we were in that region. Since we have not seen any of these islands, I feel that it is because the currents are driving us to the NE and that we might not have gone as far as the pilots say. I had Martín send the chart back to me by a line, and I worked with my pilot to establish our true position. At sunset Martín mounted the stern of the *Pinta* and with great joy called to me that he saw land and claimed the reward. When I heard this stated so positively, I fell to my knees to give thanks to Our Lord, and Martín said *Gloria in excelsis Deo* with his people. My people did the same thing, and the *Niña's* crew all climbed the mast and rigging, and all claimed that it was land. At the moment I myself was sure that it was land and reckoned that it was about 75 miles to the SW. It was getting dark as I changed course to the SW. I had only made 13½ miles today up until dark, but added another 51 miles tonight on our new course to the SW.[1] All told, we had gone about 65 miles, but I told the people we had only made 39 miles. The

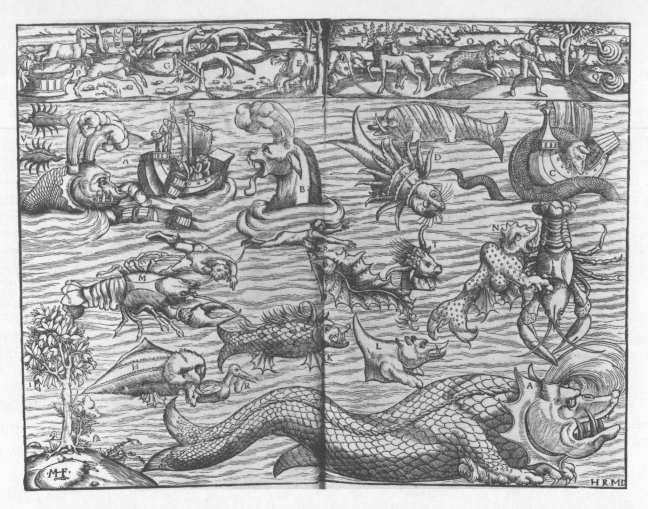

Woodcut of imaginary sea monsters from Cosmographia. *Sebastian Munster, 1550. (The British Library)*

sea is very smooth and some of the men went swimming. I saw many dorados and other fish.

----

1. The Log entry is "17 leagues (51 NM) to the SE." The course was SW, and this is a mistranscription. Las Casas also adds 4½ and 17 leagues and gets 21.

Wednesday, 26 September 1492

After sunrise[1] I realized that what we all thought was land last evening was nothing more than squall clouds, which often resemble land. I returned to my original course of west in the afternoon, once I was positive that what I had seen was not land. Day and night I sailed 93 miles, but recorded 72. The sea was like a river and the air sweet and balmy.

----

1. On the 25th, the course was SW, in the belief a squall line was land. On the 26th the error was discovered, and the original course to the west was resumed. Las Casas reverses these directions for the 26th, which is nonsensical.

Thursday, 27 September 1492

I stayed on course to the west, making 72 miles by day and night but logging only 60. Many dorados came to the ships. The men killed one. I also saw another ringtail.

Friday, 28 September 1492

I sailed to the west for 42 miles or more, but reckoned only 39. Day and night we have had calm spells. I saw very little seaweed and we caught two dorados; the other ships caught more.

Saturday, 29 September 1492

I sailed on to the west, making 72 miles by day and night, but told the crew 63 miles. I made little progress between day and night because of calms. This morning I saw a frigate bird, which makes terns vomit what they have eaten and then catches it in midair. The frigate bird lives on nothing else, and even though it is a sea bird, it does not alight on the water and never is found more than 60 miles from land. I have seen many of them in the Cape Verde Islands. A little later I saw two more terns and many flying fish. They are about a foot long and have two little wings like a bat. These fish sometimes fly above the water at about the height of a lance, rising in the air like an harquebus[1] shot. Sometimes they fall on our ships. The sea is as smooth as a river, and the breeze is delightful and pleasing; only the nightingales are lacking. On three different occasions I saw terns and another frigate bird. There is also more weed.

----

1. A gun with a flaring barrel.

Sunday, 30 September 1492

I kept my course to the west, day and night, making only 42 miles because of calms, but I told the crew 33. Four ringtails came to the ship, and the fact that they flew together has made the crew believe that land must be near. Later, four terns passed, and I saw many emperor fish, which resemble a fish called *chopo* in that they have a very hard skin and are unfit to eat. There is quite a lot of weed. I am surprised to find that the Guards[1] are near the arm on the west at night but at daybreak appear below the arm to the east. If this observation is correct, it appears that I only proceeded three lines last night, or nine astronomical hours. At nightfall the compass needle declined to the NW by a point, but at dawn it was right on the North Star. This is because the needle points true, but the star rotates. For some reason my pilots do not understand this phenomenon, and it makes them agitated and confused. These variations make them quite apprehensive, especially on a voyage of this length into strange regions. My explanation has only partly allayed their fears.

----

1. The brightest two stars in the Little Dipper, used in Columbus' day as a primitive yet effective means of telling time. For a more extensive discussion on Medieval timetelling see Prologue.

Monday, 1 October 1492

I sailed onward to the west for 75 miles, but reckoned 60. At sunrise a tern flew over the ship, and a pair flew over at 10 o'clock. It rained very hard this morning. The pilot of the *Santa María* calculated that we were 1,734 miles west of Hierro; my corrected figure that I gave him was 1,752 miles. My personal calculation shows that we have come 2,121 miles. I did not reveal this figure to the men because they would become frightened, finding themselves so far from home, or at least thinking they were that far.

Tuesday, 2 October 1492

I held course to the west night and day for 117 miles, but reckoned to the crew 90. The sea is smooth and favorable. Many thanks be given to God. Seaweed is coming from the east to the west, contrary to what we have been experiencing. There are many fish, and the crew killed one. I also saw a white bird that looked like a gull.

Wednesday, 3 October 1492

I maintained my westward course and made 141 miles, but told the men 120. There is more weed, but it is withered and appears old. There is a little fresh weed that bares something like fruit. I did not see any birds this morning and believe that I have left them astern in the islands that I have depicted on my chart and that I have passed. I could have visited those islands last week, but did not want to delay by beating windward because they were not my objective. My goal is the Indies, and it would make no sense to waste time with offshore islands.

This afternoon I assembled the pilots for another estimate of our position. The *Niña's* pilot claimed the distance made good west of Hierro is 1,620 miles; he of the *Pinta*, 1,902 miles. Allowing for the distance covered since my pilot gave me an estimate on Monday, these values are too low, for we have almost always had a stiff wind to our backs. I calculate that we have come at least 2,379 miles.

Thursday, 4 October 1492

I sailed west and between day and night made 189 miles, but reckoned 138. More than 40 petrels came to the ship at one time, along with two terns. A boy on the caravel hit one of them with a stone. A frigate bird came to the ship and a white bird that looked like a gull. So many birds are a sure sign that we are near land.

Friday, 5 October 1492

I continued to the west, at a speed of about 8¼ knots, and made some 171 miles between day and night, but reckoned 135. The wind abated somewhat during the night. The sea is pleasant and calm. Many thanks be given to God. The air is balmy and mild and there is no weed. There are many birds, especially petrels, and many flying fish flew aboard the ship.

Saturday, 6 October 1492

I maintained my course to the west and made 120 miles between day and night, but told the people 99. This evening Martín Alonso Pinzón told me that he thought it would be wise to steer to the SW by west in order to reach the island of Japan, which is marked on the chart that I had shown him. In my opinion it is better to continue directly west until we reach the mainland. Later we can go to the islands on the return voyage to Spain. My decision has not pleased the men, for they continue to murmur and complain. Despite their grumblings I held fast to the west.

Sunday, 7 October 1492

I sailed to the west and made 9 knots for 2 hours and then 6 knots for 8½ hours. I went about 69 miles up until an hour before sunset, but told the crew 54.

This morning we saw what appeared to be land to the west, but it was not very distinct. Furthermore, no one wished to make a false claim of discovery, for I had ordered that if anyone make such a claim and, after sailing three days, the claim proved to be false, the 10,000 *maravedíes*[1] reward promised by the Catholic Sovereigns would be forfeited, even if afterwards he actually did see it. Being warned of this, no one aboard the *Santa María* or *Pinta* dared call out "Land, land!" However, after we had rendezvoused this morning at sunrise (I had ordered that we assemble at sunrise and sunset because that is when there is the least haze and we can see the farthest) the *Niña*, which is a better sailer, ran ahead and fired a cannon and ran up a flag on her mast to indicate that land had been sighted. Joy turned to dismay as the day progressed, for by evening we had found no land and had to face the reality that it was only an illusion. God did offer us, however, a small token of comfort: many large flocks of birds flew over, coming from the north and flying to the SW. They were more varied in kind than any we had seen before and they were land birds, either going to sleep ashore or fleeing the winter in the lands whence they came. I know that most of the islands discovered by the Portuguese have been found because of birds. For these reasons I have decided to alter course and turn the prow to the WSW. This I did an hour before sunset, and I shall proceed on this course for two days. I added another 15 miles before darkness, making a total of 84 miles by night and by day.

---

1. 10,000 *maravedíes* equals about $540.

Monday, 8 October 1492

I sailed to the WSW, making only 35 miles day and night. The sea is like the river of Sevilla, thanks be to God. The air is as balmy as in April in Sevilla, and it is so fragrant that it is a pleasure to breathe it. Very fresh weed has been seen, and there are many land birds flying to the SW, one of which we caught. We have seen gulls, ducks, and a tern.

Tuesday, 9 October 1492

I continued on my new course to the SW and made 15 miles. The wind shifted, and I ran west by north for 12 miles. I then sailed for another 33 miles. All told, by day and night I went a little more than 60 miles, but told the men that we had gone 51 miles. All night long we heard birds passing. We must be very close to landfall, thanks be to God.

Wednesday, 10 October 1492

I held course to the WSW, running 7½ knots, and at times 9 knots, and for awhile 5¼ knots. Between day and night I made 177 miles. I told the crew 132 miles, but they could stand it no longer. They grumbled and complained of the long voyage, and I reproached them for their lack of spirit, telling them that, for better or worse, they had to complete the enterprise on which the Catholic Sovereigns had sent them. I cheered them on as best as I could, telling them of all the honors and rewards they were about to receive. I also told the men that it was useless to complain, for I had started out to find the Indies and would continue until I had accomplished that mission, with the help of Our Lord..

PART TWO

THE DISCOVERY OF THE BAHAMAS
11 October to 27 October 1492

Thursday, 11 October 1492

sailed to the WSW, and we took more water aboard than at any other time on the voyage. I saw several things that were indications of land. At one time a large flock of sea birds flew overhead, and a green reed was found floating near the ship. The crew of the *Pinta* spotted some of the same reeds and some other plants; they also saw what looked like a small board or plank. A stick was recovered that looks manmade, perhaps carved with an iron tool. Those on the *Niña* saw a little stick covered with barnacles. I am certain that many things were overlooked because of the heavy sea, but even these few made the crew breathe easier; in fact, the men have even become cheerful. I sailed 81 miles from sunset yesterday to sunset today. As is our custom, vespers were said in the late afternoon, and a special thanksgiving was offered to God for giving us renewed hope through the many signs of land He has provided.

After sunset I ordered the pilot to return to my original westerly course, and I urged the crew to be ever-vigilant. I took the added precaution of doubling the number of lookouts, and I reminded the men that the first to sight land would be given a silk doublet as a personal token from me. Further, he would be given an annuity of 10,000 maravedíes from the Sovereigns.

About 10 o'clock at night, while standing on the sterncastle, I thought I saw a light to the west. It looked like a little wax candle bobbing up and down. It had the same appearance as

"This afternoon the people of San Salvador came swimming to our ships and in boats made from one log."

a light or torch belonging to fishermen or travellers who alternately raised and lowered it, or perhaps were going from house to house. I am the first to admit that I was so eager to find land that I did not trust my own senses, so I called for Pedro Gutiérrez, the representative of the King's household, and asked him to watch for the light. After a few moments, he too saw it. I then summoned Rodrigo Sánchez of Segovia, the comptroller of the fleet, and asked him to watch for the light. He saw nothing, nor did any other member of the crew. It was such an uncertain thing that I did not feel it was adequate proof of land.

The moon, in its third quarter, rose in the east shortly before midnight. I estimate that we were making about 9 knots and had gone some 67½ miles between the beginning of night and 2 o'clock in the morning. Then, at two hours after midnight, the *Pinta* fired a cannon, my prearranged signal for the sighting of land.

I now believe that the light I saw earlier was a sign from God and that it was truly the first positive indication of land. When we caught up with the *Pinta,* which was always running ahead because she was a swift sailer, I learned that the first man to sight land was Rodrigo de Triana, a seaman from Lepe.

I hauled in all sails but the mainsail and lay-to till daylight. The land is about 6 miles to the west.

Friday, 12 October 1492
(Log entry for 12 October is combined with that of 11 October.)

At dawn we saw naked people, and I went ashore in the ship's boat, armed, followed by Martín Alonso Pinzón, captain of the *Pinta,* and his brother, Vincente Yáñez Pinzón, captain of the *Niña.* I unfurled the royal banner and the captains brought the flags which displayed a large green cross with the letters F and Y at the left and right side of the cross. Over each letter was the appropriate crown of that Sovereign. These flags were carried as a standard on all of the ships. After a prayer of thanksgiving I ordered the captains of the *Pinta* and *Niña,* together with Rodrigo de Escobedo (secretary of the fleet),

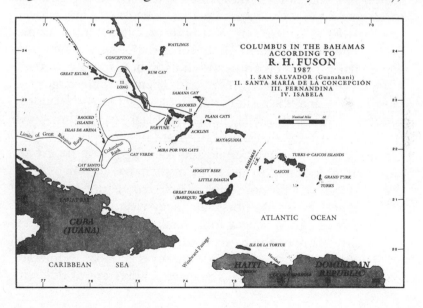

and Rodrigo Sánchez of Segovia (comptroller of the fleet) to bear faith and witness that I was taking possession of this island for the King and Queen. I made all the necessary declarations and had these testimonies carefully written down by the secretary. In addition to those named above, the entire company of the fleet bore witness to this act. To this island I gave the name *San Salvador*,[1] in honor of our Blessed Lord.

No sooner had we concluded the formalities of taking possession of the island than people began to come to the beach, all as naked as their mothers bore them, and the women also, although I did not see more than one very young girl. All those that I saw were young people, none of whom was over 30 years old. They are very well-built people, with handsome bodies and very fine faces, though their appearance is marred somewhat by very broad heads and foreheads, more so than I have ever seen in any other race. Their eyes are large and very pretty, and their skin is the color of Canary Islanders or of sunburned peasants, not at all black, as would be expected because we are on an east-west line with Hierro in the Canaries. These are tall people and their legs, with no exceptions, are quite straight, and none of them has a paunch. They are, in fact, well proportioned. Their hair is not kinky, but straight, and coarse like horsehair. They wear it short over the eyebrows, but they have a long hank in the back that they never cut. Many of the natives paint their faces; others paint their whole bodies; some, only the eyes or nose. Some are painted black, some white, some red; others are of different colors.

The people here called this island *Guanahaní* in their language, and their speech is very fluent, although I do not understand any of it. They are friendly and well-dispositioned people who bare no arms except for small spears, and they have no iron. I showed one my sword, and through ignorance he grabbed it by the blade and cut himself. Their spears are made of wood, to which they attach a fish tooth at one end, or some other sharp thing.

I want the natives to develop a friendly attitude toward us because I know that they are a people who can be made free and converted to our Holy Faith more by love than by force. I therefore gave red caps to some and glass beads to others. They hung the beads around their necks, along with some other things of slight value that I gave them. And they took great pleasure in this and became so friendly that it was a marvel. They traded and gave everything they had with good will, but it seems to me that they have very little and are poor in everything. I warned my men to take nothing from the people without giving something in exchange.

This afternoon the people of San Salvador came swimming to our ships and in boats made from one log. They brought us parrots, balls of cotton thread, spears, and many other things, including a kind of dry leaf[2] that they hold in great esteem. For these items we swapped them little glass beads and hawks' bells.

Many of the men I have seen have scars on their bodies, and when I made signs to them to find out how this happened, they indicated that people from other nearby islands come to San Salvador to capture them; they defend themselves the best they can. I believe that people from the mainland come here to take them as slaves. They ought to make good and skilled servants, for they repeat very quickly whatever we say to them. I think they can easily be made Christians, for they seem to have no religion. If it pleases Our Lord, I will take six of them to Your Highnesses when I depart, in order that they may learn our language.

----

1. Samana Cay. For a more extensive discussion of the various landfall theories, see Epilogue.

2. The "dry leaves" are not actually mentioned until the October 15 entry. At that time Columbus tells us that these highly prized dry leaves were offered to him on 12 October. It is reasonable, then, that the tobacco was part of "the many other things" cited in the Log entry.

Saturday, 13 October 1492

After sunrise people from San Salvador again began to come to our ships in boats fashioned in one piece from the trunks of trees. These boats are wonderfully made, considering the country we are in, and every bit as fine as those I have seen in Guinea. They come in all sizes. Some can carry 40 or 50 men; some are so small that only one man rides in it. The men move very swiftly over the water, rowing with a blade that looks like a baker's peel. They do not use oarlocks, but dip the peel in the water and push themselves forward. If a boat capsizes they all begin to swim, and they rock the boat until about half of

"I showed one my sword, and through ignorance he grabbed it by the blade and cut himself."

the water is splashed out. Then they bail out the rest of the water with gourds that they carry for that purpose.

The people brought more balls of spun cotton, spears, and parrots. Other than the parrots, I have seen no beast of any kind on this island.

I have been very attentive and have tried very hard to find out if there is any gold here. I have seen a few natives who wear a

Indians paddling a dugout canoe. (Benzoni, 1581)

little piece of gold hanging from a hole made in the nose. By signs, if I interpret them correctly, I have learned that by going to the south, or rounding the island to the south, I can find a king who possesses a lot of gold and has great containers of it. I have tried to find some natives who will take me to this great king, but none seems inclined to make the journey.

Tomorrow afternoon I intend to go to the SW. The natives have indicated to me that not only is there land to the south and SW, but also to the NW. I shall go to the SW and look for gold and precious stones. Furthermore, if I understand correctly, it is from the NW that strangers come to fight and capture the people here.

This island is fairly large and very flat. It is green, with many trees and several bodies of water. There is a very large lagoon[1] in the middle of the island and there are no mountains. It is a pleasure to gaze upon this place because it is all so green, and the weather is delightful. In fact, since we left the Canaries, God has not failed to provide one perfect day after the other.

I cannot get over the fact of how docile these people are. They have so little to give but will give it all for whatever we give them, if only broken pieces of glass and crockery. One seaman gave three Portuguese *ceitis* (not even worth a penny!) for about 25 pounds of spun cotton. I probably should have forbidden this exchange, but I wanted to take the cotton to Your Highnesses, and it seems to be in abundance. I think the cotton is grown on San Salvador, but I cannot say for sure because I have not been here that long. Also, the gold they wear hanging from their noses comes from here, but in order not to lose time I want to go to see if I can find the island of Japan.

When night came, all of the people went ashore in their boats.

----

1. The Log states: ". . . *y muchas aguas y una laguna en medio*

muy grande. . . ." The word is *laguna* (lagoon), not *lago* (lake). Columbus probably meant that the island had many small lakes and ponds (*muchas aguas*) and a saltwater lagoon in the middle ("halfway," "in between") on the coast he was on. This description fits Samana, not Watlings.

Sunday, 14 October 1492

At daybreak I ordered the small boats to be made ready, that is, put in tow behind, and I went along the island to the NNE, to see the other part of the east and the villages. Soon I saw two or three of them, and the people came to the beach, shouting and praising God. Some brought us water; others, things to eat. Others, seeing that I did not care to go ashore, jumped into the sea and swam out to us. By the signs they made I think they were asking if we came from Heaven. One old man even climbed into the boat we were towing, and others shouted in loud voices to everyone on the beach, saying, "Come see the men from Heaven; bring them food and drink." Many men and women came, each one with something. They threw themselves on the sand and raised their hands to the sky, shouting for us to come ashore, while giving thanks to God. I kept going this morning despite the pleas of the people to come ashore, for I was alarmed at seeing that the entire island is surrounded by a large reef. Between the reef and the island it remained deep, and this port is large enough to hold all the ships of Christendom. There are a few shoal spots, to be sure, and the sea in it moves no more than water in a well. I found a very narrow entrance, which I entered with the ship's boat.

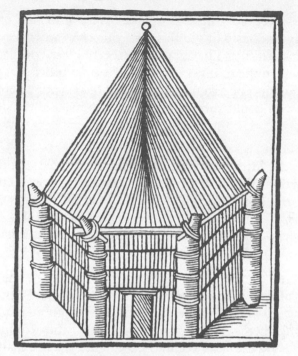

Indian house. (Oviedo, 1547)

I kept moving in order to see all of this so that I can give an account of everything to Your Highnesses. Also, I wanted to see if I could find a suitable place to build a fort. I saw a piece of land that looked like an island, even though it is not, with six houses on it. I believe that it could be cut through and made into an island in two days. I do not think this is necessary, however, for these people are very unskilled in arms. Your Highnesses will see this for yourselves when I bring to you the seven[1] that I have taken. After they learn our language I shall return them, unless Your Highnesses order that the entire population be taken to Castile, or held captive here. With 50 men you could subject everyone and make them do what you wished.

Next to the little peninsula, which looks like an island, there are groves of the most beautiful trees I have ever seen. They are as green and leafy as those of Spain in the months of April and May. And there are many ponds and lakes nearby. Also, I saw what looks like an abandoned quarry, but it is natural.

I inspected the entire harbor before returning to the ship. I made sail and saw so many islands that I could not decide where to go first. The men whom I had captured made signs indicating there were so many islands that they could not be counted, and they named, in their language, more than a hundred. All the islands I saw were level and most of them are inhabited. Finally, I looked for the largest island and decided to go there. It is probably 15 miles from San Salvador, though some of the other islands are nearer, some farther. Since it was getting late, I knew that I could not reach the island before sunset, and decided to lay-to until dawn tomorrow.

----

1. The entry for 12 October said six. Columbus is inconsistent on this point.

Monday, 15 October 1492
(The entries for 15–16 October are confused in the original Log. Both appear to have been written late on the 16th.)

I had lain-to last night for fear of approaching the shore in the dark and because I did not know if the coast were clear of rocks, and at dawn I intended to haul in sail. I discovered that the island was nearer to 21 miles from San Salvador than my first estimate of 15 miles, and the tide detained me. I did not reach the island until noon.

The coast that faces San Salvador lies in a north-south line and extends for 15 miles. The other coast, which I followed, runs east and west, and is more than 30 miles long. Having sighted from this island another larger one to the west, I hauled in the sails, for I had sailed all day until night; otherwise I would not have been able to reach the western cape. To this island I gave the name *Santa María de la Concepción*.[1]

I anchored at sunset near the cape in order to find out if there was any gold there. The men from San Salvador told me that people on this island wear big golden bracelets on their arms and legs. I really did not believe them but think they made up the tale in order to get me to put ashore so that they could escape. Nevertheless, I did stop, for I have no desire to sail strange waters at night. It is not my wish to bypass any island without taking possession, although having taken one you can claim them all.

----

1. Literally, Saint Mary of the Conception. Probably the north coast of Acklins-Crooked, which is the correct length. Morison

----

Tuesday, 16 October 1492

At daybreak I went ashore in the small boat. People met us on the beach. There were many people, and they went naked and in the same condition as those of San Salvador. They let us go anywhere we desired and gave us anything we asked.

I decided not to linger very long at Santa María de la Concepción, for I saw that there was no gold there and the wind freshened to a SE crosswind. I departed the island for the ship after a two hours' stay. Just as I was preparing to board the ship, a big dugout came alongside the *Niña*, and one of the men from San Salvador jumped overboard and escaped in it. This is the second such incident, for in the middle of last night another man leaped into the sea and escaped by dugout. Some of the men went after the boat last night, but there was no way they could catch up to it, even though they were armed. Those boats go very swiftly.

This morning some men of my company tried to catch the second dugout, but again, it outran them. They found it abandoned on the beach, and the men in it fled like chickens. The sailors brought the boat back to the *Niña*, to which had come still another boat with one man in it. He had come from another cape and wanted to trade a ball of cotton. Some sailors jumped into the sea and seized him because he would not come aboard the caravel. Watching all this from the poopdeck, I sent for him. I gave the man a red cap and some little beads of green glass, which I placed on his arm, and two hawks' bells, which I placed on his ears. I also ordered the men of the *Niña* to return his dugout and sent him ashore. I did not take the ball of cotton, even though he wished to give it to me. I could see that he was surrounded by people when he reached shore, and they held it a great marvel and were convinced that we were good people. I wanted them to think that the men who had fled had done us some harm and that was why we were carrying them along with us. Thus I used him for these reasons and gave him all the aforesaid articles in order that the people might hold us in such esteem that on some other occasion when Your Highnesses send men back here they will be well treated. All that I gave him was not worth two cents.

Not only was there a shifting wind and no gold here, I was also afraid that all the men from San Salvador would escape if I did not move on and get farther away. I wanted to go to another large island that I determined lay to the west.[1]

Judging by the clouds and the signs made by the men from San Salvador, this large island to the west was about 27 miles distant. They said that there is a lot of gold there and that the people wear it on their arms, legs, ears, noses, and necks. I do not know if this is another ruse of theirs or not, for I am beginning to believe that all they want to do is escape and they will tell me anything I want to hear.

I ordered the *Niña* to cast adrift the dugout its sailors had brought from the beach, and I departed at 10 o'clock in the morning, or maybe a little later. The wind was veering SE and south, but the sea was calm. We had been sailing west for three or four hours toward that large island when we came upon a man in a dugout. He, too, was passing from Santa María de la Concepción to that other island. He carried a bit of bread about the size of your fist and a gourd full of water. Also, he had a lump of bright red earth[2], which was powdered and kneaded, and some of those dry leaves which are much valued by these people, for they brought some to me on San Salvador as a gift. Also, he carried a basket of the style made here, in which he had a string of glass beads and two Spanish coins. These were things that I had given out at San Salvador, so I knew he had come from there and was going to the large island I saw in the west.

He came alongside the ship and I brought him aboard, as he requested. I had his boat hoisted to the deck and ordered his possessions to be guarded, after which I gave him some of our bread and honey and drink. I will take him to the very large island that has appeared in the west and to which we are going, and then I will give him back all his things. In this way he will give a good account of us when, please be Our Lord, Your Highnesses send other men here. Those who come will be made welcome and given all that they need.

The sea was very smooth, and I sailed all this day with calms. We arrived at the island just at sunset. It was too dark to see

Indian canoe. (Oviedo, 1547)

the bottom in order to find a clear place, and it is necessary to be very careful in order not to lose the anchors. The beaches are all clear, without boulders, but there are some rocks underwater near the shore, and you must keep your eyes peeled when you wish to anchor and not anchor too near shore. The water is very clear and you can see the bottom during the daylight hours, but a couple of lombard shots[3] offshore there is so much depth that you cannot find bottom. On this side of the island the coast runs NW-SE. I decided to lay-to until daylight tomorrow, but I allowed the man we had taken in mid-channel to take his dugout and go ashore.

----

1. The large island to the west was Long Island, which Columbus named *Fernandina*, for King Ferdinand. Long Island cannot be seen from Crooked Island, but it is usually covered with a bank of cumulus clouds, a certain island-indicator.

2. The "bright red earth" (*tierra bermeja*) may have been dough made from the sweet potato. *Bermeja* may also be translated as reddish, light brown, or ginger-colored.

3. A *lombard* (lombarda) was a small canon with a range of about 300 yards. Two lombard shots equals about 600 yards.

Wednesday, 17 October 1492

At first light I moved the ships closer to shore and anchored at a cape near a small village. It was to this village that the man we brought from mid-channel had gone last night. And he must have given a good account of us, for no sooner had we anchored than dugouts began to come to the ships. They brought us water and all manner of things. As was my custom, I ordered each person to be given something, if only a few beads; 10 or 12 glass ones that cost a penny or two, and some eyelets for lacing shirts and shoes. They found these things to be of great value. I also gave them honey when they came aboard.

At 9 o'clock in the morning I sent the ship's boat ashore for water, and those on the island, with very good will, showed my people where the water was. They even carried the full casks to the boat and took great delight in pleasing us.

I named this island *Fernandina*.[1] It is very big and about 24 miles due west of Santa María de la Concepción. This entire part of the island where I am anchored runs NNW-SSE. It appears that this coast I am on runs for 21 miles or more,[2] and I saw 15 miles of it, but it did not end there. It is very level without any mountains. These islands are very green and fertile and the air is balmy. There are many things that I will probably never know because I cannot stay long enough to see everything. I must move on to discover others and to find gold. Since these people know what gold is, I know that with our Lord's help I cannot fail to find its source.

Fernandina is very large and I have determined to sail around it. Although I know that Japan is to the south or SW, and that I am about to take a detour, I understand that there is a mine of gold either in Fernandina or near it. Now, as I am writing this, I have made sail with the wind from the south, in order to sail around the whole island and work my way to a place the people here call *Samoet*[3] in their tongue. This is either an island or a city where there is gold, as all those on board have told me and as I heard also on the islands of San Salvador and Santa María.

All the people I have seen so far resemble each other. They have the same language and customs, except that these on Fernandina seem to be somewhat more domestic and tractable, and more subtle, because I notice that when they bring cotton and other things to the ship they drive a harder bargain than those of the first islands visited. And also, on Fernandina I saw cotton clothes made like short tunics. The people seem better disposed, and the women wear a small piece of cotton in front of their bodies, though it barely covers their private parts. I do not recognize any religion in the people, and I believe that they would turn Christian quickly, for they seem to understand things quite well.

This is a very green, level, and fertile island, and I have no doubt that the people sow and reap grain, and also many other things, year around. I saw many trees quite different from ours. Many of them have branches of different kinds, all on one trunk;[4] one twig is of one kind and another of another,

Fernãdº rex hyspania

King Fernando, after whom the island of Fernandina was named.
(First illustrated Latin edition of the Carta de Colón, *Basel, 1493)*

and so different from each other that it is the greatest wonder of the world. How great is the diversity of one kind from the other. For example, one branch has leaves like cane, another like mastic; thus on one tree five or six kinds, and all so different. Nor are these grafted so that one can say that the graft does it, for these trees are right there in the woods, and the people do not take care of them.

Here the fishes are so unlike ours that it is amazing; there are some like dorados, of the brightest colors in the world—blue, yellow, red, multi-colored, colored in a thousand ways; and the colors are so bright that anyone would marvel and take a great delight at seeing them. Also, there are whales. I have seen no land animals of any sort, except parrots and lizards—although a boy told me that he saw a big snake. I have not seen sheep, goats, or any other beasts, but I have only been here a very short time—half a day—yet if there were any, I could not have failed to have seen some. The circumnavigation of this island I shall write about after I have done it.

I left this village at noon—the place where I was anchored and where I took in water—to sail around this island of Fernandina. The wind was SW and south, and I wanted to follow the coast of this island to the SE because it all runs NNW-SSE, and the Indians[5] whom I had aboard (and another from whom I got instructions) told me that a southerly course leads to the island they call Samoet, where the gold is. Furthermore, Martín Alonso Pinzón, captain of the caravel *Pinta*, on whose ship I had placed three of the San Salvador Indians, came to

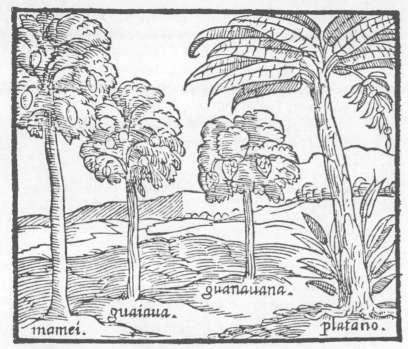

New World fruit trees: Mamey *(Mammea americana),* Guayaba *(Psidium guajava),* Guanabána *(Annona muricata),* Plátano *(Musa paradisiaca). (*Benzoni, Historia del Mondo Nuovo, *1572)*

After I had sailed six miles from the island's cape where I had been anchored, I discovered a very wonderful harbor with one entrance,[6] or rather, one may say two entrances, for there is an island in the middle. Both passages are very narrow, but once within, the harbor itself is wide enough for 100 ships. I did not think that either the entrance or the harbor was deep enough, however, nor did I feel that the bottom was clear of rocks. It seemed reasonable to me to look it over well and take soundings, so I anchored outside and went in with the small boats. It was fortunate that I did, for there was no depth at all. I did find what looked like a small river, and I ordered casks to be broken out to get water. On shore I found eight or 10 men who took us to a nearby village. I waited in the village for some two hours while my men—some armed and some with casks—went for the water.

During this time I walked among the trees, which are the most beautiful I have ever seen. I saw as much greenery, in such density, as I would have seen in Andalucia in May. And all of the trees are as different from ours as day is from night, and so are the fruits, the herbage, the rocks, and everything. It is true that some of the trees are like those in Castile, but most of them are very different. There are so many trees of so many different kinds that no one can say what they are, nor compare them to those of Castile.

The people on Fernandina are the same as the others already mentioned: of the same condition, usually nude, of the same stature, and willing to give what they had for whatever we

me and told me that one of them very definitely had led him to believe that Fernandina would be easier to circumnavigate by going NNW. Since the wind was not helping me to take the SE course that I wished, but was good for the other, I set sail to the NNW.

gave them. Some of the ships' boys traded broken glass and bowls to them for spears. The others that had gone for the water told me that they had been in the houses and found them very simple but clean, with beds and furnishings that were like nets[7] of cotton.

The houses look like Moorish tents, very tall, with good chimneys. But I have not seen a village yet with more than 12 or 15 houses. I also learned that the cotton coverings were worn by married women or women over 18 years of age. Young girls go naked. And I saw dogs: mastiffs and pointers. One man was found who had a piece of gold in his nose, about half the size of a *castellano*,[8] and on which my men say they saw letters. I scolded them because they would not exchange or give what was wanted, for I wished to see what and whose money that was, but they answered me that the man would not barter for it.

After taking on water, I returned to the ship and sailed to the NW until I had explored all that part of the island as far as the coast that runs east-west. The Indians on board began to say that this island was smaller than Samoet, and that it would be a good idea to turn around to get there sooner. The wind went calm, then began to blow from the WNW, which was contrary to the way we had come. I turned and sailed all this night to the ESE, sometimes due east and sometimes to the SE. I had to do this to keep clear of land, for there were heavy clouds and the weather was very threatening. But there was little wind and I was unable to approach land to anchor. Later it rained very hard from midnight to daylight, and it is still cloudy and threatening. We will go to the SE cape of the island, where I hope to anchor until it clears up. It has rained every day since I have been in these Indies, some times more, some less. Your Highnesses may rest assured that this land is the best and most fertile and temperate and level and good that there is in the world.

----

1. Long Island.

2. The Log states that the coast of Fernandina extended for more than 28 leagues (84 NM) and that Columbus saw 20 leagues (60 NM) of it. Sighting distances and time allowances make these distances impossible. On 12 known occasions, Las Casas wrote *leagues* in the abstract and then crossed the word out, substituting *miles*. It appears as though Columbus logged miles in the original Log and Las Casas converted these references to leagues. There is a good possibility here that Las Casas did not catch his own error, and that the original read 28 miles and 20 miles.

3. Fortune Island and (possibly) the SW part of Crooked Island; also called *Saometo* in the Log. The Indians may have been referring to the entire Ackins-Crooked-Fortune group.

4. There is no such tree, but Columbus may have seen a complex community of epiphytes and vines amidst the trees.

5. First use of term Indians (*Indios*) for native inhabitants.

6. Little Harbour, Long Island.

7. Columbus' first reference to hammocks, though he had almost certainly seen them before on San Salvador.

8. Half of a gold *ducat*, worth about $10.

Thursday, 18 October 1492

After it cleared up, I followed the wind and sailed around the island as far as I could. When it was too dark to sail, I anchored and did not go ashore.

Friday, 19 October 1492

At daybreak I hauled in the anchors and sent the caravel *Pinta* to the ESE and the caravel *Niña* to the SSE; with my own ship I went to the SE. I gave orders that these courses should be followed until noon, and at that time the *Pinta* and *Niña* should alter courses and join me if land was not sighted. Before we had sailed three hours we saw an island to the east, for which we steered, and before midday all three ships reached a small island at the north point. There is a rocky reef at this island that runs to the north, and between the reef and the large island to the north is another island. The men on board from San Salvador called this large island Samoet, but I gave it the name *Isabela*.[1]

The wind was still blowing from the north, and this small island is east of Fernandina, from which I had departed. To the NE[2] of this small island there is a great bay and many wooded places that are thick and extensive. I wanted to anchor

Portrait of Queen Isabela by Masson, Madrid, 1865. (Fiske, 1902)

in that bay and go ashore and see such beauty, but the water is shallow and I could not anchor.

The coast trends west for 12 miles from the small island[3] to a cape, and as the wind was favorable for coming to this cape, I have done so. I have named it *Cabo Hermoso*,[4] and beautiful it is. It is round and the water is deep, with no shoals offshore.

As I approached the harbor, I found some rocks and shoals at the entrance, but within, it is a sandy beach like most of this coast. I anchored here this night, Friday.

This island is one of the most beautiful I have ever seen; if the others are beautiful, then this is more so. Of what I have seen so far, the coast is almost all sandy beach. It has many large, beautiful, green trees. The island is a little higher than the others I have seen, and there is a large hill, nothing that can be called a mountain, that adds to the beauty. There are many lakes and ponds in the middle of the island.

I think that this Cabo Hermoso is on an island separate from Isabela, which the natives call Samoet, and there may even be another island between it and Isabela. I do not really care to know such detail, for I could never see it all in fifty years anyhow. I merely want to see and discover as much as possible before returning to Your Highnesses, Our Lord willing, next April. It is true, however, that should I find gold or spices in abundance, I would delay my return to Spain until I have gathered as much as possible. Accordingly, I can do nothing more than press on and try to find these things.

I simply do not know where to go next. I never tire from looking at such luxurious vegetation, which is so different from ours. I believe that there are many plants and trees here that could be worth a lot in Spain for use as dyes, spices, and medicines, but to my great sorrow I do not recognize them.

You can even smell the flowers as you approach this coast; it is the most fragrant thing on earth.

Tomorrow before I depart, I am going ashore to explore. There is no village on the coast, but the men from San Salvador tell me there is one further inland where there is a king with a lot of gold. Tomorrow I am going to find that village and talk with that king. According to the signs the Indians make, he is lord of all the neighboring islands, and he wears clothes and many golden adornments. I do not hold much faith in what they tell me, for I have been fooled before. It is possible, however, that there is a lord who wears a little bit of gold, for these Indians are so poor that any gold trinket would seem like a fortune to them.

----

1. Southern Crooked island and probably including Fortune Island; named for Queen Isabela.

2. The Log uses the word *angla*, which is used eight times during the voyage. Four times it means *cape*; four times, *bay*. Columbus was referring to the Bight of Acklins.

3. The Log reads "12 leagues to the west," but this is impossible. If the coast extended west for 12 leagues (36 miles), Columbus would have seen it on the approach from Fernandina; furthermore, he would have run aground on it when later he sailed SW for Cuba. This is another example of Las Casas transposing leagues and miles. The coast trended for 12 miles, and to the SW, not west.

4. Beautiful Cape, probably the westernmost cape of Fortune Island.

Saturday, 20 October 1492

Today I weighed anchors at sunrise and departed Cabo Hermoso. I thought that I might sail around the island to the NE and to the east, from the SE and south, where I am told by the men with me that there is a settlement and its king. But the bottom is so shallow that I cannot enter or sail to the village. I saw that if I followed a SW course, it would be a very long way around, so for this reason I decided to return by the way I had come, to the NNE from the west part, and sail around the island from there. The SW cape of the island of Saometo I named *Cabo de la Laguna*.[1]

Because of the wind I could only sail at night, and I did not dare approach the coast in the dark. The *Pinta* and the *Niña* did anchor near the coast, but I stayed clear and lay-to all night, even though they made signals as they were accustomed to do and thought I would anchor, but I did not wish to.

----
1. Cape of the Lagoon, probably at the SE tip of Fortune Island.

Sunday, 21 October 1492

At 10 o'clock in the morning I arrived at *Cabo del Isleo*[1] and anchored, as did the other two ships. After having eaten, I went ashore and found no settlement except one house. I found no one; the inhabitants must have fled in fear, for all their housewares were left behind. I did not permit my men to touch a thing, and I went with my captains to see the island. If the other islands are very green and beautiful and fertile,

this is much more, with great and green groves of trees. There are some large lakes and above and around them is the most wonderful wooded area. The woods and vegetation are as green as in April in Andalucía, and the song of the little birds might make a man wish never to leave here. The flocks of parrots that darken the sun and the large and small birds of so many species are so different from our own that it is a wonder. In addition, there are trees of a thousand kinds, all with fruit according to their kind, and they all give off a marvelous fragrance. I am the saddest man in the world for not knowing what kind of things these are because I am very sure that they are valuable. I am bringing a sample of everything I can.

While going around one of the lagoons I saw a serpent,[2] which we killed with lances, and I am bringing Your Highnesses the skin. When it saw us, it went into the lagoon, and we followed it in because the water is not very deep. This serpent is about 6 feet long. I think there are many such serpents in these lagoons. The people here eat them and the meat is white and tastes like chicken.

I recognized the aloe[3] here, and tomorrow I am going to have 1,000 pounds of it brought to the ship because they tell me that it is very valuable. Also, while looking for good water, we stumbled onto a settlement about two miles from where we are anchored. When the people sensed our coming, they left their houses and fled, hiding their clothing and other things they had in the woods. I did not allow my men to take anything, not even something the value of one pin. Eventually

Iguana. (Oviedo, 1547)

sail around Isabela until I find the king and see if I can get from him the gold which I hear that he wears. Then I shall sail for another great island which I strongly believe should be Japan, according to the signs made by the San Salvador Indians with me. They call that island *Colba*,[4] where they say there are many great ships and navigators. And from that island I intend to go to another that they call *Bohío*,[5] which is also very large. As to any others that lie in between, I shall see them in passing, and according to what gold or spices I find, I will determine what I must do. But I have already decided to go to the mainland and to the city of Quisay,[6] and give Your Highnesses' letters to the Grand Khan and ask for a reply and return with it.

----

1. "Cape of the Island."

2. An iguana.

3. Columbus was probably confusing *Agave americana* (or one of its close relatives) with either *Aloe vera* or with *lignum aloe*. The former is grown as an ornamental indoor plant that serves as a readily accessible burn remedy. It is native to the Mediterranean area and was certainly known to Columbus. *Lignum aloe* is mentioned by Marco Polo. It is a fragrant, resinous wood used as incense. Columbus used the term *lignaloe*, which is a common name for this wood today.

4. The reference is the first to Cuba, but the name *Cuba* is not used until 23 October.

5. The Indian name for Española.

some of the men came to us, and I gave one of them some hawks' bells and some small glass beads. He left very contented and very happy. And in order that our friendship might grow, and that something be asked of them, I requested water. Later, after I returned to the ship, they came to the beach with their gourds filled and were very delighted to give it to us. I ordered that they be given another string of glass beads, and they said they would return in the morning. I wanted to top off all of the ships' water casks while I had the chance.

If the weather permits, I shall depart this Cabo del Isleo and

Monday, 22 October 1492

I was here all last night and today waiting to see if the king on this island, or some other persons, would bring gold or something else substantial. And there came many of these people, similar to the others on the other islands, also naked and also painted. Some are painted white, some red, some black; others are in different colors. They brought spears and balls of cotton which they traded with some sailors for pieces of glass, broken cups, and pieces of clay bowls. A few brought pieces of gold hanging from their noses, which, with good will, they gave for a hawk's bell or small glass beads. It is so little that it is nothing. But it is true that they will trade anything they have for what little thing we may give them.

These people hold our arrival with great wonder and believe that we have come from heaven. We have been getting our water from a lake near the Cabo del Isleo, and in that lagoon Martín Alonso Pinzón, captain of the *Pinta,* killed another serpent like the one that was killed yesterday. It was about the same length. I have taken as much of the aloe as I could find.

Tuesday, 23 October 1492

I want to leave today for the island of Cuba,[1] which I believe to be Japan, according to the signs these people give of its magnificence and wealth. I do not want to tarry here any longer or explore this island looking for a settlement, even though I had originally planned to do this. I am not going to waste any more time looking for this king or lord, since I know there is no gold mine here. Furthermore, to sail around these small islands would require winds from many directions, and it does not blow that way; usually the wind is from the east or NE. And since I must go where there might be great commerce, it is foolish to delay. I must move on and discover many lands, until I come across a very profitable one. This island of Isabela may have many valuable spices, but I do not recognize them, and this causes me a great deal of sorrow, for I see a thousand kinds of fruit trees, each of which is as green now as in Spain during the months of May and June; there are also a thousand kinds of plants and herbs, and the same with flowers. And I know nothing except this aloe which I am carrying to Your Highnesses in great quantity.

I cannot sail today for Cuba because there is no wind; it is dead calm. It has rained a lot today, as yesterday, but it has not gotten cold; rather, the days are hot and the nights moderate, as in May in Spain and Andalucía.

1. This is the first correct spelling of the Indian name. It is one of the few native place-names that has survived.

Wednesday, 24 October 1492

At midnight I weighed anchors from the island of Isabela, from Cabo del Isleo which is in the north part, in order to go to the island of Cuba, which the Indians tell me is very large and has much commerce; gold, spices, ships, and merchants.

The Indians indicated that I should sail to the SW to get to Cuba, and I believe them because all my globes and world maps seem to indicate that the island of Japan is in this vicinity and I am sure that Cuba and Japan are one and the same.

I sailed all night in the rain to the WSW. At dawn the wind calmed, but the rain continued. There was little wind until past noon, when it began to blow very gently. I set all my sails—mainsail and two bonnets, foresail and spritsail, mizzen and topsail. I even set the sail of the small boat on the poop-deck. Thus I went on course until dusk. And then the green cape of Fernandina,[1] which is on the SW part of that island, bore to the NW 21 miles.

Because the wind blew strongly now, and I did not know how far it might be to Cuba, I did not want to look for it at night. It is very deep off all these islands, there being no bottom at all except at a distance of two cannon shots, and near the land the bottom is dotted with rocks and shoals. One cannot anchor where it is so deep, and one cannot anchor where it is shallow with security, except by sight. I lowered all sails except the foresail and sailed with it. In a little while the wind increased greatly and the ship made great headway on a dubious course. And there was rain and threatening weather. Eventually I had to lower the foresail. I did not make six miles this night.

---

1. South Point, Long Island.

Thursday, 25 October 1492

After sunrise the weather cleared somewhat, and I sailed WSW. By 9 o'clock in the morning I had gone 15 miles. Then I changed course to the west and went at a speed of 6 knots until 1 o'clock and 4½ knots until 3 o'clock, or a total of 33 miles since 9 this morning. At 3 o'clock I saw land. There were seven or eight islands, all in a line from north to south, about 15 miles distant.

Friday, 26 October 1492

I have been anchored about 15 to 18 miles south of those islands that I call the *Islas de Arena*,[1] and it is all shallow between them and me. The Indians indicated that it is a journey of a day-and-a-half from there to Cuba in their dugouts,[2] little boats made of a single log, with no sail.

---

1. Sand Islands, now called the Ragged Islands.

2. The Indian word *canoa* appears in the manuscript, but was probably introduced at this point by Las Casas, not Columbus. See Log entry for October 28.

Saturday, 27 October 1492

I hauled up the anchor at sunrise and departed for Cuba, which I am told is magnificent, with gold and pearls. I am now certain that Cuba is the Indian name for Japan. I made 6 knots from sunrise until 1 o'clock in the afternoon, to the SSW. I added another 21 miles before nightfall on the same course, for a total of 51 miles. Just before sunset I saw land, but it rained so hard that we had to beat about all this night.

PART THREE

THE DISCOVERY OF CUBA
28 October to 5 December 1492

Sunday, 28 October 1492

At sunrise I approached the coast and entered a very beautiful river,[1] which was free from dangerous shoals and other obstructions. The water all along this coast is very deep and clear right to the shore. The mouth of the river I entered is 12 fathoms deep and quite wide enough to beat about in. I anchored inside, at about the distance of one lombard shot.

I have never seen anything so beautiful. The country around the river is full of trees, beautiful and green and different from ours, each with flowers and its own kind of fruit. There are many birds of all sizes that sing very sweetly, and there are many palms different from those in Guinea or Spain. Some are of medium height without any bark at the base, and the leaves are very large. The Indians cover their houses with these leaves. The land is very level.

I took the small boat ashore and approached two houses that I thought belonged to fishermen. The people fled in fear. In one of the houses we found a dog that did not bark,[2] and in both houses we found nets made of palm threads; cords; fish-hooks made of horn; harpoons made from bone; and other fishing materials. There were many fire hearths; and I believe that many people live together in each house. I ordered that not one thing be touched, and thus it was done.

The grass here is as tall as it is in Andalucía in the months of April and May. I found a lot of purslane[3] and wild amaranth.[4]

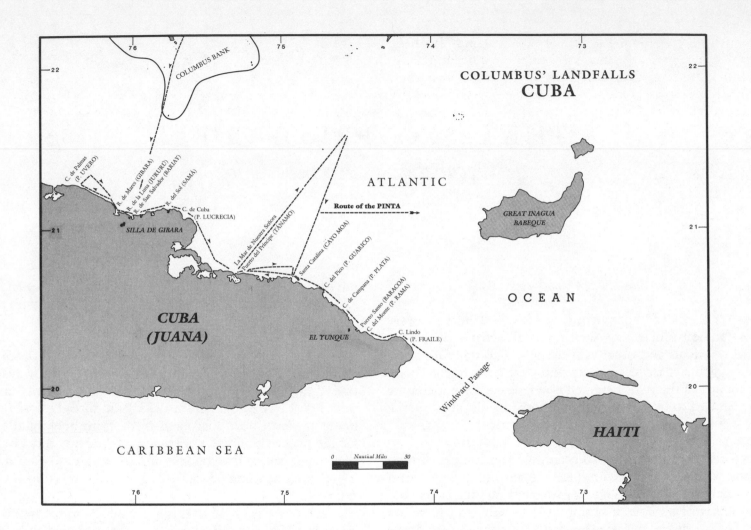

COLUMBUS' LANDFALLS
CUBA

COLUMBUS BANK

ATLANTIC

Route of the PINTA

GREAT INAGUA
BABEQUE

OCEAN

C. de Palmas
(P. UVERO)
R. de Mares (GIBARA)
R. de la Luna (JURURÚ)
R. de San Salvador (BARIAY)
R. del Sol (SAMÁ)
C. de Cuba
(P. LUCRECIA)
SILLA DE GIBARA

La Mar de Nuestra Señora
Puerto del Príncipe (TÁNAMO)
Santa Catalina (CAYO MOA)
C. del Pico (P. GUARICO)
C. de Campana (P. PLATA)
Puerto Santo (BARACOA)
C. del Monte (P. RAMA)
C. Lindo
(P. FRAILE)

*CUBA
(JUANA)*

EL YUNQUE

Windward Passage

HAITI

CARIBBEAN SEA

0   *Nautical Miles*   30

THE LOG OF CHRISTOPHER COLUMBUS

« 94 »

I returned to the boat and went up the river a good distance. It was such a great pleasure to see the verdure and those groves and the birds that it was hard to leave them. This island is the most beautiful I have seen, full of very good harbors and deep rivers, and it appears that there is no tide because the grass on the beach reaches almost to the water, which does not usually happen when there are high tides or rough seas. So far I have not experienced rough seas in any of these islands.

This island is filled with very beautiful mountains, although they are not very long, only high. All the other land is high like Sicily. According to what I can understand from the Indians from Guanahaní that are with me, this land is full of rivers. They told me by signs that there are 10 large rivers and that the island is so large that they cannot circumnavigate it with their canoes[5] in 20 days.

When I first arrived at this river, I sent the small boat ahead to take soundings in order to find the proper place to anchor. Just before the men entered the small boat, two canoes came out to see the ship, but when they saw my men get in the small boat, they fled.

The Guanahaní Indians said that in this island there are mines of gold and pearls. I saw a good place for the pearls and for shellfish, which is an indication of them. I also was given to understand that large ships belonging to the Great Khan came here, and from here to the mainland it is a 10 days' journey. I named this river and harbor *San Salvador.*

---

1. *Bahía de Bariay,* Cuba. The depth and the description positively identify this site.

2. This reference continues to baffle scholars. Some have argued for raccoons, but this seems unlikely, for the Spaniards surely knew a dog when they saw one. Perhaps it is a species now extinct.

3. An herb, used as a salad plant.

4. Pigweed; called *bledo* today, as by Columbus, at least three different species are eaten. One of the amaranths was probably native to Cuba; the plant is indigenous to Central America.

5. *Canoa,* an Arawak word. Columbus may have used it here for the first time, instead of the Spanish term *almadía* (raft or dugout) used earlier. On 26 October both terms are used in the Log, but it appears that Las Casas amended Columbus' words at that point, providing the Indian name.

Monday, 29 October 1492

I weighed anchors this morning to sail westward from this harbor, in order to go to the city where, according to the Indians, the king dwells. One point of the island projected to the NW 18 miles from there. Another point projected to the east 30 miles. After I went three miles, I saw a river with a narrower entrance than the one at San Salvador. To this one I have given the name *Río de la Luna*.[1]

I continued sailing until the hour of vespers, when I saw yet another river, very much larger than the others—or so the Indians told me with signs; near this river were attractive villages of houses. I named this river the *Río de Mares*.[2]

I sent my men in the small boats to a village to talk with the Indians, including in the party one of the Indians from Guanahaní. I did this because the Indians from Guanahaní

"It was such a great pleasure to see the verdure and those groves and the birds, that it was very hard to leave them to return."

already understand these other Indians somewhat, and this would show the people that the Indians with me were pleased with us Christians. Even so, all the men, women, and children fled, abandoning their houses and everything they had. I ordered that nothing left behind be touched.

These houses are more beautiful that any I have seen, and I believe that the nearer I approach the mainland the better they become. They are constructed like pavilions, very large, and look like royal tents in a campsite without streets. One is here and another, there. Inside they are very well swept and clean, and the furnishings are arranged in good order. All are built of very beautiful palm branches.

We found many statues of women and many head-shaped masks, all very well made. It is not known whether the people have them because of their beauty or whether they worship them. There are barkless dogs and in the houses small, wild birds that have been tamed. There are wonderful collections of nets, fishhooks, and other fishing equipment. Not one thing was touched. I believe that all the Indians on this coast are fishermen; because this island is very large, they carry the fish inland.[3]

There are trees with wonderful-tasting fruit. There must be cows and other herds of animals on this island because I saw skulls that look to me like the skulls of cows. There are birds of all sizes and the crickets sing all night, which pleases everyone. The breeze is soft and pleasant at night, neither cold nor warm. It is much warmer on the other islands, but here it is as temperate as May. I think the other islands are hotter because they are so level and the wind blows to them from the south.

The water in the rivers I have seen is salty at their mouths, and I do not know where the Indians get the water they drink, but they have fresh water in their houses.

The ships are able to turn around in this river to enter or leave, and there are good landmarks. The water is seven or eight fathoms deep at the mouth and five within. It seems to me that the sea must always be as calm as the river at Sevilla, and the water suitable for the growth of pearls. I found some large tasteless snails,[4] not like those we have in Spain.

The mountains are beautiful and high, like the *Peña de los enamorados*[5] near Granada. One of them has another little mount at the summit like a beautiful little mosque.[6] Southeast of this river and harbor are two very round mountains, and to the WNW there is a beautiful low cape.

----

1. Moon River (or River of the Moon); now known as *Bahía de Jururú*.

2. *Bahía de Gibara*. Columbus probably named this *Río de Marte* (Mars River, or River of Mars), and *Mares* is an error on the part of either Columbus or the copyist of the original Log. Las Casas questioned this term in his abstract, striking through it once and placing quotation marks around it on another occasion. Las Casas thought it might be *martes* (Tuesday), but it was named on Monday. Mars is logical, for Columbus had just

named one harbor for the moon, and on 12 November he names a neighboring harbor after the sun.

3. Columbus probably means that the coastal fishermen supply the interior people; the latter are too far away to fish because the island is so big.

4. Conchs.

5. Literally, Cliff of the Lovers—"Lover's Leap."

6. The very distinctive *Teta de Bariay,* which helps locate this site.

Tuesday, 30 October 1492

I departed Río de Mares to the NW, and after having gone 45 miles, I saw a cape covered with palms and named it the *Cabo de Palmas.*[1] The Indians who were in the *Pinta* said that behind that cape was a river, from which it was four days' journey to Cuba. The captain of the *Pinta* understood that Cuba was a city, and that it was on the mainland, a very large land that extends far to the north. He also understood that the king of Cuba was at war with the Great Khan, whom they call *Cami* and whose country or city they call *Faba* and many other names.

I intend to approach that river and send a present to the king of this land, as well as the letter from the Sovereigns. I have a sailor who has been on a similar mission in Guinea and some Indians from Guanahaní who want to go with him, so that afterwards they might return home.

I took a reading with the quadrant and Río de Mares is 21 degrees north of the Equator.[2]

I must try to go to the Great Khan, for he is in the vicinity or at the city of Cathay, which is the city of the Great Khan. This is a very great city, according to what I was told before leaving Spain.

This entire country is low and beautiful, and the sea is very deep.

----

1. Palm Cape (Cape of Palms); now known as *Punta Uvero*.

2. Columbus was misreading his quadrant (see Prologue). The Log gives 42 degrees, and there is no way that Columbus thought he was at this latitude. The reading is the arc-tangent of 21 degrees, the correct latitude.

Wednesday, 31 October 1492

All last night I beat to windward and saw a river that I could not enter because the mouth was too shallow. The Indians thought that ships could enter as their canoes did. Sailing onward, I found a cape that extended quite far out and was surrounded by shoals. I saw an inlet or bay where small ships could lie, but I could not reach it because the wind shifted entirely to the north and all the coast extends to the NNW and SE, with yet another cape ahead projecting even farther out. For this reason, and because the sky indicated a squall brewing, I had to return to Río de Mares.

"This evening I took the altitude with my quadrant, and Rio de Mares *is 21 degrees north of the Equator."*

Thursday, 1 November 1492

At sunrise I sent the boats ashore to the houses there and found that all the people had fled. After a while a man appeared. In order to reassure him, I ordered that he should be left alone, and the boats returned. After eating, I sent one of the Indians ashore, who called to the people from a distance, saying that they should not be afraid because the Spaniards were good people who did no harm to anyone. Also, the Indian told them that we were not from the Great Khan; rather, we had given away many of our possessions in the many islands where we had already been. This Indian jumped in and swam ashore, and two of the Indians there took him by the arms and led him to a house, where they questioned him. When they were sure that no harm would come to them, they came out to the ships—16 canoes with spun cotton and other little things of theirs. I ordered that nothing be taken so that they would know that I sought nothing except gold, which they call *nucay*. And thus all day long they came and went from the land to the ships, and my men went to the land in great safety. I did not see any of them with gold, but I did see one of them with a piece of wrought silver hanging from his nose, which indicated that there was silver in the country.

By signs the Indians indicated that within three days merchants would come from inland to buy things from the Christians, and that they would bring news from the king of the country who, according to what I could understand from the signs they made, was distant a four days' journey from there. The Indians had sent many people throughout the country to tell the people about us. These people are of the same type and have the same customs as the others we have found. They have no sect that I know of, for up until now I have not seen any of the Indians I have brought with me make a prayer. Instead, they say the *Salve* and the *Ave María* with their hands raised to Heaven as they are shown, and they make the sign of the cross. Their language is one and they are all friends; I believe that all these islands are friendly with each other. But they are at war with the Great Khan, whom they call *Cavila*,[1] and with the province *Bafan*. They also go naked like the others.

The river is very deep, and the ships can approach the banks at the mouth. The water is not fresh within three miles of the mouth, but upstream of that it is very fresh.

I am certain now that this is the mainland and that I am before Zayto and Quinsay,[2] 300 miles distant, more or less. This is indicated by the sea, which comes in a different manner from how it has come up to now. Yesterday, as I was going NW, I found that it was becoming cold.

----

1. Columbus is having difficulty understanding the Indians. Now he believes the Khan is called *Cavila;* earlier he had thought it was *Camí. Faba,* a region mentioned earlier, is now thought to be called *Bafan.*

2. Zayto (Zaytun) is from Marco Polo and on most 15th century charts. It is probably Zhao'an, China. Quinsay (sometimes Quisay) is modern Hangzhou, China.

Friday, 2 November 1492

I decided to send an embassy into the country, consisting of two Spaniards and two Indians. One of the Christians was Rodrigo de Jérez, from Ayamonte; the other, Luis de Torres,[1] who had lived with the Adelantado of Múrcia and knew how to speak Hebrew, Chaldean, and even some Arabic. With these men I sent one of the Indians from Guanahaní and one from those houses situated on the river here. I gave them strings of beads to trade for something to eat, if necessary, and told them to return within six days' time. I also gave them specimens of spices so that they would recognize the same if they came across them. I instructed them as to how they should ask for the king of that land and what they should say on the part of the Sovereigns of Castile. That is, I told them to explain how the Sovereigns had sent me, in order that I might give to the king, on their behalf, their letters and a gift, and in order that I might learn of his condition and win his friendship. I told my men to tell the king that I would appreciate anything he could do to assist them, especially in learning of certain provinces, harbors, and rivers of which I have information, and how far away these things are.

This evening I took the altitude with my quadrant and find that I am 21 degrees north of the Equator. I have calculated that I have come 1,142 leagues, or 3,426 miles, from the island of Hierro. I am certain that this is the mainland.

----

1. Luis de Torres was a converted Jew, who had served Juan Chacon, the Governor (*Adelantado*) of Múrcia (a province of southern Spain), as the latter's Hebrew interpreter. Múrcia had a large Jewish population, but with the expulsion of the Jews there was no longer need for an interpreter.

Saturday, 3 November 1492

The river here forms a great lake at its mouth, which makes a very remarkable harbor. It is very deep and free from rocks, and there is a good beach to run the ships aground in order to clean the hulls. There is also a great deal of wood.

This morning I took the small boat and went up the river until I reached fresh water, which might be about six miles. I beached the boat and went ashore, climbing a slight elevation in order to learn something about this country, but I could not see anything because of the thick forest, which was very fresh and fragrant. I have no doubt that there are many aromatic herbs here. Everything is so beautiful that the eyes never weary of seeing such a sight, nor could one ever tire of the songs of the birds, both large and small.

Today many canoes came to the ships to trade things made of spun cotton, including the nets in which these people sleep, called hammocks.

Sunday, 4 November 1492

At dawn I took the small boat and went ashore to hunt some of the birds that I had seen the day before. After I returned, Martín Alonso Pinzón came to me with two pieces of cinnamon and said that a Portuguese sailor on his ship had seen an Indian who was carrying two very large handfuls of it, but that he had not dared to trade with him for it because of the prohibition I had placed on trading. He also said that the Indian

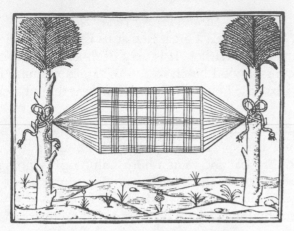

Indian hammock. (Oviedo, 1547)

I also understand that, a long distance from here, there are men with one eye and others with dogs' snouts who eat men. On taking a man they behead him and drink his blood and cut off his genitals.

I decided to return to the ship and await the return of the men I had sent inland before starting to search for those lands to the SE, for my men may bring some good news of what I desire.

These people are very meek and shy: naked, as I have said, without weapons and without government. These lands are very fertile. They are full of *niames,*[1] which are like carrots and taste like chestnuts. They have beans very different from ours, and a great deal of cotton, which they do not sow and which grows in the mountains to the size of large trees. I believe that they can gather it anytime, for I saw pods already open and others just opening, and flowers all on one tree and a thousand other kinds of fruit which I cannot describe, but which should all be very profitable.

---

1. This is the common sweet potato. Later, Columbus is confused by a number of the tubers he encounters. See Epilogue.

---

had some bright reddish things like nuts. The boatswain of the *Pinta* said that he had found trees of cinnamon. I went to see for myself and found that it was not cinnamon. I showed samples of cinnamon and pepper, which I had brought with me from Castile, to some Indians there. They recognized these spices and indicated by signs that there was a great deal of it nearby, toward the SE. I showed them gold and pearls, and certain old men replied that in a place they call *Bohío* there was an infinite amount of gold. They said that people there wore it around the neck, in the ears, and on the arms and the legs, and that they also had pearls. I further understood them to say that there were large ships and merchandise, all of this to the SE.

Monday, 5 November 1492

At dawn I ordered the *Niña* beached in order to clean the hull. I shall do the *Pinta* next and then the *Santa María*. It is my intention that two should remain in service all the time for security reasons, although here people are very safe and I could beach all three ships together without fear.

While the *Niña* was beached, its boatswain came to me to beg a reward for finding mastic.[1] But he did not bring a specimen because he had lost it. I promised him the reward and sent Rodrigo Sánchez and Master Diego to the trees, and they brought a little of it, which I kept to carry to the Sovereigns. I also kept some of the tree, for I knew that it was mastic. Although it must be gathered at the right time of the year, there is enough in this vicinity to procure 50 tons a year. An Indian told me by signs that mastic is good for the stomach-ache. I also found a great deal of aloe.

Puerto de Mares is one of the best harbors in the world, and it has the best climate and the friendliest people. Inasmuch as it has a point formed by a high, rocky hill, a fortress can be built, so that if rich and great things are ever produced in this country the merchants would be secure from any other nations whatsoever. May Our Lord, in whose hands are all victories, ordain all that is for His service.

----

1. Columbus thought that he had found *Pistacia lentiscus,* the mastic familiar to him from the island of Chios. This is a small, evergreen tree that yields an aromatic, astringent resin. It was a principal export from Chios, and of great commercial value. The tree in Cuba was probably the gumbo-limbo (*Bursera simaruba*), with a bright reddish bark and gnarled limbs. This is further evidence that Columbus was a poor botanist.

Tuesday, 6 November 1492

Last night the two men I had sent inland to see the country returned and told me how they had gone 36 miles, to a village of 50 houses where there were a thousand inhabitants, as a great many live in one house. These houses are like very large pavilions.

The Spaniards said that the Indians received them with great solemnity, according to Indian custom, and all the men and women came to see them and lodged them in the best houses. The Indians touched them and kissed their hands and feet in wonderment, believing that we Spaniards came from Heaven, and so my men led them to understand. The Indians gave them to eat what they had.

The men said that on their arrival, the most distinguished persons in the village took them on their shoulders and carried them to the principal house and gave them two chairs in which to sit, and all the Indians seated themselves on the floor around them. These were most peculiar chairs. Each was made in one piece and in a strange shape, resembling a short-legged animal[1] with a tail as broad as the seat. This tail lifted up to make a back to lean against. These seats are called *dujos* or *duchos* in their language.

The Indians who had gone with my men, that is, the one from Guanahaní and the one from here, told the people how the Christians lived and how we were good people. Afterwards

The dress of an Indian woman. (Benzoni, Historia del Mondo Nuovo, 1572)

My men showed the Indians the cinnamon and pepper and other spices I had given them, and they were told by signs that there were many such spices nearby to the SE, but that they did not know if they had those things there in their own village. Having seen that there were no rich cities, my men returned to Puerto de Mares.

If my men had desired to make a place for those who wished to come along, more than 500 men and women would have made the trip because they thought they would be going to Heaven. Three Indians, however, did return with my men: one of the principal men, his son, and one of his men.

I talked with these three Indians and paid them great honor, and one Indian (the principal one) indicated to me that there are many lands and islands in these parts. I wanted to bring these men to the Sovereigns, but I could not interpret what one of them wanted. It appears that he was fearful and wanted to go ashore during the darkness of the night. Since I had my ship beached for maintanence, and not wishing to irritate him, I let him go. He said that he would return at daybreak, but he never did.

On the way inland, my two men found many people who were going to different villages, men and women, carrying a charred, hollow wood in their hands and herbs to smoke in this wood, which they are in a habit of doing. My men did not find a village on the way of more than five houses, and

the men left, and the women seated themselves in the same manner around them, kissing their hands and feet, trying to see if they were of flesh and bone like themselves. The women pleaded with them to stay there longer, at least for five days.

everyone gave them the same welcome. They saw many kinds of trees and grasses and fragrant flowers, as well as many different kinds of songbirds. Except for partridge and nightingales,[2] they were unlike those of Spain. And they saw geese; of these there is a very great number here. They saw no four-footed beasts except dogs that do not bark. The land is very fertile and well cultivated with those niames, beans very different from ours, and panic grass.[3] They saw a great quantity of cotton that had been gathered and spun and worked—in one house alone more than 12,000 pounds of it. Two hundred tons could be had there each year.

I have already mentioned that they apparently do not plant this cotton and that it bears fruit all year. It is very fine and has a large pod.

All that these people have they will give for a very ridiculous price; they gave one great basket of cotton for the end of a leather strap. These people are very free from evil and war. All the men and women are as naked as their mothers bore them. It is true that the women wear a cotton swatch only large enough to cover their private parts and no more. They are modest, nevertheless, and are not as dark as the people of the Canaries.

I have to say, Most Serene Princes, that if devout religious persons knew the Indian language well, all these people would soon become Christians. Thus I pray to Our Lord that Your Highnesses will appoint persons of great diligence in order to bring to the Church such great numbers of peoples, and that they will convert these peoples, just as they have destroyed those[4] who would not confess the Father, Son, and Holy Spirit. And after your days, for we are all mortal, you will leave your realms in a very tranquil state, free from heresy and wickedness, and you will be well received before the Eternal Creator, Whom may it please to grant you a long life and a great increase of larger realms and dominions, and the will and disposition to spread the Holy Christian religion, as you have done up until this time. Amen.

Today I will launch the ship and prepare to depart Thursday, in the name of God, to go to the SE and seek gold and spices and discover land.

---

1. The animal chair was the *dujo*. Several excellent ones are on display in the Museo del Hombre Dominicano, Santo Domingo, Dominican Republic.

2. The partridge (*perdiz*) known to Columbus was *Perdix perdix,* the gray partridge. He may have seen a bobwhite (*Colinus virginanus*). What he thought was a nightingale (*Luscinia megarhyncha*) was actually a mockingbird (*Mimus polyglottos*). There were no geese in Cuba, but it is possible he saw a turkey or even the muscovy duck.

3. Literally, *panizo,* a synonym for millet. The reference is to corn (maize), which was unfamilar to the Spaniards.

4. Columbus is referring to the defeat of the Moors, not to the expulsion of the Jews.

Wednesday, 7 November 1492

(There are no Log entries for 7–11 November. This reconstruction of 7–10 November is derived from Fernando's Historie *and interpolation by the author. November 11 is mostly from the Log entry of 12 November.)*

I was not able to complete caulking and cleaning the caravels, and the wind is contrary. I still intend to depart tomorrow for the SE in search of Bohío.

Thursday, 8 November 1492

Our work on the caravels is not complete, and the winds are still contrary. I therefore have postponed my departure and will remain here until the ships are ready. The wood we have been burning during the caulking is of the mastic tree. Although the leaves and fruit of this tree appear to be those of the lentiscus, the tree here is much larger than the trees on Chios. I ordered many of the trees tapped in order to get resin. I could only get a little bit since it has rained every day, but I am bringing it to Your Highnesses. Also, it may not be the season to tap them. I think it should be done after winter, just as they are about to flower. Here the fruit is almost ripe. There is also a lot of aloe, but it is the mastic that is worth paying attention to, for it is found only on Chios and they derive over 50,000 ducats[1] a year from it, as I recall. The great quantity of cotton here could be sold to the large cities of the Great Khan, which will be discovered.

----

1. Approximately $1,000,000.

Friday, 9 November 1492

The winds are contrary for departing toward the SE and Bohío, which these Indians have indicated by signs to be a very rich land. I went ashore in order to learn more of the people. Those roots that taste like chestnuts are their principal food, and much land is planted to it.

Saturday, 10 November 1492

The ships are ready, but the winds remain contrary. I am anxious to go to the SE and, with the help of Our Lord, shall do so at the first opportunity.

Sunday, 11 November 1492

I shall depart tomorrow to the SE for Bohío,[1] which is also called *Babeque* by some here. I do not know for certain whether one is a province of the other or not, but all these people indicate by signs that there is an abundance of gold, pearls, and spices to the east.

It appears to me that it would be well to take some of these people dwelling by this river to the Sovereigns, in order that they might learn our language and we might learn what there is in this country. Upon return they may speak the language of the Christians and take our customs and Faith to their people. I see and know that these people have no religion whatever, nor are they idolaters, but rather, they are very meek and know no evil. They do not kill or capture others and are without weapons. They are so timid that a hundred of them flee from one of us, even if we are merely teasing. They are very trusting; they believe that there is a God in Heaven, and they firmly believe that we come from Heaven. They learn very quickly any prayer we tell them to say, and they make the sign of the cross. Therefore, Your Highnesses must resolve to make them Christians. I believe that if this effort commences, in a short time a multitude of peoples will be converted to our Holy Faith, and Spain will acquire great domains and riches and all of their villages. Beyond doubt there is a very great amount of gold in this country. These Indians I am bringing say, not without cause, that there are places in these islands where they dig gold and wear it around the neck, in the ears, and on the arms and the legs—and these are very heavy bracelets. Also, there are precious stones and pearls, and an infinite quantity of spices.

Today there came to the side of the ship a canoe with six youths in it, and five came aboard. These I ordered held and am bringing them with me. Afterwards I sent some of my men to a house west of the river, and they brought seven women, small and large, and three children. I did this so that the men I had taken would conduct themselves better in Spain than they might have otherwise, because of having women from their own country there with them.

On many occasions in the past I have taken men from Guinea to Portugal in order that they could learn the language, with the thought that when they returned, they might be made good use of, especially because of the good company they had enjoyed and the gifts that had been bestowed upon them. But this did not prove to be the case. So with these people, if I let them have their wives they will be willing to undertake what is desired of them, and these women will teach our people their language, which is the same throughout these islands of India. Everyone understands one another, and they all travel about in their canoes. This is not the case in Guinea, where there are a thousand languages and one does not understand the other.

Tonight there came to the ship the husband of one of the women and the father of the three children, a male and two females. He asked that I might let him come with us, and it pleased me greatly, and all of the people on board are now consoled, so they must be relatives. He is a man of 45, or a little older.

1. Columbus has heard of two islands to the east: Bohío (Española) and Babeque (Great Inagua Island, Bahamas). He is confusing the two. The name Babeque was soon to vanish, being replaced by a Spanish corruption of *iguana* (the large native lizard).

Monday, 12 November 1492

I left the harbor and the Río de Mares at dawn to go to an island which the Indians aboard positively declared was Babeque. They indicated by signs that the people on that island gather gold by candlelight at night in the sand and then with a hammer make bars of it. In order to go to this island it was necessary to turn the prow to the east by south.

After having gone 24 miles forward along the coast I found a river, and after 12 more miles I found another river, which appeared very rich and larger than any of the others I have seen. I did not wish to stop or enter either of them on two accounts: first, the weather and wind were favorable to go in search of Babeque; second, if there were any large or famous city in this land, it would be on the coast. Also, to enter any of these rivers would require small vessels, which these ships were not, and I would lose a lot of time. These rivers are a thing to be explored separately. This entire coast is mainly populated near the river, to which I have given the name *El Río del Sol*.[1]

It is somewhat cold and therefore it would not be wise to sail north in the winter in order to make discoveries. I sailed this Monday until sunset 54 miles, to the east by south, as far as a cape, which I named *Cabo de Cuba*.[2]

------

1. Sun River, or River of the Sun; now known as *Bahía de Samá*.

Tuesday, 13 November 1492

All last night I was standing off the coast, beating to windward and making no headway, in order to see a gap in the mountains that I had first sighted just at sunset. I had seen two large mountains, and it seemed that the land of Cuba was separate from that of Bohío. The Indians with me confirmed this by signs.

Daylight having arrived, I sailed toward the land and passed a point which at night had appeared about six miles distant. Fifteen miles to the SSW, I entered a large gulf with another 15 miles still remaining to the cape, where between two large mountains there was an opening. I could not determine whether the sea had an entrance or not. Since I wanted to go to the island they call Babeque, where I have been given to understand that there is much gold, and which is east of me, and since I saw no large villages where I could seek shelter from the wind, which increased more than ever, I decided to make for the sea and go east with the wind, which was north. I made 6 knots, and from 10 o'clock in the morning when I took that course, until sunset, I went 42 miles from Cabo de Cuba to the east. This other land of Bohío, which I think is separate from Cuba, I left to the leeward. I discovered 60 miles of that coast from the Cabo de Cuba to the east, and all this coast extends ESE and WNW.

Wednesday, 14 November 1492

All last night I beat about and went cautiously, for it is unwise to sail among these islands at night until they have been examined.[1] I had to stand by until this morning because the wind became light and I could not steer to the east, certainly no better than east by south. The Indians told me yesterday that it is about a three days' journey from the Río de Mares to the island of Babeque, which must be understood as three days' journey for their canoes, which average 21 miles a day.

At sunrise I determined to search for a harbor because the wind has shifted from the north to the NE. If I cannot find a harbor, it will be necessary to turn back to one of the harbors on the island of Cuba.

I reached land, having gone last night 18 miles east by south. I went to the south 6 miles to land, where I saw many inlets and many small islands and harbors. Inasmuch as the wind was strong and the sea heavy, I did not dare attempt to enter. Rather, I ran along the coast to the NW by west, searching for a harbor; I saw many but they were not clear to enter. After having sailed another 24 miles (or 48 all told), I found a very deep inlet about 1,000 feet wide, and a good harbor and river, very wide and deep. I entered and turned the prow to the SSW, and afterward to the south until I reached the SE.

I saw so many islands I could not count them all, of good size and very high, their terrain covered with different trees of a thousand varieties and an infinite number of palms. I am amazed to see so many high islands, and, Your Highnesses, it seems to me that there are no higher mountains in all the world than those I have seen in the last few days. They are beautiful and clear, without fog or snow, and at their base the sea is very deep. I believe that these islands are those countless ones that appear on world maps in the far east. I believe that there are many great riches and precious stones and spices in these islands, which extend very far to the south and spread out in all directions.

I have named this place *La Mar de Nuestra Señora*,[2] and the harbor near the entrance to these islands I have named *Puerto del Príncipe*.[3] I did not enter but observed all of this from outside.

Your Highnesses will have to pardon me for repeating myself concerning the beauty and fertility of this land, but I can assure you that I have not told a hundredth part. Some of the mountains appear to reach Heaven and are like points of diamonds; others of great height seem to have a table on top; and the sea is so deep that a ship can approach some of them right up to the base. They are all covered with forests and are without rocks.

----

1. The Log gives *descubierto* ("discovered"), usually translated as "explored." "Examined" is a better meaning. These strange islands, with coral reefs, had to be examined before sailing among them in order to explore.

2. The Sea of Our Lady.

Thursday, 15 November 1492

I decided to sail among these islands with the ships' boats. I found mastic and a great quantity of aloe. Some of these islands are covered with the roots from which the Indians make their bread, and I found several places where there had been campfires. I found no fresh water, but I did see some people, who fled. Everywhere I went I found a depth of 15 and 16 fathoms, and the bottom underneath is sand, not rock, which sailors greatly desire because rock cuts the lines of the ships' anchors.

Friday, 16 November 1492

In every place I have entered, islands and lands, I have always planted a cross. I took the ship's boat and went to the mouth of those harbors, and on a point of land I found two very large tree trunks, one larger than the other, which I placed one upon the other to make a cross. A carpenter could not have made it in better proportion. After praying before the cross, I ordered a very large, high cross made of the same timbers.

I found canes[1] along that beach, and although I cannot be certain where they came from, I believe that some river has brought them and cast them upon the beach. Within the entrance of the harbor to the SE, I came upon a creek, a narrow inlet where sea water enters the land. There the land forms a peninsula of stone and rock, like a cape, and at the base the sea is very deep—so deep that the largest ship in the world could lie against the land. There was also a place or corner where six ships could remain without anchors, as in a cove. It appears to me that a fortress could be built here at small cost, if in the future any notable commerce should come about in this sea from these islands.

When I returned to the ship, I found that the Indians with me were fishing for conchs, which are found in these seas, and I made the people dive and search for *nacaras,* which are the oysters where pearls are formed. They found many oysters but no pearls; I attribute this to the fact that pearl-bearing oysters are not in season, which I believe is May and June. The sailors found an animal that appears to be a badger.[2] They also fished with nets and found a fish, among many others, that looked like a real hog,[3] not at all like a porpoise—all shell and very hard, with nothing soft except the tail and the eyes, and an opening underneath to expel its superfluities. I have ordered this fish to be salted so that I might take it to the Sovereigns to see.

----

1. Reeds, or bamboo.

2. There were no badgers in Cuba. The animal might have been a *hutía* (*Capromys pilorides* or *C. melanurus*). This is a large, rabbit-sized rodent, still found in the Bahamas and Greater Antilles. It is now on the endangered species list, along with the Bahamian iguana.

3. *Lactophrys guadicornus;* cowfish or trunkfish.

"I decided to sail among these islands with the ships' boats."

PART THREE THE DISCOVERY OF CUBA *28 October to 5 December 1492*

« III »

Saturday, 17 November 1492

I took the ship's boat this morning and went to the SW to see the islands I had not yet seen. I saw many others that were very fertile and delightful, and between them the sea is very deep. Some of them are separated by streams of fresh water, which I think comes from springs that rise in the mountain ranges on the islands. Continuing on, I found a very beautiful river of fresh water that flowed very cold. I saw a very pretty meadow and many palms, much taller than those I had seen before. I found large nuts like those of India, and large rats, also like those of India, and very large crawfish. I saw many birds and smelled a powerful odor of musk, which leads me to believe that there must be some hereabouts. Today, of the six youths I had taken at the Río de Mares and who were on the *Niña,* the two oldest ones escaped.

Sunday, 18 November 1492

I went out again in the small boats, along with many people from the ships, and placed the great cross, which I had ordered made of the two timbers, at the mouth of the entrance to the said Puerto del Príncipe in a clear and very visible location. It is high and commands a very beautiful view. The sea here rises and falls much more than in any other harbor I have visited in this land, and that is not odd because of the many islands. The tide is the reverse of ours:[1] when the moon is SW by south, it is low tide here. I did not depart today because it is Sunday.

----
1. A correct statement. When it was low tide at Bahía de Tánamo, it was high tide at Palos at the same time.

Monday, 19 November 1492

I departed in a light breeze before sunrise, and after midday it blew somewhat to the east. I sailed to the NNE and at sunset Puerto del Príncipe bore to the SSW, about 21 miles distant. I saw the island of Babeque due east, about 45 miles distant. I sailed slowly all night to the NE and went about 45 miles.

Tuesday, 20 November 1492

By 10 o'clock this morning I added another 9 miles, which means that altogether, last night and this morning, I sailed 54 miles in the direction of NE by north.

Babaque, or the islands of Babeque, now bear to the ESE, from which direction the wind blows, which is contrary. Because the wind did not shift and the sea was becoming rough, I decided to make a short run back to Puerto del Príncipe, whence I had come, a distance of 75 miles.

I did not wish to seek anchorage at the small island of Isabela, 36 miles away, for two reasons: one, I see two islands to the south which I want to see, and two, Guanahaní (which I call San Salvador) is 24 miles from Isabela and the Indians I have taken from there might get away, and I have need of them and want to bring them to Castile. They understand[1] that when I find gold, I shall allow them to return to their country.

I approached Puerto del Príncipe but could not enter the harbor because it was dark and the currents pushed me to the NW. I turned the prow to the NE, with a stiff breeze. Later it calmed and the wind shifted about 3 o'clock the next morning. I turned the prow east by north. The wind was SSE, and at dawn, it shifted entirely to the south, then veered to the SE.

At sunrise I reckoned Puerto del Príncipe to be SW and almost SW by west, 36 miles distant.

----

1. It is unclear whether deceit is intended or not. Columbus seems to be saying that *they* think they will be released when gold is found, but that is not his intention.

Wednesday, 21 November 1492

At sunrise I sailed to the east with the wind south. I made little headway because of the contrary sea. Up until the hour of vespers I had gone 18 miles. Then the wind shifted to the east, and I went south by east. By sunset I had gone another 9 miles.

I took a fix with my quadrant and found myself 21 degrees[1] north of the Equator, the same as in the harbor of Mares. I have abandonned the use of the quadrant until I reach land in order to repair it. It does not appear to me that I can be so far north.

This day Martín Alonso Pinzón sailed away with the caravel *Pinta,* without my will or command. It was through perfidy. I think he believes that an Indian I had placed on the *Pinta* could lead him to much gold, so he departed without waiting and without the excuse of bad weather, but because he wished to do so. He has done and said many other things to me.

----

1. Arc-tangent; see note for 30 October, above.

Thursday, 22 November 1492

Last night I sailed south by east, with the wind east and almost calm. About 3 in the morning it blew NNE. I was still going to the south in order to see the country that lay in that direction, but when the sun rose I found myself as far away as yesterday because of the contrary currents; The land was a distance of 30 miles from me.

Last night, after Martín Alonso departed for the east and the island of Babeque, I could see him for a long time, until he was 12 miles away. I sailed all night toward the land, but took in some of the sails and even showed a light because it seemed that Pinzón was coming toward me. The night was very clear and the light wind favorable for him to sail in my direction if he had so chosen.

Friday, 23 November 1492

I sailed all this day toward the land to the south, always with light wind, and the current never letting me reach land. At sunset I was as far away from land as I was in the morning. The wind was ENE and favorable to sail south, but it was almost calm. Beyond the cape, visible in the distance, is another land or cape that extends to the east. The Indians aboard

"This morning Martín Alonso Pinzón sailed away with the Pinta, without my will or command."

call this Bohío and say it is very large and has people there with one eye in the forehead, as well as others they call cannibals,[1] of whom they show great fear. When they saw I was taking that course, they were too afraid to talk. They say that the cannibals eat people and are well armed. I believe there is some truth in this, although if they are armed they must be an intelligent people. Perhaps these people may have captured some of the other Indians; when the captives did not return to their own country, it was said that they were eaten. The Indians we have encountered believed the same thing at first about us Christians.

----

1. *Canibales,* the people of *Caniba* who eat other people. This is the first recorded usage of this term, which is a Taino Indian word.

Saturday, 24 November 1492

I sailed all night, and up until 9 o'clock this morning, when I made landfall at the low island, in the same place I had been last week when I was on my way to the island of Babeque. At that time I did not dare to approach the coast because the sea broke heavily in that bay surrounded by mountains. Finally, I arrived at the Mar de Nuestra Señora, where there are many islands, and entered the harbor near the mouth of the entrance to the islands. If I had known about this harbor before and had not occupied myself with seeing the islands of the Mar de Nuestra Señora, it would not have been necessary to turn around, although I consider it time well spent in having seen the islands.

Upon arriving, I sent the small boat to survey the harbor and found it to be a very good one, 6 fathoms deep and sometimes 20, clear and with a sandy bottom. I entered and turned the prow to the SW and then to the west leaving the low island to the north. The low island, together with another near it, makes a lagoon, in which all the ships of Spain could lie and be safe from all winds without anchoring. This entrance on the SE side, found by turning the prow to the SSW, has a way out to the west. It is very deep and very wide, so whoever might come from the sea to the north can pass between these islands and acquire a knowledge of them, as it is the direct passage along this coast.

These islands are at the base of a great mountain that runs lengthwise from east to west and is exceedingly long, higher and longer than any of the other mountains on this coast, where there is an infinite number. A rocky reef extends outside and along the said mountain like a bar, reaching as far as the entrance. All this is on the SE part. On the side of the low island there is also another reef, although it is small. Between the two there is great width and great depth.

At the entrance on the SE side, inside the harbor, there is a large and very beautiful river, with more water than I have seen up till now. The water in the river is fresh right up to the sea. It has a bar at the entrance, but inside there is good depth, 8 or 9 fathoms. The land is covered with palms and has many other trees.

I took the small boat before sunrise and went to see a cape to the SE of the low island, a distance of about 4 miles, because it appeared to me that there ought to be a good river there. At the entrance to the cape on the SE side, at a distance of two crossbow shots, I saw a large stream of very fine water, which descended from a mountain and made a great noise. I went to the river and saw in it some stones, glittering like gold, and I remembered that in the Río Tejo, at its mouth near the sea, gold was found. It appeared to me that there certainly must be gold here, and I ordered certain of those stones to be gathered for the Sovereigns.

While we were at this place, the ship's boys cried out that they saw pines.[1] I looked toward the mountains and saw them, so large and wonderful that I cannot exaggerate their height and straightness, like spindles, both thick ones and slender ones. I knew that ships could be made from these, and there is a great quantity of timber and masts for the largest vessels of Spain. I saw oak trees and arbutus, and a good river and the materials necessary for sawmills. The land and the air were more temperate than before because of the height and beauty of the mountain ranges.

Along the beach I saw many stones the color of iron, and others which some said were from silver mines, carried down by the river. Here I had cut a lateen yard and a mizzen mast for the caravel *Niña*.

I went to the mouth of the river, and at the foot of that cape on the SE side I entered a bay which was very large and deep and which could contain 100 ships without lines or anchors. Eyes have never seen such a harbor. The mountain ranges are very high, from which many fine streams descend; all the ranges are covered with pines; and everywhere there are the most varied and beautiful groves of trees. There are also two or three other rivers lying behind me.

I just cannot express to you, my Sovereigns, what a joy and pleasure it is to see all this, especially the pines, because there could be built here as many ships as desired, simply by bringing the necessary implements—except the wood and fish, of which there are enormous quantities. I have not praised it a hundredth part of what it deserves, and it pleases Our Lord to continually show me something better, for always in what I have discovered up to the present it has been a matter of going from good to better, as well in the trees and forests and grasses and fruits and flowers as in the people, and always in a different manner, first in one place and then in another. The same is true with regard to the harbors and waters. When one who has seen all of this wonders at it so greatly, how much more wonderful will it be to those who merely hear of it, and no one will be able to believe all of this until he sees it.

----

1. They *were* pines. Columbus finally found a plant he knew.

Monday, 26 November 1492

At sunrise I weighed anchors from this harbor that I have

named *Santa Catalina*,[1] from behind the low island, and I sailed along the coast before a light SW wind in the direction of *Cabo del Pico*,[2] which lay to the SE. I reached the cape late because the wind died down. Once I arrived, I saw another cape to the SE by east, approximately 4½ miles distant;[3] from there I saw another cape bearing SE by south, which appeared to be about 15 miles away. I named this one *Cabo de Campana*[4] and could not reach it before sunset because the wind calmed again altogether. I went during this entire day about 24 miles.

Within that distance I noted and marked nine very remarkable harbors, which all the sailors considered wonderful, and five large rivers, because I sailed close to the coast all the time in order to see everything well. This entire country consists of very high and beautiful mountains that are not dry or rocky but all accessible; there are also the most delightful valleys. The valleys as well as the mountains are covered with tall and verdant trees, so that it is a pleasure to look at them, and it appears that there are many pines. Also, beyond the said Cabo del Pico on the SE side, there are two small islands, each about six miles around; within them there are three marvelous harbors and two great rivers. On all this coast I saw no town whatsoever from the sea. There might have been some people, for their are signs of them. Whenever I am on land, I find signs of habitations and many fires.

I think that the land I see to the SE of Cabo de Campana is the island the Indians call Bohío, because the cape is separated from that land.

"*When I returned to the ship, I found that the Indians with me were fishing for conchs.*"

All the people I have encountered up until this time greatly fear the people of Caniba or Canima, whom they say live on this island of Bohío. This island appears to be very large, and I believe that the people on it go and take the other Indians and their lands and houses, because the ones I have seen are very cowardly and know nothing about arms. It is for these reasons that I think the Indians I am taking with me are not accustomed to settling on the coast. The Indians with me continued to show great fear because of the course I was taking and kept insisting that the people of Bohío had only one eye and the face of a dog, and they fear being eaten. I do not believe any of this. I feel that the Indians they fear belong to the domain of the Great Khan.

---

1. Saint Catherine; now known as *Cayo Moa*.

2. Cape of the Peak; now known as *Punta Guarico*.

3. The Log states "*60 millas*" (15 leagues, or 45 NM). This is an obvious error for "6 miles" (1.5 L, or 4.5 NM). Columbus could not see 45 NM, and the capes located agree with the 4.5 NM distance.

4. Cape of the Bell; now known as *Punta Plata*.

Tuesday, 27 November 1492

Yesterday at sunset I arrived in the vicinity of Cabo de Campana, but did not anchor even though the sky was clear and the wind light and there were five or six wonderful harbors to the leeward. Whenever I enter one of these harbors, I am detained by sheer pleasure and delight as I see and marvel at the beauty and freshness of these countries, and I do not want to be delayed in pursuing what I am engaged upon. For all these reasons, I stood off the coast last night and beat about until day.

The rapid currents[1] last night carried me 15 or 18 miles farther SE than my position at sunset. I could now see beyond Cabo de Campana to a great inlet that apparently divided one country from another, and that seemed to have an island in the middle of it. I decided to turn back, with the wind SW. When I reached the opening I had seen I found that it was only a large bay, at the head of which, on the SE side, was a point rising to a high, square mountain; it is this that had appeared to me as an island.

The wind shifted to the north, and I again took a course to the SE in order to go along the coast and discover what might be there. I saw at the foot of Cabo de Campana a marvelous harbor and a large river; ¾ mile from there, another river; 1½ miles from there, another river; 1½ miles from there, another river; 3 miles from there, another river; 3 miles from there, another river; ¾ mile from there, another river; and another 3 miles from there, another river. From this last river to Cabo de Campana is about 15 miles, the river lying SE of the cape.

Most of these rivers have large mouths, wide and clear, with wonderful harbors for very large ships. They are free from rocks, sand bars, and reefs.

Coming thus along the coast in a SE direction from the last river, I found a large village, the largest I have found up until the present time. A great number of people came to the shore, crying out loudly, all naked, and with spears in their hands. I wanted to speak with them, so I lowered the sails and anchored. I sent the boats from the ship and the caravel in an orderly manner, so that the Spaniards might not do any harm to the Indians or receive any harm from them. I commanded the men to give some trifles to the Indians for their articles of barter. The Indians made a pretense of not allowing the sailors to land and of resisting them. But when they saw that the boats approached nearer to the land and that the Spaniards were not afraid, the Indians withdrew from the shore. Believing that if two or three men got out of their boats the Indians would not be afraid, three Christians landed and spoke in Indian language (they had picked up a bit of it from conversation with the Indians we were taking with us) telling these people not to be afraid. But the Indians ran, and not an adult or child remained. When the three Christians went to the houses, which are made of straw and of the same shape as the others we have seen, they found no one there and nothing in any of them. The men returned to the ships, and we spread sail at midday to go to a beautiful cape which lay to the east, some 24 miles away.

After sailing 1½ miles along the same bay, I saw to the south a very remarkable harbor, and to the SE some incredibly beautiful land, similar to a rolling valley surrounded by mountains. There was a lot of smoke and a number of large villages there, and the land was intensely cultivated. Because of this I decided to enter this harbor and see if I could communicate with these people. If I have praised other harbors, then this one deserves more, along with the land and surroundings and the temperate climate and the population. It is a beautiful place, with pines and palms and a rolling plain extending to the SSE. There are low, smooth mountains on the plain and many streams flowing from the mountains. It is the most beautiful thing in the world.

I anchored the ship and jumped into the boat in order to take soundings in the harbor, which is shaped like a small hammer. When I was facing the entrance to the south, I found the mouth of a river that was wide enough for a galley to enter and so situated that it could not be seen until it was reached. Within a boat's length of the entrance it was 5 fathoms and 8 fathoms in depth.

As I went along the river it was marvelous to see the forests and greenery, the very clear water, the birds, and the fine situation, and I almost did not want to leave this place. I told the men with me that, in order to make a report to the Sovereigns of the things they saw, a thousand tongues would not be sufficient to tell it, nor my hand to write it, for it looks like an enchanted land. I want many other persons who are prudent and have the proper credentials to see this, so as to be certain that they do not praise these things less than I do.

I do not need to write how great the benefits will be from here. It is certain, Lords and Princes, that where there are such lands there must be an infinite quantity of profitable things. But I do not linger in any harbor because I want to see as many lands as I can, in order to tell Your Highnesses about them. Also, I do not know the language, and the people of these lands do not understand me, nor do I or any other person I have with me understand them. And these Indians I am taking with me misunderstand things many times; besides, I do not trust them very much because they have attempted to escape several times. But now, Our Lord willing, I shall see all

I can, and little by little I will investigate and learn, and will have this language taught to persons of my house because I see that the language is all one up to this time. Then the benefits will be known, and one will labor to make all these people Christian, since it can easily be done. They have no sect nor are they idolaters; Your Highnesses will order a city and fortress built in these regions, and these countries will be converted. And I certify to Your Highnesses that it does not seem to me that there can be more fertile countries under the sun, or any more temperate in heat and cold, with a greater abundance of good, pure water—unlike those rivers of Guinea, which are all pestilent. Praise be to Our Lord, so far there has not been a single one of my people who has had a headache or who has been in bed because of sickness, except for one old man through pain from kidney stones, from which he has suffered all his life—and even he became well at the end of two days. I say this in regard to all three ships. So may it please God that Your Highnesses may send learned men here, or that they shall come, and they will see that everything I say is true.

I have already spoken of a village site or fortress on the Río de Mares, on account of the good harbor and the surrounding territory, and it is certain that all I have said is true, but there is no comparison between that place and this, neither with the Mar de Nuestra Señora. Here there must be large villages and a dense population inland and things of great profit, for here, and in all the other lands I have discovered or hope to discover before I return to Castile, I say that Christendom will enter into negotiations, but most of all with Spain, to which all these lands should be subject. And I say that Your Highnesses must not allow any foreigner to set foot here or trade, except Catholic Christians, since it was the beginning and the end of this enterprise that it should be for the increase and the glory of the Christian religion. No one should come to these regions who is not a good Christian.

I went up the river there and found some branches of it, and going around the harbor, I found at the river's mouth some very pleasant groves, like a delightful orchard; there I also found a canoe made of a log as large as a rowboat with 12 benches for the rowers. It was very beautiful and tied up under a shed made of wood and thatched with palm, so that neither the sun nor the rain could damage it. This is a good place to build a village or city and fortress because of the excellent harbor, good water, good land, good surroundings, and great quantity of wood.

----

1. Columbus assumed "rapid currents" because of his 15–18 mile drift during the night. See Map for location.

Wednesday, 28 November 1492

I remained in this harbor today because it rained and was very dark and cloudy. I could have run along the coast with the wind, which was SW and at my stern, but visibility was poor, and since I was not familiar with this section of the coast, I determined that it was dangerous to the ships, so I did not depart.

The crew went ashore to wash their clothes, and some of them went inland a little ways. They found large villages, but all of the houses were empty because the people had fled. They returned by way of another river, larger than the one where we are in the harbor.

Thursday, 29 November 1492

The rain continued today and the sky was overcast, so I chose not to depart. Some of the men went to another village nearby, to the NW, and found nothing. On the way they met an old man who could not flee. They took him and told him they meant him no harm. They gave him some trifles from the articles of barter and left him. I wished they had brought him to me because I would have liked to talk with him and clothe him. The men found a cake of wax in one of the houses, which I am bringing to the Sovereigns. If there is wax here, there must be a thousand other things. In one house the sailors found a human skull in a little basket, covered with another little basket and hanging from a post in the house. They found another one just like it in another village. These must be the skulls of some family ancestors because the houses are such that many people live in each, and they must all be related and descended from the same ancestor.

Friday, 30 November 1492

Again I was not able to depart this harbor. The wind is east, contrary to my course. I sent ashore eight well-armed men and two of the Indians who were with us, in order to see the villages and talk with the inhabitants. They found a lot of

houses, but in each case, these were empty. They did see four youths digging in their fields, but when these youths saw the sailors they fled and could not be caught. The men covered a good deal of territory and saw many settlements and fertile ground, all cultivated, and large rivers. Near one river they found a canoe that was over 60 feet long, made of one log and very beautiful. It could be navigated with 150 people.

Saturday, 1 December 1492

I did not depart because the wind was still contrary and it rained hard. I placed a large cross in some rocks at the entrance to this harbor, which I have named *Puerto Santo*.[1] The cross sets on the point on the SE side of the harbor entrance, but whoever wishes to enter must approach nearer to the point on the NW than to this one on the SE. Although at the foot of both points, next to the rock, there are 12 fathoms of very clear water, off the SE point, there is a rock that rises above the water. It is far enough from the SE point that one could pass between it and the point if necessary, since at the base of the rock and the cape there is everywhere 12 or 15 fathoms. At the entrance you should turn your bow to the SW.

----
1. Holy Port; now known as *Baracoa*.

Sunday, 2 December 1492

The wind is still contrary and I cannot depart. Every night there is a land breeze, and every ship that may come here need have no fear of any storm whatever. Storms cannot reach the ships inside because of a rocky shoal at the entrance of the harbor. At the river's mouth one of the ship's boys found certain stones that appear to contain gold, and I am bringing them to show to the Sovereigns. There are large rivers within a lombard shot from here.

Monday, 3 December 1492

The wind continued to blow contrary and I did not depart this harbor. I decided to go and see a very fine cape, ¾ mile from the harbor to the SE, taking with me the boats and some armed men. At the foot of the cape is the mouth of a good river. I turned the boat to the SE in order to enter and found the mouth to be 100 paces wide. At the entrance itself the depth was one fathom, but inside it was 12 fathoms, and 5 and 4 and 2, and it could contain as many ships as there are in Spain.

Passing a branch of that river, I went to the SE and found a small bay or inlet, in which I saw five very large boats that the Indians call canoes. They are like rowboats, and very beautiful, and carved so that it is a pleasure to see them. I saw that at the foot of the mountain the land was all cultivated. We were following a path through a thick forest, when we came across a very well-arranged boathouse. It was covered so that neither sun nor rain could do any damage, and in it there was another canoe, made of one log like the rest, that had 17 benches for the rowers. It was a pleasure to see how it was constructed and to admire its beauty.

I climbed a mountain and came to level ground, which was sown with many different crops and with gourds, and it was a delightful thing to see. In the midst of all this was a large village. I came suddenly upon the people of the village, who saw us and started to flee. The Indians with us reassured the people of the village that they need not be afraid as we were good people. I gave them hawks' bells and brass rings, and little green and yellow glass beads, with which they were much pleased. I saw that they had no gold or any other precious thing and that it was sufficient to leave them alone. The whole area is inhabited, but the others fled through fear. I assure the Sovereigns that 10 men cause 10,000 Indians to flee. They are such cowards and so fearful, and they carry no weapons but spears, which have a small, hardened, sharp stick on the end. I decided to return to the ship, but first I easily took away all of their spears by trading for them.

After returning to the place where I had left the boats, I sent a few men to the mountain I had climbed, because I thought I had seen a large beehive. While these men were gone many Indians gathered and came to the boats, where all of my men were together. One of them went into the river near the stern of the boat and made a long speech, which I did not understand, except that the other Indians, from time to time, raised their hands to Heaven and shouted loudly. I though they were reassuring me and that my presence pleased them. But I saw that the Indian I was taking with me changed countenance. He turned the color of yellow wax and trembled greatly. He said by signs that I must leave the river because these Indians wished to kill me and my men. He approached one of the sailors who had a loaded crossbow and showed it to the Indians, telling them, I understand, that it would kill them all because a crossbow went a long way and killed. He also took a sword and drew it from the scabbard, showing it to them and saying the same thing. When they heard that, they all commenced to flee, leaving the Indian with us still trembling through cowardice and lack of courage, even though he was a strong man and of good stature.

I refused to leave the river, but rather made them row inland toward the place where the Indians were, who were in great number, all stained with red, and naked as their mothers gave them birth. Some of them had feathers upon their heads and other plumes, and they all had handfuls of spears. I approached them, gave them some pieces of bread, and demanded their spears. I gave them different things for their spears; hawks' bells, cheap little brass rings, worthless little beads. They all quieted down and came to the boats and gave us whatever they had for whatever was given to them. The sailors had killed a tortoise, the pieces of whose shell lay in the boat; the boys gave the Indians a piece as large as a fingernail, and the Indians gave them a handful of spears. These people are like the others I have found and have the same belief: they believe that we come from Heaven, and whatever they have they trade for whatever is offered them, without ever saying it is too little. I believe they would do the same thing with spices and gold if they had them.

Caribs. (Epistola Albericij, De Nouo Mundo, Rostock, 1505)

I saw and entered a beautiful house, not very large and with two doors, such as they are all built. I saw a wonderful arrangement of chambers, built in a way that I do not know how to describe. The chambers were formed by mats and shells hanging from the ceiling. I thought it was a temple, and I called them and asked by signs if they prayed in it and they said no. One of them went overhead[1] and gave me all they had there, and I took some of it.

----

1. They had a loft, quite common in those houses. This is called a *jorón*.

Tuesday, 4 December 1492

I made sail with a light wind, departing Puerto Santo. At a distance of 6 miles I saw that river that I spoke of yesterday. I went along the coast and found that all the land beyond the said cape ran ESE and WNW as far as *Cabo Lindo*,[1] which is east by south of *Cabo del Monte*,[2] and that it is 15 miles between the two capes. Four and one-half miles from Cabo del Monte is another large river, somewhat crooked, which appears to have a good entrance and to be very deep. Two and one-quarter miles from there I saw another very large river that must flow from a long distance. It is a good 100 paces wide at the mouth, and there is no bar in it; it is 8 fathoms deep and has a good entrance. I know these things because I sent a boat to investigate it and to take soundings. The water is fresh for some distance into the sea and it is one of the largest rivers that I have found. There must be large villages along its course. Beyond Cabo Lindo there is a large bay[3] that extends some distance to the ENE and SE and SSW.

----

1. Beautiful Cape; now known as *Punta Fraile*.

2. Cape of the Mountain; now known as *Punta Rama*.

3. The Windward Passage, separating Cuba and Haiti.

Wednesday, 5 December 1492

I beat almost all night off Cabo Lindo, where I was at sunset yesterday, in order to see the country that extends toward the east. At sunrise I saw another cape 6 or 7 miles to the east. I sailed past that and found that the coast turned to the south and inclined to the SW. I then saw a very high and beautiful cape on my course, 21 miles to the SW. I would like to have gone there had it not been such a detour, for I am desirous of going to the island of Babeque, which lies to the NE, according to what the Indians with me have indicated.

I found that I could not go to the island of Babeque to the NE because the prevailing wind was from the NE. While going along more-or-less toward the east, I looked to the SE and saw land. It was a very great island, which I had already been informed of by the Indians with me. They call it Bohío[1] and say that it is inhabited. The people of Cuba (which I have named *Juana*[2]), and those of all the other islands I have visited, are very much afraid of the people of Bohío. They believe that those of Bohío eat people. The Indians also told me many other fantastic things, by signs, but I do not believe them. I think that the Indians of Bohío must be more astute and intelligent in order to capture those in Cuba and the islands, as those are very much lacking in courage.

As the wind was NE and turning north, I decided to leave Cuba or Juana, which up until now I have thought to be the mainland on account of its extent, because I have sailed along its coast for at least 360 miles. I departed to the SE by east. Since the land that I saw lay to the SE, I took this precaution, because always the wind veers from the north to the NE, and then to the east and SE. The wind changed greatly and I carried all my sails. The sea was calm and the current helped me, so from morning until one o'clock I made 6 knots, and that was not quite 6 hours because the nights are about 15 hours.[3] Afterwards I made 7½ knots, and in this manner I went until sunset 66 miles, all to the SE.

Since it was getting dark, I ordered the caravel *Niña* to go ahead and find a harbor by daylight, since she was a faster sailer than the *Santa María*. As it was already night by the time they reached the harbor, which was like the Bay of Cádiz, the *Niña* sent her small boat, carrying a light, to take soundings.

Before I reached the place where the *Niña* was beating about, awaiting a signal from the small boat, the light went out. The *Niña* then showed a light and came up to me to explain what had happened. While this was going on the men in the small boat rekindled the light. The *Niña* was able to go to it, but I was afraid to attempt this at night with the large ship. So I beat about all night, remaining where I was.

----

1. Columbus now realizes that Babeque and Bohío are two different islands, and he has Babeque correctly located to the NE. The "very great island of Bohío" is Española, and he is looking directly at Haiti.

2. This is the first mention of naming Cuba *Juana,* after Prince Juan, heir to the throne. Columbus must have named it before this time.

3. The correct value is closer to 13. See Prologue.

"The current was so strong that I had to throw a line on land and have some of the sailors pull the boat against the current."

PART FOUR

THE DISCOVERY OF ESPAÑOLA
6 December 1492 to 15 January 1493

Thursday, 6 December 1492

t dawn I found myself 12 miles from the harbor, which I named *Puerto María*.[1] I saw a lovely cape to the south by west which I named *Cabo de la Estrella*.[2] and it appears to me that this is the last land of this island to the south, and that it is about 21 miles away. Another land appeared to the east, seemingly an island of no great size, at a distance of about 30 miles. Another very beautiful, well-formed cape, which I named *Cabo del Elefante*,[3] lay to the east by south, 40½ miles away. Yet another cape lay to the ESE, about 21 miles away, and I named it *Cabo de Cinquín*.[4] There is a large opening or arm of the sea that appears like a river, 15 miles to the SE, tending slightly to the SE by east. It appears to me that between Cabo del Elefante and Cabo de Cinquín there is a very wide channel; some of the sailors said that it was a division of the island. I named that the *Isla de la Tortuga*.[5] This big island appeared to be very high, not encircled by mountains but level like beautiful fields. It appears to be all cultivated, or at least a large part of it, and the crops look like wheat in the month of May in the vicinity of Córdoba. I saw many fires last night and today there is a lot of smoke, as if coming from watch towers that have been set up to guard against people with whom they might be at war.

All the coast of this land extends to the east.

At the hour of vespers we entered a harbor that I named *Puerto de San Nicolás*,[6] in honor of St. Nicholas because it was his feast day. As I approached the entrance of this harbor, I marveled at its beauty and excellence. Although I have praised

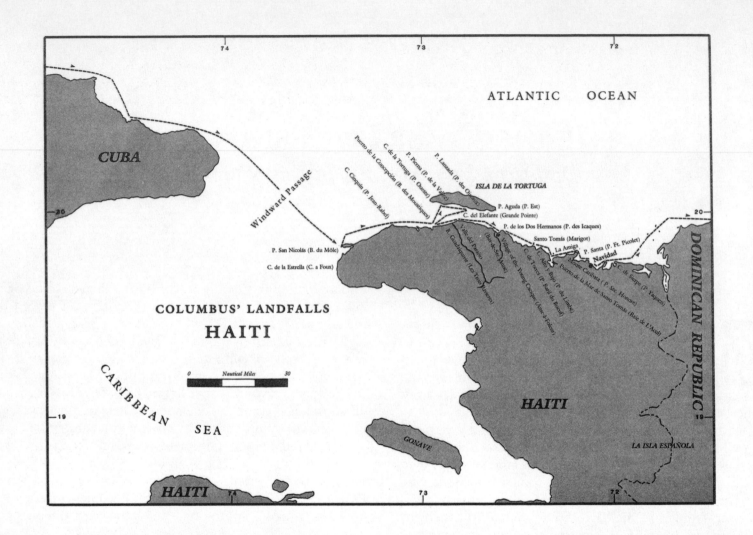

ATLANTIC OCEAN

CUBA

Windward Passage

C. Cinquin (P. Jean-Rabel)

Puerto de la Concepción (B. des Moustiques)

C. de la Tortuga (P. Ouest)

P. Pierna (P. de la Vallée)

P. Lanzada (P. des Oyeaux)

ISLA DE LA TORTUGA

P. Aguda (P. Est)

C. del Elefante (Grande Pointe)

P. de los Dos Hermanos (P. des Icaques)

Santo Tomás (Marigot)

La Amiga

P. Santa (P. Ft. Picolet)

Navidad

P. San Nicolás (B. du Môle)

C. de la Estrella (C. a Foux)

Valle del Paraíso (Baie de Ste-Marie)

R. Guadalquivir (Le Trois Rivieres)

Village of the Young Cacique (Anse-à-Foleur)

C. Alto Bajo (P. Baril du Boeuf)

C. de Torres (P. Barú du Limbe)

Monte Caribata (P. Ste. Honoré)

(Puerto de la Mar de Santo Tomás (Baie de L'Acul))

C. de Sierpe (P. Yaquesi)

DOMINICAN REPUBLIC

COLUMBUS' LANDFALLS
HAITI

CARIBBEAN SEA

0   Nautical Miles   30

HAITI

GONAVE

LA ISLA ESPAÑOLA

HAITI

the harbors of Cuba greatly, this one is even superior, and none of them is similar to it. At the mouth and entrance it is 4½ miles wide, and one should sail to the SSE, although on account of the great width the prow can be turned wherever desired. It extends to the SSE 6 miles, and at its entrance toward the south there is something like a promontory. From there it is level as far as the cape, where there is a very beautiful beach and a grove of trees of a thousand kinds, all loaded with fruit. I think these are spices and nutmegs, but since they are not ripe I do not recognize the kind. There is a river in the middle of the beach.

The depth of this harbor is tremendous: for the distance of a lombard shot the lead did not touch bottom at 40 fathoms, and from the shore to this deep part there is up to this stretch of water a depth of 15 fathoms. The water is very clear and, within one pace from any point on the shore, 15 fathoms deep. Likewise, all the water along this coast is very deep and clear, and not a single shoal appears. At the foot of the land, about the distance of a boat's oar from it, it is still 5 fathoms deep. Beyond the confines of the harbor, which extends to the SSE and in which a thousand ships could beat about, there is an inlet that runs inland to the NE for a good 1½ miles, and at a constant width as if measured by a cord. It is so situated that when one is in that inlet (which is 25 paces wide) the mouth of the large entrance cannot be seen, so that the harbor appears enclosed. The depth of the inlet from one end to the other is 11 fathoms, and the entire bottom is sandy. It is 8 fathoms deep up to where the ships can touch land. All the harbor is very breezy and unsheltered, and there are no trees around it. This island appears to have more rocks than the others I have found. The trees are smaller, and many of them are the same kind that are in Spain, such as oaks, arbutus, and others; the same thing is true in regard to the grasses. The land is very high and quite level, and the breezes are refreshing. It has not been as cold anywhere as here, although it is only cold in comparison with the other islands I have visited, and not really cold.

Opposite the harbor there is a beautiful plain, and in the center of it the river I have mentioned. There must be a lot of people in this region, since I have seen so many canoes. Some of them are as large as a rowboat, with 15 benches for the rowers. All the Indians fled when they saw our ships. Those Indians I have with me from the small islands are so desirous of returning to their lands that they think I will take them back after I leave this place. They are already suspicious because I have not taken the route toward their homes. Because of this I do not believe what they tell me; I do not understand them nor do they understand me. And they are scared to death of the people on this island. In order to have had conversation with the people here it would have been necessary for me to remain for several days. I did not stay because there is so much that I have not seen, and I am not sure that the good weather will continue. I hope in Our Lord that the Indians I am carrying will learn my language and I will learn theirs. Then I can return and talk with these people. I hope to God that I can have some good trade in gold before I return to Spain.

1. Port Mary. The name changed immediately to *Puerto de San Nicolás* (see below).

2. Cape of the Star; now known as *Cap à Foux*.

3. Elephant Cape; now known as *Grande Pointe*.

4. Fifth Cape; now known as *Pointe Jean-Rabel*.

5. Tortoise Island; now known as *Ile de la Tortue*. This is the large island off the NW coast of Haiti.

6. Port of St. Nicholas; now known as *Baie du Môle*. This is the same harbor as was earlier named *Puerto María*.

Friday, 7 December 1492

At dawn I made sail and departed Puerto de San Nicolás. I sailed with the SW wind 6 miles to the NE, as far as a point that the beach makes. A small cape lay to the SE, and Cabo de la Estrella lay to the SW, 18 miles distant. From there I sailed to the east along the coast as far as Cabo Cinquín, a distance of about 36 miles. Fifteen miles of this extended to the east by north. The coast is very high and the water very deep—20 and 30 fathoms right up to the edge of the land, while at a distance of a lombard shot from land the bottom cannot be reached. I confirmed all of this today, much to my pleasure, with the wind SW.

The above-mentioned cape reaches within a lombard shot of Puerto de San Nicolás, and if it were cut off and made an island it would have a circumference of about 2 or 3 miles.[1] This entire country is very high and does not have large trees, only evergreens, oaks, and arbutus, the same as in Castile. Before Cabo Cinquín, and within 6 miles of it, I discovered a small opening, like a cut in the mountain, through which I discovered a very large valley. It was all sown with something resembling barley, and I thought that there must be a large population. The valley is surrounded by large, high mountains.

When I reached Cabo de Cinquín, Cabo de la Tortuga lay to the NE, about 24 miles away. Off Cabo de Cinquín at the distance of a lombard shot there is a rock in the sea which stands out and can be seen very well. To the East by South lay Cabo del Elefante, some 50 miles distant, all of it mountainous. At a distance of 18 miles I saw a large bay and beyond it extensive valleys and planted fields and mountains, all like those in Castile. At a distance of 6 miles I found a very deep, crooked river. One vessel could enter it very well, since the mouth is free from banks and shoals. At a distance of 12 miles I found a very wide harbor, so deep that I could not find the bottom at the entrance; only three paces from the shore it was 15 fathoms. It extends inland three-quarters of a mile.

Although it was still very early (1 o'clock in the afternoon) and the wind was strong at my stern, I decided to stop at this harbor because the sky looked as though it would rain very hard, and it was very dark and cloudy. If poor weather conditions are dangerous in a familiar country, they are much more so in unfamiliar surroundings. I named this harbor *Puerto de la Concepción*.[2]

I took the ship's boat and entered a small river at the end of the harbor. This river flows through a plain that is cultivated and a beautiful thing to behold. I took a net with me to fish; before I reached land a mullet like those in Spain jumped into the boat. Until this moment no fish had been seen like those in Castile. The sailors caught mullets and soles and other fish like those in Castile. I went a short distance along that river, and all the land is cultivated. I heard nightingales sing and other small birds like those of Castile. I saw five men but they fled. I found myrtle and other trees and grasses like those in Castile, and the mountainous country looks like Castile.

----

1. The Log records "34" miles, clearly an error for 3 *or* 4 Columbian miles (approximately 2 or 3 nautical miles).

2. Port of the Conception; now known as *Baie des Moustiques*.

Saturday, 8 December 1492

It rained very hard, and the north wind blew very strong. The harbor is safe from all winds except from the north, although it cannot damage a vessel because there is a strong surge, or undertow, that does not permit the ship to drag its anchors, nor does the wind disturb the water in the river. After midnight the wind shifted to the NE and afterward to the east.

This harbor is well sheltered from these winds by the island of Tortuga, which fronts this island for 27 miles.

Sunday, 9 December 1492

It rained today, and the weather was wintry like October in Castile. I have seen no village except one very beautiful house in Puerto de San Nicolás. It was constructed better than those I have seen in other places. This island is very large; it is no exaggeration to say that it is 600 miles around. It is all well cultivated. I believe that all the villages lie inland, some distance from the sea, and that the villagers can see me approaching. The people light signal fires, take all of their possessions, and flee before I land.

This harbor, Puerto de la Concepción, is 1,000 paces wide at the mouth, which is equal to three-quarters of a mile. In it there are no banks or shoals, but rather, the bottom can barely be found until you go toward the shore. Inside, it is 3,000 paces long, clear of rocks, and with a sandy bottom. Any ship whatsoever can anchor in it without fear and can enter without danger. At the head of the harbor the mouths of two rivers discharge a small quantity of water. Opposite there are some of the most beautiful plains in the world, almost like the lands of Castile, only better. Because of this I have named this island *La Isla Española*.[1]

----

1. The Spanish Island. The island that today contains Haiti and the Dominican Republic is called *Española* (in Spanish) and Hispaniola (in English), but both are incorrect. Columbus said the island looked like the lands of Castile, only better, and

named it accordingly. He never referred to the island as simply *La Española* (the Spanish). Shortly after the First Voyage the incorrect corruption was concocted.

Monday, 10 December 1492

The wind blew hard from the NE and caused the anchors to drag half the length of their lines. This surprised me, but it must have been because I am anchored quite near land and the wind blew toward it. Since the wind was contrary for me to depart, I sent six well-armed men ashore, with orders to go 6 to 9 miles inland to see if they could find anybody. They went and returned without finding any people or houses. They did find a few huts, some very wide roads, and places where many fires had been built. They saw some of the best land in the world and found many mastic trees. They brought some of it and said that there was a great deal, but now is not the time to gather it, for it is not ready to form into gum.

Tuesday, 11 December 1492

I was unable to depart this harbor because the wind was still east and NE. In front of this harbor, as I have said, is the Isla de la Tortuga. It seems to be a large island, and the coast extends almost in the same direction as that of La Isla Española. It may be, at the most, 30 miles long. I would like to examine the strait between these two islands in order to get a better view of La Isla Española, which is the most beautiful thing I have ever seen. Also, according to what the Indians with me say, one must go to Tortuga to reach the island of Babeque. These Indians tell me that Babeque is a very large island with high mountains and many rivers and valleys, and they say that the land they call Bohío is larger than Juana, (which they call Cuba). They indicate that there is continental land behind La Isla Española, which they call *Caritaba*.[1] They say that it is of infinite extent, which supports my belief that these lands may be harassed by a more astute people, because the inhabitants of all these islands live in great fear of the people of *Caniba*. So I repeat what I have said before, the Caniba are none other than the people of the Great Khan, who must be very near here. They have ships that come to these lands to capture these people and take them away. Since the people never return, it is believed that they have been eaten. Each day we understand these Indians better, and they, us; although many times they may have misunderstood us, and vice versa.

I sent some men to the land, where they found a great deal of mastic that was not coagulated. I believe this is because of the rains. On the island of Chios they gather it in March, but here they could gather it in January because it is so temperate. We caught many fish like those in Castile: dace, salmon, hake, dory, pompano, mullet, conger eels, and shrimp. We also saw sardines and found a great deal of aloe.

----

1. Columbus has misunderstood the Indians. *Caritaba* is the region (or province) including and surrounding the *Cap Haitien* area.

Wednesday, 12 December 1492

The wind remains contrary, and I am unable to depart. I

placed a large cross at the entrance to the harbor, on a little rise the western side. This is a sign that Your Highnesses possess this land as your own and especially as an emblem of Jesus Christ, Our Lord, and in honor of Christianity. After erecting the cross, three sailors started up the mountain to see the trees and plants; and they heard a large crowd of people. These people were all naked like the others they had seen, and my men called to them and went after them, but the Indians fled. Finally they caught one woman who could go no farther: in doing so, they were carrying out my orders to take some of the Indians in order to show them honor and cause them to lose their fear of us. I also wanted to see if these Indians had anything worthwhile; it appeared that it could not be otherwise, judging from the beauty of the country.

So they brought the woman to the ship, a very young and beautiful girl, and she talked with those Indians with me, since they all have the same language. I clothed her and gave her glass beads, hawks' bells, and brass rings, and sent her back to land, very honorably, the way I always do. I also sent some people from the ship with her, including three of the Indians with me, so that they could talk with those people. The sailors who took her to land said that she did not wish to leave the other Indian women on the ship, the ones we had taken at Puerto de Mares on the island of Juana.[1] All the Indians who had accompanied this Indian woman originally had come in a canoe, which is their caravel that they navigate everywhere; when they entered the harbor and saw the ships, they fled from my men, leaving the canoe, and ran back to their village overland. The Indian woman showed us the location of the village. She wore a small piece of gold in her nose, which is an indication that there is gold in this island.

---

1. Here the Log states: ". . . the island of *Juana de Cuba*" (Juana of Cuba).

Thursday, 13 December 1492

The three men I sent with the woman returned at 3 o'clock in the morning. They did not go all the way to the village, either because it was too far or because they were afraid. They said that the next day many people would come to the ships, so by now these people must already be reassured by what the woman has told them. I was anxious to learn whether or not there was anything of value here and, also, to hold conversation with these people. Their land is so beautiful and fertile, and they might be disposed to serve the Sovereigns. So I decided to send men to the village yet again, trusting that by this time the Indian woman would have spread the news that we are good people. For this purpose I selected nine men, well armed and used to such an expedition. I also sent one of the Indians who was with us. They went to the village, which was a little over 12 miles to the SE, located in a valley and unoccupied. Everyone had fled when they heard we were coming, leaving behind whatever they had. The village consisted of more than 1,000 houses and must have had a population of over 3,000. The Indian and the men ran after the occupants, telling them not to be afraid, that they were not from Caniba but rather from Heaven, and that they gave beautiful things to everyone they met. The Indians were so much impressed with what they heard that more than 2,000 assembled. They all came to my men and placed their hands upon my men's heads, which is a sign of great reverence and friendship, but they continued to tremble until they were reassured. After they were calmed down, they all went to their houses and each one brought food. They brought the bread of *niamas*,[1] which are tubers and look like large radishes. These are planted in all their fields and are their staff of life. They make bread from them and boil and roast them, and they taste like chestnuts—anyone who eats them will say that they taste like chestnuts.

They gave my men bread and fish and whatever they had.

The Indians on my ship had told the Indian accompanying the sailors that I wanted a parrot, and he passed the word on to these other Indians. They brought many parrots and required no payment for them. The Indians begged my men not to leave that night and offered them many other things that they had in the mountains. When all these people were together, the sailors saw a great multitude of Indians coming with the husband of the woman whom I had honored and returned. They were carrying this woman on their shoulders, coming to thank me for the honor I had done her and the presents I had given her.

My men told me that these people were more handsome and of better disposition than any that we had seen up to now, but I do not know how this is possible. As to their appearance, the sailors said that there is no comparison with the ones we have seen before, either men or women. They are whiter than the others—indeed, they saw two young girls as white as any to be seen in Spain. As to the country, the best in Castile in beauty and fertility cannot compare with this. This land is as different from that surrounding Córdoba as day is from night.

All the land around the village is cultivated, and a river flows through the middle of the valley. It is very large and wide and could irrigate all the lands around. All the trees are green and full of fruit, and the plants are in flower and very tall. The roads are wide and good, and the breezes are like those in Castile in the month of April. The nightingales and other small birds sing as they do in Spain in the same month, and it is the greatest pleasure in the world. Small birds sing sweetly during the night, and one can hear many crickets and frogs. The fish are the same as in Spain. There are many mastic trees and aloes and cotton trees. No gold has been found, but this is not surprising since we have been here such a short time.

I have ascertained that there are 10 hours of daylight, by measuring with a glass of half-hour duration. It takes 20 of these *ampolletas* to make a day, unless some error was made because the glass was not turned quickly enough or because some of the sand did not run through. I found by means of the quadrant that I am 20 degrees north[2] of the Equator.

----

1. These were probably *niamas,* manioc. See Note for 16 December, below.

2. Once again, Columbus gives the arc-tangent reading of the correct latitude; true position was approximately 19 degrees 54 minutes.

Friday, 14 December 1492

I departed Puerto de la Concepción with a land breeze, which calmed after a little bit. Afterward the wind became east. I sailed in this wind to the NNE and reached the Isla de Tortuga, where I saw a point that I named *Punta Pierna*,[1] ENE of the head of the island and at a distance of maybe 9 miles. From there I discovered another point, which I called *Punta Lanzada*,[2] on the same course to the NE, about 12 miles away. Thus, from the head of the Isla de Tortuga, as far as *Punta Aguda*,[3] it is about 33 miles, to the ENE. On that course there are some long expanses of beach. The island of Tortuga is very high but not mountainous, and it is very beautiful and populated the same as the Isla Española. The land is so completely cultivated that it is like looking at the fields around Córdoba. Because the wind was contrary for going on to the island of Babeque, I returned to Puerto de la Concepción. I tried, but was unable, to reach a river 6 miles east of this harbor.

----

1. Leg Point; now known as *Pointe de la Vallée*.

2. Spear Thrust Point; now known as *Pointe des Oiseaux*.

3. Sharp Point; now known as *Pointe Est*.

Saturday, 15 December 1492

I again departed from Puerto de la Concepción. As we left the harbor the wind blew strongly from the east, which was contrary to my course, and I turned and went back to the *Isla de la Tortuga*. From there I went to see the river that I had not been able to reach yesterday. Once again I was not able to fetch it, but I did anchor a mere three-quarters of a mile to the leeward at a beach with a good, clear harbor.

I went with the boats to see the river, but first entered a bay that was not the mouth, but three-quarters of a mile nearer. I came back and found the mouth, which was not even a fathom deep and which had a very strong current. I entered with the boats in order to reach the villages my people had seen the day before yesterday. The current was so strong that I had to throw a line on land and have some of the sailors pull the boat against the current, and by this means I was able to go upstream a distance of two lombard shots, but no farther.

I saw some houses and the large valley where the villages are; never have I seen a more beautiful sight. That river flowed right through the middle of the valley. I also saw people at the entrance to the river, but they all fled. These people must be hunted, for they live in constant fear. Whenever we arrive, at any spot, they build signal fires from towers that they have erected throughout the land, and at this warning all the people flee inland. They do this much more on this Isla Española and on Tortuga, which is also a large island, than in any of the other places I have left behind. I named this valley the *Valle del*

Paraíso,[1] and the river, *Guadalquivir,*[2] because it flows as strongly as the Guadalquivir by Córdoba. There are beautiful stones along its banks and it is navigable.

1. Valley of Paradise.

2. Now known as *Les Trois Rivières*.

Sunday, 16 December 1492

I departed at midnight, to get out of that bay taking advantage of a very light land breeze. Coming from the coast of the Isla Española, I sailed close to the wind, because later, by 9 o'clock the next morning, the wind blew from the east. In the middle of that bay I found a canoe with a solitary Indian in it. I wondered how he was able to keep himself afloat when there was such a high wind. I brought him and his canoe on board and pleased him greatly by giving him glass beads, hawks' bells, and brass rings. I took him in the ship to a coastal village 12 miles distant. I found a good anchorage there next to the village, which appeared to be newly constructed, for all the houses were new. I let the Indian go ashore in his canoe and trusted that he would spread the word that we Christians are good people. They already knew this, however, from information they had received where my six men had gone before; soon more than 500 men came to the beach, where they gathered near the ships, for we were anchored very near to the shore. After a little while, their King came.

One by one, and in small groups, they came to the ship without bringing anything with them, although some of them wore grains of very fine gold in their ears and noses, which they gave away willingly. I ordered that everyone be treated honorably because they are the best and gentlest people in the world, and above all because I have great hope in Our Lord that Your Highnesses will convert all of them to Christianity and they will all belong to you, for I regard them as yours now.

I saw that they all showed respect for the King, who was on the beach. I sent him a gift, which he received with much ceremony. He is a young man, about 21 years of age. He had an old governor or advisor and other counselors who advised him and spoke for him. He himself said very few words. One of the Indians with me spoke with the King and told him how we had come from Heaven, and that we were searching for gold and wished to see the island of Babeque. He replied that this was good, and that there was a great deal of gold on that island. He showed my master-at-arms who had delivered my gift, the course that must be followed to reach Babeque and said that it could be reached in two days' time from where we were anchored. He also said that if we needed anything in his country, he would give it to us willingly.

The King and all the others went about as naked as they were born, and the women, too, without any shyness, and they are the handsomest men and women I have found up until now. They are exceedingly white, and if they wore clothing and were protected from the sun and the air they would be almost as white as the people in Spain.

This country is very cool and the best that language can describe. It is very high, and upon the highest mountain plowing could be done with oxen and everything could be transformed into fields and pastures. In all Castile there is no land that can be compared to this in beauty and fertility. All this island and the Isla de la Tortuga are entirely cultivated like the plain of Córdoba.

These fields are planted mostly with *ajes*.[1] The Indians sow little shoots, from which small roots grow that look like carrots. They serve this as bread, by grating and kneading it, then baking it in the fire. They plant a small shoot from the same root again in another place, and once more, it produces four or five of these roots. They are very palatable and taste exactly like chestnuts. The ones grown here are the largest and best I have seen anywhere. I have also seen them in Guinea, but those that grow there are as thick as your leg.

All the people here are strong and courageous and not feeble like the others I have found before. They converse very easily and have no religion. The trees are so luxuriant that the leaves are not green but very dark in color. It is a wonderful thing to see these valleys and rivers and good water and the lands suitable for bread-foods and herds of animals, of which they have none, and suitable for orchards and anything on earth a man might wish.

Making cassava (manioc) bread. (Benzoni, Historia del Mondo Nuovo, 1572)

Later in the afternoon the King came to the ship, and I paid him the honor that was due him, and, through my Indians on board, told him that we came from the Sovereigns of Castile who were the greatest Sovereigns in the world. But neither the Indians with me, who are my interpreters, nor the King believed this. They believe that we are from Heaven and that the realms of the Sovereigns of Castile are in Heaven and not in this world. I gave the King some of our Castilian food. He ate a mouthful and afterward gave the rest to his advisors and to the governor and the others who were with him.

Your Highnesses may rest assured that these lands are so extensive and good and fertile, and especially these of this Isla Española, that there is no one who can describe it, and no one who can believe it if he does not see it. And Your Highnesses may believe that this island and all the others are as much yours as is Castile, and all that is needed here is to build a town and order the Indians to do your bidding. I, with the people I have with me, who are not many in number, could go through all these islands without any opposition. I have already seen three of my sailors go ashore where there is a great number of Indians, and the Indians have all fled without anyone wishing to do them any harm. They have no arms and are naked, and have no knowledge of arms and are very timid. A thousand of them would not face three Christians, and so they are suitable to be governed and made to work and sow and do everything else that shall be necessary, to build villages and be taught to wear clothing and to observe our customs.

----

1. The description is identical to that for *niamas*. See Epilogue.

The wind blew strongly last night from the ENE, but the sea did not get very rough because the Isla de la Tortuga is in front and protects this harbor. I did not depart today, but sent some of the sailors to fish with nets.

The Indians mixed freely with us and brought some arrows that belonged to the people of Caniba, the Canibales. These arrows are quite long, made of spikes of canes; they use little sharp, hardened sticks for their tips. The Indians showed us two men who had lost some chunks of flesh from their bodies and said that the Canibales had bitten out the pieces. I do not believe this.

Again I sent some men to the village, and by trading some worthless little glass beads they obtained some pieces of gold that had been beaten into the form of a thin leaf. I saw one man that they call *Cacique,* whom I take to be governor of the province, who had a piece of that gold leaf as big as your hand, and it appeared that he wished to trade it. While the others remained in the plaza, he went to his house and broke that leaf into very small pieces. He brought a piece at a time and traded for each. After it was all gone, he indicated by signs that he had sent for more and would bring it the next day to me. All these things—and their manner, their customs, their meekness and behavior—show these people to be more alert and intelligent than the other Indians I have seen until now.

In the afternoon a canoe came here from the Isla de la Tortuga, carrying 40 men, and on reaching the beach all of the inhabitants of the village who were together seated themselves as a sign of peace. Most of those in the canoe came ashore. The Cacique stood up by himself, and, with words that sounded threatening, made them get back in the canoe. He splashed water on them and threw stones from the beach at them, and they obediently departed. The Cacique then handed a stone to my master-at-arms, whom I had sent ashore with my secretary and others to see if they could bring back anything of value, and indicated that he should throw it at the men in the canoe. This the master-of-arms would not do. The Cacique indicated quite clearly that he favored me. The canoe departed, and they told me after its departure that there was more gold in Tortuga than here is the Isla Española, because it is nearer Babeque. I do not think that there are any mines in either the Isla Española or Tortuga, but that the gold comes from Babeque. They only bring a little here because these people have nothing to give for it. This land is so rich that it is not necessary to work much to feed themselves or clothe themselves, so they all go naked. I believe that I am very near the source of this gold and that Our Lord is about to reveal its location. I was told that from here to Babeque is a four days' journey, which must be about 90 or 120 miles. I could make that in one day with a good wind.

Tuesday, 18 December 1492
I remained anchored at this beach today because there was no wind. Also, the Cacique had said that he was going to bring more gold today. It was not the amount of gold that I was interested in, for I know that there is no mine here, but I wanted to know where it comes from.

At dawn I ordered the ships to be decorated with arms and banners for the feast of *Santa María de la O,* or the commemoration of the Annunciation. We fired many lombard shots.

The Cacique of the Isla Española had arisen early, for his house must be 4 or 5 miles[1] from here, as best as I can judge, and he reached the village by 9 o'clock in the morning. Some of my men were already in the village by then to see if any gold was brought. More than 200 men came with the Cacique and four men carried him on a litter. The Cacique arrived while I was eating below the sterncastle. Without doubt his demeanor and the respect which they all show for him would appeal to Your Highnesses, even though they are naked. As he entered the ship, he saw that I was eating and came quickly to seat himself beside me, but he would not allow me to rise or interrupt my meal. I thought he might like to eat some of our food, so I ordered that something be brought for him.

When he entered under the sterncastle he signed with his hand that his entourage should stay outside, and they did so with all haste and respect, seating themselves on the deck, except for two mature men whom I took to be his counsellors and governors, who seated themselves at his feet. Of the food I

Left: imaginary islands discovered in the New World. **Middle:** Columbus in the New World. **Right:** La Navidad, the first settlement in the New World. First illustrated Latin edition of the Carta de Colón, *Basel, 1493. (Courtesy Rare Book Division, New York Public Library, Astor, Lenox, and Tilden Foundations)*

placed before him, he took a little of each thing, as a salutation, and then sent the rest to his people. They all ate some of it. He did the same thing with the drink, which he only touched to his mouth. He gave it to the others in the same manner; it was all done in a ceremonial style, with very few words. Whatever he said, according to my understanding, was very formal and prudent, and the two with him spoke with him and for him with great respect. After the meal a servant brought a belt, shaped like those in Castile but made differently. He gave this to me, along with two very thin wrought pieces of gold. I believe that they get very little of this here, but I also believe that we are very near the place it comes from and that there is a great deal of it there. I saw that a cover on my bed pleased him, so I presented it to him, along with some very good amber beads that I wore around my neck. I also gave him some red shoes and a flask of orange flower water. This pleased him wonderfully. He and his governors and counsellors were very sorry that they could not understand me, nor I them. Nevertheless, I understood he told me that if anything here would please me, the whole island was at my command. I sent for some beads of mine, on which, as a pendant, I have a gold coin with the images of Your Highnesses engraved on it, and showed it to him. I again told him that Your Highnesses command and rule over the best part of the world and that there are no other such great Princes. I also showed him the royal banners and the other banners that have a cross on them, which he admired greatly. He told his counsellors that Your Highnesses must be great Lords, since you sent me here from so far without fear. And many other things were said that I did not understand, except that I very well saw that everything was wonderful.

Since it was getting late and he wished to leave, I sent him ashore in the boat with great honors and fired a salute with the cannons. When he reached land he got into his litter and went away with his 200 men and more, and his son was carried behind him on the shoulders of an Indian, a very honorable man.

After that, whenever the Cacique encountered the sailors from the ships, he ordered that something to eat should be given to them and that they should be shown a great deal of honor. One sailor said that he had met the Cacique returning from the ship and had seen all the things I had given him. Each item was carried before the Cacique by one of his most important aides. His son was following behind the Cacique at some distance with the large number of people in the entourage, and likewise a brother of the Cacique, except that the brother was on foot and two of the principal men were leading him by the arms. This brother had come to the ship after the Cacique, and I had given him some things from the same articles of barter. It was then that I learned that the king, in their language, is called Cacique.

Today I traded for only a small quantity of gold, but I learned from an old man that there were many islands in the vicinity—at a distance of 300 miles or more, according to what I was able to make out—in which a lot of gold is found. I was told that on some of these islands there is so much gold that the whole island is gold. On others they gather it and sift it with sieves and melt it to make bars, and work it in a thousand ways. I was shown, by signs, how this is done. The old man indicated to me the course to take to get to those islands and the place where they may be found. I decided to go there, and if the old man had not been one of the principal persons belonging to the king, I would have taken him along. If I had known the language, I would have begged him to accompany me, and I believe that we are on such good terms that he would have gone along of his own free will. But since I already consider that these people belong to the Sovereigns of Castile, it is not right to offend them. So I decided to leave him alone.

I placed a very large cross in the center of the plaza of that village, and the Indians assisted me greatly in this work. They said prayers and worshipped it, and from their actions I trust in the Lord that all these islands are to be Christianized.

---

1. The Log mistakenly records 5 leagues. The locations are known.

Wednesday, 19 December 1492

I made sail during the night to get out of that gulf which the Isla Española and Tortuga define, but when day arrived the wind shifted to the east. Because of the contrary wind I was unable to clear this gulf between the two islands, nor could I reach a harbor I saw before sunset. I saw four points of land near here and a large bay and river, and from this place I also saw a very large cape and a village. Behind the village there is a valley between very high mountains, covered with trees that seem to be pines. One of the points I named the *Dos Hermanos*,[1] upon which there is a very high mountain range that extends from NE to SW. Another cape I named the *Cabo de Torres*,[2] and to the ESE of it is a small island I named *Santo Tomás*,[3] for tomorrow is his vigil. All around this island there are capes and marvelous harbors, according to what I can judge from the sea. In the forepart of the island, on its western side, there is a cape that is partly high and partly low projecting far out into the sea. For this reason I named it *Cabo Alto y Bajo*.[4] Forty-five miles to the east by south from Cabo de Torres there is an even higher mountain that extends seaward; it appears to be an island unto itself because of a low connecting isthmus on the land side. I named this *Monte Caribata*[5] because this province is called Caribata. It is very beautiful and covered with trees of bright green leaves, without snow or mists. The weather here, with respect to the breezes and temperature, is the same as it is in Castile in March. In respect to the trees and plants, it is like May in Castile. The nights are 14 hours' duration.

---

1. Two Brothers; now known as *Pointe des Icaques*.

2. Cape of Towers; now known as *Pointe Baril du Boeuf*.

3. St. Thomas Island; now known as *Ile de Marigot*.

4. High and Low Cape; now known as *Pointe du Limbé*.

5. Mount Caribata; now known as *Mont Haut du Cap*.

Thursday, 20 December 1492

Today at sunset I anchored in a harbor that lies between Santo Tomás and the Cabo de Caribata.[1] This harbor is very beautiful, and all the ships in Christendom could be contained herein. Its entrance appears impossible from the sea to those who have not entered it, on account of some obstructing rocks that extend from the mountain almost as far as the island. There is no pattern to these rocks; some are in the sea, some are by the land, one here, another there. Because of this it is necessary to be watchful in order to choose one of the entrances that is wide and safe. The water is all 7 fathoms deep, and after one gets by the rocks it is 12 fathoms deep inside. The ship can be secured with any kind of line against any winds that there may be. At the entrance to this harbor there is a channel lying to the west of a small, sandy island covered with trees. Up to the shoreline there are 7 fathoms, but there are many shoals in this vicinity and it is necessary to keep your eyes open until the harbor is entered. Once in, there is no fear from any storm in the world.

From this harbor a very large valley could be seen, all cultivated. It descends to the harbor from the SE and is surrounded by high mountains that seem to reach Heaven. They are very beautiful and covered with trees. Without doubt there are mountains here that are higher than the island of Tenerife[2] in the Canaries, which is said to be the highest that can be found.

At a distance of 3 miles from this part of the Isla de Santo Tomás there is another small island and, nearer than that, another. In all, these are wonderful harbors, but it is necessary to look out for the shoals. I saw villages and the smoke that they made.

----

1. Cape Caribata; now known as *Pointe Saint Honoré.*

2. Columbus was mistaken about the elevations. *El Pico de Teide,* the volcano on Tenerife, Canary Islands, has an elevation of 12,198 feet; Mt. Duarte, Dominican Republic, 10,400 feet. Six peaks in Italy are higher than *El Pico.*

Friday, 21 December 1492

Today I went with the ships' boats to see this harbor, which surpasses any other harbor[1] I have seen before. I have praised the others so much that I do not know how to rate this one highly enough. I fear that I will be accused of stretching the truth to an excessive degree when I say that this is the finest harbor I have encountered in these islands. Still, there are experienced men with me who will confirm that everything I have said about the other harbors is true, but that this is much finer than any of the others.

I have been sailing the seas for 23 years, without laying off for any time long enough to be counted, and I have seen all the East and West (as it is called in going to the north, which is England), and I have traveled through Guinea, but in all those regions harbors as perfect as these will never be found. And it has been the case that each harbor I have come to has been better than the last one. I have considered what I have written very carefully, and I assert I have written correctly and that now this harbor surpasses all the others. All the ships of the world could be contained in it, and it is so sheltered that the oldest line on the ship would hold it fast.

It is 4½ miles[2] from the entrance to the innermost point. I saw well-cultivated fields, although they are all like that. I ordered two men to get out of the boats and go climb a hill to see if there was a village since none could be seen from the sea. I know that the area is inhabited with many people because of the extensive fields; moreover, last night, about 10 o'clock, some Indians came to the ship in a canoe to see us, believing that we are supernatural. I gave them some of the articles of barter, with which they were greatly pleased.

My two men returned and told me they had seen a large village not far from the sea. I ordered them to row ashore as near as they could to where the village was. Soon I saw some Indians approaching the shore, apparently in fear; because of that I ordered the boats stopped and told the Indians with me to speak to them and tell them that no injury would be done to them. The Indians then drew nearer to the shore, and I drew nearer to the land. As soon as they were reassured that we meant them no harm, they came in great numbers, covering the beach and offering a thousand thanks, the men as well as the women and children. Some ran here and other there to bring us some of that bread that they make from niames,[3] which they call ajes. This bread is very white and good. They also brought us water in gourds and in clay pitchers shaped like those of Castile. They brought us all that they had in this world, knowing what I wanted, and they did it so generously and willingly that it was wonderful. It cannot be said that they gave this to us freely only because it was of little value, for they gave us pieces of gold in the same way, as liberally as those who gave us a gourd of water. It is easy to recognize when something is given very willingly and eagerly.

These people have no spears, arrows,[4] or any other arms, nor have the other inhabitants of this island, which I believe to be very large. They are as naked as their mothers gave them birth, men as well as women—unlike the people of Juana and the other islands, where the women wore in front pieces of cotton, something like men's drawers, with which they covered their private parts, especially after the age of 12. But here neither young nor old wore anything. In the other places we have been the men made the women hide from us, through jealousy, but here they do not, and there are some very pretty women. They were the first who came to give thanks to Heaven and bring whatever they had, especially things to eat, such as bread made from ajes, peanuts, and five or six kinds of fruit. I ordered some of the fruit preserved in order to take it to the Sovereigns. The women in the other places did the same thing before the men concealed them.

I ordered that at no time were any of my men to annoy any of these people in any manner—to be on guard against it—and that no one was to take anything from them against their will. For everything we received we traded something in return. I cannot believe that we have found a people with such good hearts, so liberal in giving, and so timid, that they strip themselves of everything to give all that they have to us and, upon arrival, run to bring us everything.

I sent six sailors to explore the village, and the people showed them all the honor they knew how to show and gave them whatever they had, utterly convinced that I and all my people came from Heaven. The Indians I had brought from the other islands also believed this, even though what they *ought* to believe in this respect had already been explained to them. After my six men had returned, some canoes came carrying people who begged me, on the part of their Chief,[5] to go to his village when I left here.

Since the Chief's village was situated on a point of land right on the way, and since he was waiting for me with many of his people, I went there. But before I started, so many men, women, and children came to the shore that it was alarming. They were all crying loudly that I must not leave. But the Chief's messengers who had come to invite me were waiting in their canoes, so I went to see him.

When I arrived where the Chief was waiting for me, he ordered all his people to be seated. They brought us many things to eat and took food to our boats. After they saw that I had received what they had brought, most of them ran back to the village, which must have been near, in order to get more food, which they offered, along with parrots and other things, with such generosity that it was amazing. I gave them glass beads, brass rings, and hawks' bells, not because they asked for anything but because it seemed to me to be the right thing to do and, above all, because I already consider them to be Christians and subjects of the Sovereigns of Castile. They belong to the Sovereigns even more than do the people of Castile. Nothing is lacking except knowledge of their language in order to give them commands because they do whatever they are told, without contradiction. When I departed for the ships all the men, women, and children cried out for us to remain. And even as we were departing, canoes filled with Indians followed us to the ships. I treated them with every courtesy and gave them things to eat and other items I had with me. Another Chief had come previously from the west, and many people even came swimming out to us, though the ship was more than a mile from land.

The Chief that I mentioned had departed, and I sent a few men to see him and question him about these islands. He received my men very well, taking them to his village and giving them some large pieces of gold. They came to a large river that the Indians swam across, but my men were not able to do so and came back.

In this region there are very high mountains that seem to reach Heaven; the mountains of Tenerife appear to be nothing in comparison with them in height and beauty. They are all green and forested, and they surround very pleasant plains. At the foot of this harbor to the south there is one such great plain without an obstructing mountain. The end of this plain

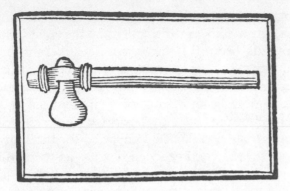

Indian hatchet. (Winsor, 1886, from Oviedo, 1547)

cannot be seen; it must be 45 or 60 miles long. A river flows through it, and it is all populated and cultivated and is as green now as if it were in Castile in May or June, although the nights are 14 hours long and the land is quite far north. This harbor is very good, well sheltered from any winds, and deep. And the entire country is inhabited by very good and gentle people, without arms, either good or bad. And any ship whatever may be free from fear in this harbor, for no ship can come in at night and attack it. Although the mouth is more than 6 miles wide, it is very restricted by two rocky reefs that are hardly visible above water. There is a very narrow entrance in this reef that looks as though it could only have been made by hand, leaving an opening wide enough for ships to enter. In the mouth it is 7 fathoms deep to the foot of a small level island, which has a beach and trees on its shore. The entrance is on the west, and a ship can approach near enough to reach shore without fear. There are three islands to the NW and a large river 3 miles from the head of the harbor. It is the best

harbor in the world and I have named it the *Puerto de la Mar de Santo Tomás,* because this day is his feast day. I called this a sea because it is so large.

----

1. The harbor was Acul Bay. Columbus named the vast approach to the bay *La Mar de Santo Tomás* (The Sea of St. Thomas). The bay itself was named the *Puerto de la Mar de Santo Tomás* (Port of the Sea of St. Thomas).

2. Las Casas mistakenly records 5 leagues. It is 5 Columbian miles from the entrance to the innermost point, not 5 leagues.

3. This was not sweet potato bread, but probably from the *yuca.* See Epilogue.

4. Columbus (or Las Casas) is mistaken. The natives had no bows and arrows, but spears were seen on San Salvador; on 3 December Columbus had even calmed hostile Indians by trading for their spears.

5. Literally, "*Señor,*" i.e., "Lord," or "Chief" in this context.

Saturday, 22 December 1492
(The Log becomes convoluted at this point. The entry for 22 December also contains material for 23 December, as well as additional commentary by Las Casas, omitted in this translation. Even with events assigned to their correct sequence, the account of the visit of Columbus' secretary to the village seems to be told twice, in parallel but slightly varied accounts.)

I set sail at dawn in order to go on my course in search of the islands that the Indians said contained a great deal of gold.

Some are said to have more gold than is to be found on the mainland. But the weather was not favorable, and I had to anchor again. I sent the boat to fish with nets.

The Chief[1] of this country, who lives near here, sent a large canoe full of people, among whom was one of his principal advisors. He begged me to go with the ships to his country and said that he would give me anything he had. He sent me a belt which had hanging from it, in place of a purse, a mask with two large ears, a tongue, and a nose of hammered gold. These people are so generous; they give whatever is asked of them, willingly, and it seems that you are doing them a favor to request something from them.

The Indians in the canoe met the boat from the ship and gave the belt to a boy and came with their canoe alongside the ship. Quite a bit of time was spent trying to communicate with each other, because the Indians with me had difficulty understanding these Indians. There is some difference in the names of things.[2] Finally, through the use of signs, I understood the invitation they were extending, and I determined to start for the Chief's village tomorrow, although I am not in the habit of leaving port on Sunday. This is solely on account of devotion and has nothing to do with any superstition whatever. Furthermore, I am striving to please these people and be agreeable to them because the good will they display makes me hope that they will be converted to Christianity. I trust that this will be accomplished by the Sovereigns of Castile because I already consider that they belong to the Sovereigns and that they may serve the Sovereigns with zeal.

---

1. The first reference to the great *Cacique,* Guacanagari.

2. Columbus makes the first reference to a language change. He is approaching the linguistic frontier of Taino, or Island Arawak.

Sunday, 23 December 1492

Because there was no wind, I did not depart today for the country of the Chief who had sent me an invitation; instead, I sent my secretary and five men to a very large village 9 miles to the east.

At the same time, I sent two of the Indians with me to the villages near the place where we are anchored. Later they returned to the ships with a Chief, and with the news that in this Isla Española there is a great quantity of gold and that people from other places come here to buy it. They said that there is as much gold as we desire. Others came who confirmed that there is much gold on the island, and they showed me the manner of obtaining it. I understood all this with great difficulty, but I felt certain that there was a very large amount of gold and that if I found the source I could get it very cheaply, or even for nothing. In the three days that I have been in this harbor I have received good pieces of gold, and I cannot believe that it is brought from another country. May Our Lord, Who has all things in His hands, assist me and give me whatever may be for His service.

When my secretary and the five men accompanying him

reached the place where the Chief's messengers led them, the Chief took the secretary by the hand and conducted him to his house, accompanied by a great throng of people. He had the people give my men something to eat, and the Indians also brought balls of spun cotton and many things made of cotton. Later in the afternoon, the Chief gave my men three very fat geese and some small pieces of gold.

A great many Indians came back with the sailors, carrying for them all the gifts and items of trade. They contended among themselves for the honor of carrying my people on their shoulders and actually did carry them across some rivers and swampy places. I ordered that some things should be given to the Chief, and he and all his people were greatly pleased, believing that we had come from Heaven and that they were fortunate in seeing us. More than 120 canoes came to the ships today. They all brought something, especially their bread and fish, small earthen jars of water, and seeds of many good kinds of spices. Some of these seeds they put in a gourd full of water and drank it, and the Indians with me said that is very healthy.

I think that more than 1,000 persons came to the ship, all bringing something from what they possessed. Even before these canoes reached the ship, at a distance of half a crossbow shot, the Indians arose and held up what they were bringing, saying, "Take, take." I think that another 500 swam to the ships because they did not have canoes, and we were anchored 3 miles from land! I judge that five princes, sons of chiefs, with all their servants, including women and children, came to see us. I ordered something given to everyone, for it was well spent. May Our Lord in His mercy direct me until I find this gold—this mine—because I have many people here who say that they know where it is.

My secretary and the boats arrived during the night, saying that they had travelled a great distance, and that at the mountain of Caribatan they had found many canoes with a great many people who were coming from the place to which we were headed. I consider it certain that, if I can be in that harbor for Christmas, everyone on this island will come there to see us, and I estimate that this island is larger than England. My men tell me that this village is larger and with better arranged streets than any others we have passed and discovered up to now. The village is about 9 miles SE of *Punta Santa*.[1]

Since the canoes go rapidly with oars, they went on ahead to inform the Cacique that we were coming. I have not been sure, up until now, whether *Cacique* meant king or governor. They also have another word for a nobleman, *nitayno*. I do not know if this means *hidalgo,* governor, or judge.

When my secretary and his men were in the Cacique's village, he finally came to them, and all the people of the village, more than 2,000 of them, came together in the plaza, which was very clean. This King[2] paid great honors to the men, giving them food and drink. Then the King gave each one some cotton cloths such as the women wear, and parrots for me, and some gold. The common people also gave the sailors some of the same cloths and other things from their houses in exchange for the little trifles that were given them. Judging by the way they received them, it seemed as though these items were of great value. In the afternoon, when my men wished to leave, the King begged them to stay, as did all of the people. But when they saw that my men were determined to depart, many of the Indians went with them, carrying on their backs the gifts from the King and from the people, as far as the boats, which remained at the entrance of the river.

----

1. Holy Point; now known as *Pointe Fort Picolet*. On 4 January he calls this *Cabo Santo* (Holy Cape).

2. Columbus uses *este rey* here ("this king"). He frequently interchanges king, lord, chief (*cacique*), etc.

Indian life as depicted in a 16th century woodcut. La Historia. *Benzoni, 1572. (Courtesy Rare Book Division, New York Public Library, Astor, Lenox, and Tilden Foundations)*

Monday, 24 December 1492

Before sunrise I weighed anchors with a land breeze. Among the many Indians who had come to the ship yesterday, telling us about gold on the island and where it could be found, was one who appeared to be better disposed and more friendly. I flattered him, and asked him to go with me to show me the gold mines; he accepted the invitation, bringing with him a companion, or relative. Among the other places they named where gold could be found was Japan, which they call *Cibao*.[1] They said that there is a great quantity of gold there and that the Cacique carries banners of hammered gold, but that it is a great distance to the east.

Your Highnesses may believe that in all the world there cannot be better or more gentle people. Your Highnesses must be greatly pleased because you will soon make them Christians and will teach them the good customs of your realms, for there cannot be a better people or country. The people are so numerous and the country so great that I do not yet know how to describe it. I have already spoken in the superlative degree of the people and the country of Juana, which they call Cuba. But there is as much difference between the people of this country and the people of Juana as there is between day and night. Neither do I believe that any other person who saw this would have done or said less than I have said. Indeed it is true that the things here are marvelous, and so also are the great villages of this Isla Española, as I have named it, and which they call Bohío. And all the people behave in a remarkably friendly manner and speak softly, not like the other Indians, who appear to threaten when they speak. And the men and women are of good statue and are not black. It is true that they all paint themselves, some black, some other colors, but mostly red. I have learned that they do this on account of the sun,[2] which does not injure them as much if they are painted. And the houses and settlements are very attractive, governed by a chief or judge whom all obey, and it is a marvel. And all these chiefs are men of few words and have fine manners, and their orders are usually given by a sign of the hand, and then it is understood, which is a marvel.

Whoever has to enter La Mar de Santo Tomás must put in a good 3 miles above the mouth of the entrance toward a small flat island, which I have named *La Amiga*[3] and which is in the middle of the entrance, and he should turn the prow toward it. After arriving within a stone's throw of the island, he must go west, leaving the island to the east, and he must keep near it and not go to the other side, because there is a very large reef to the west. Also, in the sea outside it there are three shoals, and this reef reaches within a lombard shot of La Amiga. He will then pass in the middle and will find at the most shallow place 7 fathoms of water, with gravel underneath; inside he will find a harbor for all the ships in the world where they can remain without anchors. There is another reef and more shoals that extend from the east toward the said island of La Amiga. These are very large, extending far out into the sea and reaching almost within 6 miles of the cape. But it appears that there is an entrance between them at a distance of two lombard shots from La Amiga. At the foot of Monte Caribatan on its west side there is a very good and large harbor.

---

1. This is the beautiful interior valley of the Dominican Republic, also known in the Log as *Civao*.

2. This may be the first reference in history to suntan lotion!

3. The Girlfriend; now known as *Ile des Rats*.

Tuesday, 25 December 1492 — Christmas Day

I sailed in a light wind yesterday from La Mar de Santo Tomás to Punta Santa, and at the passing of the first watch, 11 o'clock at night, I was 3 miles east of the point. I decided to lie down to sleep because I had not slept for two days[1] and one night. Since it was calm, the sailor who was steering the ship also decided to catch a few winks and left the steering to a young ship's boy, a thing which I have always expressly prohibited throughout the voyage. It made no difference whether there was a wind or calm; the ships were not to be steered by young boys.

I felt secure from shoals and rocks because on Sunday, when I had sent the boats to that King, they had gone a good 10 miles to the east of Punta Santa, and the sailors had seen this entire coast and the shoals that extend from Punta Santa a good 9 miles to the ESE, and they saw where we could pass. This is something I had not done before on this voyage.

Our Lord willed that at midnight, when the crew saw me lie down to rest and also saw that there was a dead calm and the sea was as in a bowl, they all lay down to sleep and left the helm to that boy. The currents carried the ship upon one of these banks. Although it was night, the sea breaking on them made so much noise that they could be heard and seen at a 3-mile distance. The ship went upon the bank so quietly that it was hardly noticeable.[2] When the boy felt the rudder ground and heard the noise of the sea, he cried out. I jumped up instantly; no one else had yet felt that we were aground. Then the master of the ship, Juan de la Cosa,[3] who was on watch, came out. I ordered him to rouse the crew, to launch the small boat we carry on our stern, and to take an anchor and cast it at the stern. The master and many others jumped into the small boat, and I assumed they were going to follow my orders. Instead, their only thoughts were to escape to the *Niña*, which was a 1½ miles to the windward. The crew of the *Niña* would not receive them, which was correct, and therefore they returned to the ship. But the boat from the *Niña* reached the ship before my own boat did!

When I saw that some of my own crew were fleeing and that the sea was becoming more shallow, with my ship broadside to it, I did the only thing I could. I ordered the mast cut and the ship lightened as much as possible, to see if it could be refloated. But the water became even more shallow, and the ship settled more and more to one side. Although there was little or no sea, I could not save her. Then the seams opened, though she remained in one piece.

I took my crew to the *Niña* for their safety, and as there was a light land breeze and still half the night ahead of us, and since I did not know how far the banks extended, I beat about till daybreak and then went inside the bank to the ship. I also dispatched Diego de Arana, master-at-arms of the fleet, and Pedro Gutiérrez, representative of the Royal Household, to take the small boat and go directly to the King that had last Saturday invited me to his village. I instructed them to beg the King to come to this harbor with his boats.

The village of this King is about 5 miles beyond this bank. My men told me that the King wept when he heard of the disaster. He sent all his people from the village with many large canoes to help us unload the ship. The King displayed great haste and diligence, and everything was unloaded in a very brief space of time. He himself personally assisted the unloading, along with his brothers and relatives, and guarded what was taken ashore in order that everything might be completely secure.

From time to time the King sent one of his relatives to me, weeping, to console me, and they said that I was not to be troubled or annoyed, for the King would give me whatever he possessed. I certify to Your Highnesses that in no part of Castile could things be so secure; not even a shoe string was lost!

"Although there was little or no sea, I could not save her."

THE LOG OF CHRISTOPHER COLUMBUS

« 152 »

The King ordered everything placed near the houses, even emptying some in order that everything could be stored and guarded. He ordered armed men placed around the houses to guard everything all night. He, with all his people in the village, wept a great deal. They are an affectionate people, free from avarice and agreeable to everything. I certify to Your Highnesses that in all the world I do not believe there is a better people or a better country. They love their neighbors as themselves, and they have the softest and gentlest voices in the world and are always smiling. They may go naked, but Your Highnesses may be assured that they have very good customs among themselves, and the King maintains a most marvelous state, where everything takes place in an appropriate and well-ordered manner. It is a pleasure to see all of this. These people have good memories and want to see everything; they ask what things are and for what purpose they are used.

----

1. Columbus had been extremely busy with the multitude of Indians coming and going, and he probably did a little celebrating on Christmas Eve, just before the grounding. Too much "partying" may be the simple explanation of the accident that was to follow.

2. Columbus used the term *banco* (bank), where the *Santa María* grounded, not his term for coral reef (*restinga de piedras*). The ship appears to have missed the reef, where the waves made the noise Columbus heard, and gently eased into a sand bank. The ship was not really damaged very much, merely hopelessly stuck.

3. Juan de la Cosa, owner of the *Santa María*, was the same man who made (or compiled) the famous chart of the New World

in 1500. He sailed again with Columbus on the second voyage; made an expedition to South America with Alonso de Ojeda and Amerigo Vespucci (1499); and was the pilot for Rodrigo de Bastidas in 1500–1501 (when Vasco Nuñez de Balboa was aboard and the coast between Cartagena, Colombia, and Porto Belo, Panama, was first explored). In 1504 he returned to Santo Domingo to serve as Ojeda's lieutenant in the colonization of what is now Colombia (called *Nueva Andalucía*). In 1509, in a fight with the Caribs, Juan de la Cosa died from a poisoned arrow.

Wednesday, 26 December 1492

Today at sunrise the King of this country came to the *Niña*, where I was, and almost in tears told me not to be dismayed because he would give me whatever he had. He had already given two very large houses to my men, and he would give us more if we needed them. And yesterday he gave us as many canoes as we needed and the labor to unload the ship, and not even a breadcrumb was taken. They are so loyal and so respectful of the property of others, and this King is even more honest than the others.

While we were talking, another canoe came from some other place and brought some pieces of gold, which the Indians wished to trade for a hawk's bell, for they valued hawks' bells above everything else. The canoe had not even reached the *Niña*'s side when they called out and showed the pieces of gold, saying, "*Chuque, chuque,*" which means hawks' bells, which they are crazy about. When they saw the difficulty we were having, these Indians from the other place departed, begging me to keep a hawk's bell for them until tomorrow. They said that they would bring four pieces of gold as large as the hand. I was pleased to hear this. Then a sailor who had come from land told me that the wonderful pieces of gold my men were trading for in the village were costing practically nothing. For a leather thong the Indians gave pieces of gold worth more than two *castellanos,* and by the end of the month things should get even better.

The King was delighted to see me happy, and he understood that I desired a great deal of gold. He indicated by signs that he knew where there was a lot of it nearby and that I should be of good cheer, for he would give me as much of it as I desired. He told me all about this gold, specifically, that it is found in Japan, which they call *Cibao.* The people there have so much of it that they place no value on it at all and will bring it here. Also, the King told me, there is much gold here in the Isla Española, which they call Bohío, and in the province of Caribata.

The King dined with me on the *Niña* and afterwards went ashore with me, where he paid me great honor. Later we had a meal with two or three kinds of ajes, served with shrimp, game, and other foods they have, including their bread; which they call *cazabe.*[1] Then the King took me to see some groves of trees near the houses, and fully 1,000 people, all naked, went with us. The King was already wearing a shirt and a pair of gloves which I had given him, and he was more excited about the gloves than anything else that had been given him.

By his manner of eating, his decent behavior, and his exceptional cleanliness, he showed himself to be of good birth.

After the meal we remained at the table for some time, and we were brought some herbs with which to rub our hands—I believe they use these to soften the skin. We were also given water for our hands. Later, after we had eaten, the Indians took me to the beach, and I sent for a Turkish bow and a handful of arrows. I had a man from my company who was a skilled archer shoot the arrows. Inasmuch as the King did not know what arms are, since his people neither possess nor use them, the demonstration impressed him very much. This all came about because we had had a conversation about the people of Caniba, whom they call *Caribes,*[2] who come to seize them and who carry bows and arrows without iron tips. Nowhere in these lands is there knowledge of iron or steel, nor of any other metal except gold and copper, and I have seen very little of the latter. I told the King by signs that the Sovereigns of Castile would order the destruction of the Caribes, commanding the Caribes to be brought before them with their hands tied.

I ordered that a lombard and a musket be fired, and the King was spellbound when he saw the effect of their force and what they penetrated. When the people heard the shots, they fell to their knees. They brought me a large mask, which had large pieces of gold in the ears and eyes and in other places, which the King himself presented to me. He placed this, along with other jewels of gold, on my head and around my neck. They also gave many things to the men with me. I derived a great deal of pleasure and consolation from these things, and when I realized that this mitigated the trouble and affliction I had experienced by losing the ship, I recognized that Our Lord had caused me to run aground at this place so that I might establish a settlement here. And so many things came to hand here that the disaster was a blessing in disguise. Certainly, if I had not run aground here, I would have kept out to sea without anchoring at this place because it is situated inside a large bay containing two or three banks of shoals. Neither would I have left any of my people here on this voyage; even if I had desired to leave them, I could not have outfitted them well enough, nor given them enough ammunition, provisions, and materials for a fort. It is quite true that many of the people with me have pleaded with me to permit them to remain here.

Now I have ordered that a tower and a fortress be constructed,[3] very well built, with a large moat. This is not because I believe this to be necessary with these Indians, for I am sure that I could subjugate the entire island—which I believe is larger than Portugal with twice the population—with the men that I have in my company. These Indians are naked, unarmed, and cowardly beyond help. But it is right that this tower be built, and what must be, must be. Since these Indians are so far from Your Highnesses, it is necessary that the people here know your people and what they can do, in order that the Indians may obey Your Highnesses with love and fear.

The men remaining have timbers with which to construct the fortress and provisions of bread and wine for more than a year, as well as seeds for sowing, and the ship's boat. I am leaving a caulker, a carpenter, a gunner, and a caskmaker among the many men who desire zealously to serve Your Highnesses and who will please me greatly if they find the mine where the gold comes from. Thus, everything that has happened was for this purpose, that this beginning may be made.

All this was the will of God: the ship's running aground so easily that it could not be felt, with neither wind nor wave; the cowardice of the ship's master and some of the crew (who were mostly from his part of Spain), who refused my order to cast the stern anchor to draw the ship off and save it; the discovery of this country.

Without God's intervention this country would not have been known as it has come to be known during our time here, and as it will be known by the people I intend to leave here. I had been sailing all the time with the intention of making discoveries and not remaining anywhere longer than a day unless there was no wind because the *Santa María* was very cumbersome and not suited to the work of discovery. The reason I took that ship in the first place was due to the people of Palos, who did not fulfill to me what they had promised the King and Queen. I should have been given ships suitable for this journey, and the people of Palos did not do that. Of the *Santa María*'s contents, not a leather strap was lost, nor a board, nor a nail, because the ship remained as sound as when she started except that we chopped and split her some in order to remove

"I ordered that a lombard and a musket be fired, and the king was spellbound when he saw the effect of their force."

the large casks and all the cargo. All these things have been placed on land and are well secured.

I hope to God that when I come back here from Castile, which I intend on doing, that I will find a barrel of gold, for which these people I am leaving will have traded, and that they will have found the gold mine, and the spices, and in such quantities *that within three years[4] the Sovereigns will prepare for and undertake the conquest of the Holy Land. I have already petitioned Your Highnesses to see that all the profits of this, my enterprise, should be spent on the conquest of Jerusalem, and Your Highnesses smiled and said that the idea pleased them, and that even without this expedition they had the inclination to do it.*

----

1. Manioc bread. For a more extensive discussion of roots and breads, see Epilogue.

2. First mention of these feared cannibals using the name by which they are known today. Native to South America, they had followed the Taino migrations northward through the Lesser Antilles to Puerto Rico. By 1492 they were raiding Española. Their name also survives in the name Caribbean Sea.

3. For a more extensive discussion of *La Navidad,* the first Spanish town in the New World, see Epilogue.

4. Author's italics. According to John Boyd Thacher, this is Columbus' Grand Design: the conquest of the Holy Land, financed by the wealth obtained from the enterprise.

Thursday, 27 December 1492

At sunrise the King of this land came to the *Niña* and told me that he had sent for gold and wanted to cover me from head to foot with it before I departed, and he begged me not to leave before this. He ate with me, as did his brother and another close relative. Both the brother and his relative told me that they wished to go to Castile with me. At this time it was reported by an Indian messenger that the caravel *Pinta* had come to a river at the end of this island. This was the first report of its whereabouts since the night of 22 November, when it sailed east for the island of Babeque. The Cacique, who loved me so much that it was a marvel, instantly dispatched a canoe there, and one of my men went with it. I was already preparing to return to Castile as soon as possible.

Friday, 28 December 1492

I went ashore in order to hasten the construction of the fortress and to put on any final touches. Also, I wanted to establish a chain of command and instructions for those who were to remain. Apparently, the King saw me going to the boat. He entered his house quickly, pretending to ignore my arrival on land, but sent one of his brothers to receive me. He led me to one of the houses that had been given to us, which was one of the largest and best in the village. In this house the Indians had prepared a raised platform made from the inner bark of a palm tree, and here they sat me. Then the brother sent one of his pages to inform the King that I was there, as though the King did not already know it. I realize now that the King was pretending ignorance of all of this in order to pay me even more honor. When the page told the Cacique, he came running to me and placed a large plate of gold around my neck, which he had carried in his hands. He stayed there with me until afternoon, considering what was to be done.

Saturday, 29 December 1492

At sunrise, a nephew of the King, a very young boy of good judgment and courage, came to the ship. Since I always attempted to learn where the gold came from, I questioned everyone I could, and I already understood something by means of signs. In this manner the boy told me that at a distance of four days' journey to the east there was an island called *Guarionex,* and others which they called *Macorix, Mayonic, Fuma, Cibao,* and *Coroay,*[1] in which there was an infinite amount of gold. I wrote down these names, and a brother of the King, upon learning that the nephew had told me this, rebuked him, according to what I understood. Also, I had felt at other times that the King was trying to keep me in ignorance of the places where the gold was to be found and collected, so that I might not go to trade for it and buy it elsewhere. But there is so much of it and in so many locations on this Isla Española that it is wonderful. After dark the King sent a large mask of gold and begged me for a handbasin and pitcher. I believe that he asked for these so that he could copy them and make others, and therefore I sent them to him.

----

1. These were all Indian provinces, not islands. Some of the names have survived, almost without change, such as *Cibao* and *Macoris.*

Sunday, 30 December 1492

I went ashore to eat and arrived at the time when five kings, who were subjects of this Guacanagari,[1] arrived. They all wore crowns as an indication of their high rank, and Your Highnesses would be pleased to witness their bearing. When I came ashore, the King took me by the arm and led me to the same house where I was yesterday, where he had the raised platform and the chair for me to sit in. He then took off his crown from his own head and placed it upon mine, and I took from around my neck a necklace of good bloodstones—very beautiful beads of fine colors, excellent in every way—and placed them around his neck. I then took off a cloak of fine scarlet cloth that I was wearing that day and clothed the King with it. I also sent for some colored boots, laced with leather thongs, and made him put them on, and I placed upon his finger a large silver ring. I had been told that he had seen a silver ring on one of my sailors and desired it very much. The King was joyful and overwhelmed, and two of these kings who were there with Guacanagari came to me, each presenting me with a large gold plaque.

In the midst of these festivities, an Indian arrived with the news that two days ago he had left the caravel *Pinta* in a harbor to the east. I returned to the *Niña* with this information, and while there, the *Niña*'s captain, Vincente Yáñez Pinzón, told me that he had seen rhubarb on the island of Amiga, which is at the entrance of La Mar de Santo Tomás, 18 miles from here; he recognized the leaves and roots. They say that rhubarb sends small shoots out of the ground and bears fruits that look like green mulberries, almost dry. The stalk that grows from the root is yellow and as fine as the best color there can be to paint. Underground the root grows like a large pear.

----
1. This is the first time Columbus has used the cacique's formal name.

Monday, 31 December 1492

Today I occupied myself with seeing that water and wood were taken aboard in preparation for the departure for Spain, in order to give speedy information to the Sovereigns, so that they may send ships to discover that which remains to be discovered. This enterprise already appears to be so great and of such importance that it is wonderful. I would like to see all the land to the east of here before departing, and to go all along this coast in order to learn its distance from Castile, so as to bring cattle and other things here. But I have only one ship remaining, and it does not appear reasonable to expose myself to the dangers that might occur in making these discoveries. All this trouble and inconvenience has arisen because the *Pinta* deserted me.

Tuesday, 1 January 1493

At midnight I sent a boat to the island of *Amiga* to fetch the rhubarb. It returned at vespers with a basketful. They did not bring more because they did not carry a spade with them to dig it. I am carrying what they brought to the Sovereigns as a specimen. The King of this country has sent many canoes for

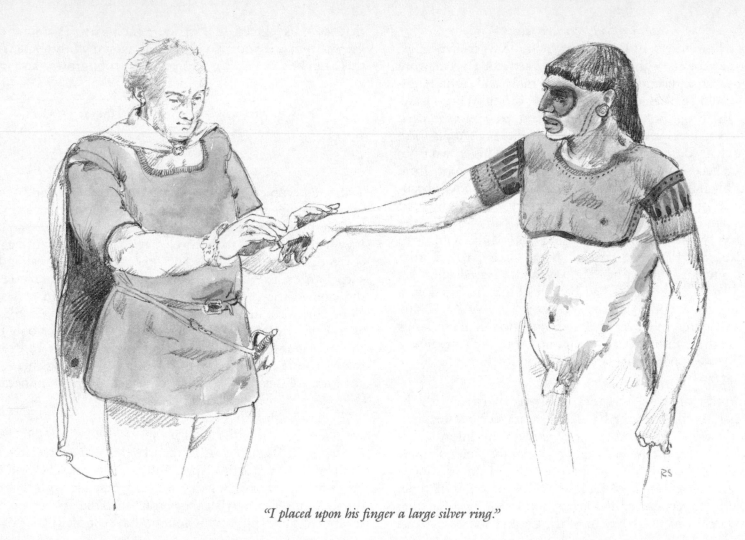

"I placed upon his finger a large silver ring."

THE LOG OF CHRISTOPHER COLUMBUS

gold. The sailor who had been sent with the Indian canoe to look for the *Pinta* returned without finding anything. This sailor told me that at a distance of 15 miles[1] from there he had seen a king who wore upon his head two large gold plates, and when the Indians in the canoe spoke to him he took them off; the sailor said he also saw other persons with a great deal of gold. I think that King Guacanagari has prohibited everyone from trading gold to us, so that it might all pass through his hands. But I have learned about places where there is so much gold that they do not assign a price to it. I have also learned where there are spices in large quantities, worth more than pepper or allspice. The people remaining here have been ordered to obtain as much of these as they can.

----

1. 20 leagues (60 NM) in the Log, an obvious mistake for 20 miles (15 NM).

Wednesday, 2 January 1493

I went ashore this morning to take leave of King Guacanagari and to depart in the name of the Lord. I gave the King one of my shirts and showed him the force of the lombards and their effect. For this purpose I ordered one loaded and fired at the side of the *Santa María,* which was aground. This all came about as a result of a conversation about the Caribes, with whom they were at war. The King saw how far the lombard shot reached and how it passed through the side of the ship. I also had the people from the ship fight a mock battle with their arms, telling the Cacique not to fear the Caribes if they came. I did all this so that the King would consider those I am leaving as friends, and also that he might fear them. The King escorted me and the men with me to his house to eat with him.

I left on this Isla Española, which the Indians call Bohío, 39 men in the fortress, under the command of three officers, all of whom are very friendly with King Guacanagari. In command is Diego de Arana, a native of Córdoba, whom I have given all of the powers I have received from the Sovereigns, in full. Next in line, if something should happen to him, is his lieutenant, Pedro Gutiérrez, the representative of the Royal Household. Next in the line of succession is the lieutenant Rodrigo de Escobedo, secretary of the fleet and a native of Segovia, nephew of the friar Rodrigo Pérez.[1]

I have left with them all the merchandise which the Sovereigns had ordered purchased for trading, of which there is a large quantity. With this they may trade and barter for gold, together with everything the grounded ship carried. I also left them sufficient biscuits for a year and wine and much artillery. I also left the ship's boat, since most of them are sailors, so they can go find the gold mine when they see that the time is favorable. In this manner, when I return, I might find a lot of gold waiting and a place to establish a settlement, for this harbor is not to my liking. Since the gold that is brought here comes from the east, the more they went to the east the closer to Spain they would be. I also left seeds for sowing, and I left my officers, including the secretary and the master-at-arms, and among the others a ship's carpenter, a caulker, a good gunner who knows a great deal about machines, a caskmaker, a physician, and a tailor. All these men are also seamen.

Many times I charged Diego de Arana, Pedro Gutiérrez, and Rodrigo de Escobedo to see that everything was well ruled and governed for the service of God and Your Highnesses. I gathered my men together, the ones I was leaving, and addressed them.[2] First, I charged them to consider the great blessings that God has bestowed upon me and upon all of them up until now, and the benefits he has offered them, for which they must always give Him endless thanks and dedicate themselves to His goodness and mercy, taking care not to offend Him and placing all their hope in Him. They must pray to Him for my return, which, with His aid, I promised them would be as soon as possible—which, I trust to God, would please everyone. Second, I begged them and charged them and ordered them, on the part of Your Highnesses, to obey their Captain as myself, as I am confident of his merit and loyalty. Third, they should greatly respect King Guacanagari and his chiefs and principal men, or nitaynos, and other inferior chiefs. And they should avoid as they would death annoying or tormenting the Indians, bearing in mind how much they owe these people, and why it is necessary to keep them content, since they are remaining in Indian land and under Indian dominion. They should strive, by their honest and gentle speech, to gain the good will of the Indians, keeping their friendship and love, so that our relationship with them will be as friendly and pleasant, and more so, when I return. Fourth, I ordered them and begged them earnestly to do no injury or use any force toward any Indian—man or woman—nor take from them anything against their will. Especially, they should be on guard and avoid doing injury or using violence toward the women, by which they would cause scandal and set a bad example for the Indians, and expose our own infamy, we whom the Indians are certain come from Heaven. Fifth, I charged them not to scatter themselves or go inland, but to stay together until I return, and most of all, not to leave the land and dominion of that King who loves them so much and has been so good and merciful to them. Sixth, I encouraged them to suffer their solitude, which is only a little less than exile, although they willingly have chosen it. Seventh, I charged them that, when they saw it was fitting, to beg the King to send some Indians with them in canoes, and to take the ship's boat along the coast to see if they could discover the mines of gold, for it seems to me that the gold comes from the east. Also, they should look for a good place to build a village because I am not pleased with this harbor. Further, if they find any gold they can barter for, they should do so, discreetly, so that when I return I shall find a great quantity of it. Eighth and last, I promised them that I would petition the Sovereigns to grant them special favors, which they truly merit, and which they will see fulfilled when they are rewarded by the Sovereigns and, with the favor of God, by me when I return.

The Cacique demonstrated much love for me and great emotion over my departure, especially when he saw that I was ready to embark. A favorite of the King told me that he had ordered a statue of pure gold made as large as me and that at the end of 10 days they were to bring it to me. I embarked, with the intention of departing then, but the wind would not allow me to do so.

----

1. See Epilogue for the names of those remaining at *La Navidad*. The friar was Juan (not Rodrigo) Pérez. He was the one who had intervened with Queen Isabela on Columbus' behalf in 1491.

2. This speech, with its eight points, is from Las Casas' *Historia*, and was certainly a part of the original Log. It does not, however, appear in the abstracted Log.

Thursday, 3 January 1493

I did not leave today because last night three of the Indians who had come with me from the other islands and remained here on land, reported to me that other Indians and their wives were coming today at sunrise. The sea had also changed somewhat, and the small boat could not go ashore. I determined to depart tomorrow, the grace of God permitting.

If I had had the *Pinta* with me, I would certainly have obtained a cask of gold because I would have been willing to follow the coasts of these islands. But being alone, I would not dare risk this, as I do not want anything to befall me and prevent my returning to Castile and informing the Sovereigns of everything I have found. If I were certain that the *Pinta* would reach Spain in safety with Martín Alonso Pinzón, I would not hesitate to continue the exploration. But because I do not know if this will happen, and since Pinzón would be able to lie to the Sovereigns to avoid the punishment he deserves for leaving me without permission and preventing all the good that might have come about and all that might have been learned at this time, I feel confident that Our Lord will give me good weather and everything will be remedied.

Friday, 4 January 1493

At sunrise I weighed anchors in a light wind. I sent the small boat ahead on a course to the NW to get outside of the reef, using a wider channel than the one by which I had entered. This channel and others are very suitable for going to the *Villa de la Navidad;*[1] the least depth is 3 fathoms, and it ranges up to 9 fathoms. This channel extends from the NW to the SE along the reefs that extend from *Cabo Santo*[2] (Punta Santa) to *Cabo de Sierpe,*[3] a distance of more than 18 miles, and that reach out into the sea a good 3 miles[4] beyond Cabo Santo. Three miles beyond Cabo Santo the water is not more than 8 fathoms deep, and inside the cape to the east there are many shoals and channels to pass through. This entire coast extends NW and SE and is all beach, and the land is very level for a distance of 12 miles inland. After that there are very high mountains, and it is all well populated with large villages and good people, as we have seen.

I sailed to the east toward a very high mountain that looks like an island but is not. It is connected to the land by a low isthmus and is shaped like a very beautiful tent. I named this mountain *Monte Cristi*[5] and it is exactly east of Cabo Santo at a distance of about 24 miles. Since there was a very light wind

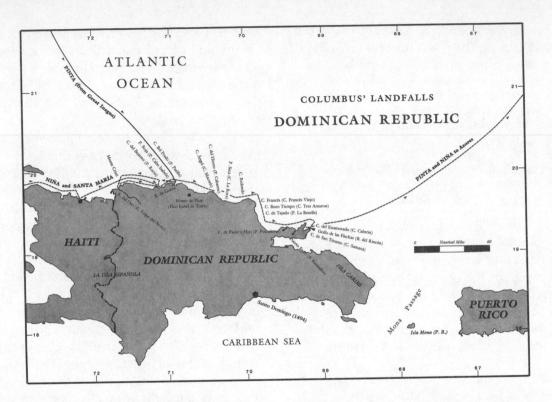

ATLANTIC OCEAN

COLUMBUS' LANDFALLS
DOMINICAN REPUBLIC

HAITI

DOMINICAN REPUBLIC

PUERTO RICO

Santo Domingo (1494)

CARIBBEAN SEA

Mona Passage

Isla Mona (P. R.)

today, I was only able to get within 18 miles of Monte Cristi. I found four very low, small, sandy islets with a reef projecting well out toward the NW and extending to the SE. Inside there is a large gulf that extends to the SE from the mountain a good 60 miles, and that seems to be very shallow and have many shoals. Inside this gulf, along the coast, there are many rivers that are not navigable, although the sailor I had sent with the Indians to look for the *Pinta* said that he had seen a river where ships could enter.

I anchored here for the night, 4½ miles from Monte Cristi[6] and in 19 fathoms of water, having put out to sea a little in order to avoid the many shoals and banks. Whoever is obliged to go to the Villa de la Navidad must take his bearing from

Monte Cristi at a distance of 6 miles on the sea. I am certain that Japan is on this island and that there is a great deal of gold and a great quantity of spices, mastic, and rhubarb.

----

1. This is the first mention of the name of the village established by Columbus. Because it was founded on Christmas Day (*Navidad* means Nativity), its name is most fitting. For a more extensive discussion, see Epilogue.

2. Punta Santa, already mentioned in the entry for 23 December.

3. Cape of the Serpent; now known as *Pointe Yaquezi*.

4. The Log again confuses miles and leagues. In point of fact, the reefs are 3 miles offshore at this location.

5. Christ Mountain. The name survives in the town of the same name. The Log states that Monte Cristi is 18 Leagues (54 NM) from Cabo Santo. Another error: 8 leagues (not 18), or about 24 NM.

6. The Log entry, "6 leagues," again confuses leagues and miles. The correct reading is "6 Columbian miles, or 4½ NM.

Saturday, 5 January 1493

Just before sunrise I made sail with a land breeze. It then shifted and blew from the east and I saw to the SSE, between Monte Cristi and a small island, what appeared to be a good harbor in which to anchor tonight. I took the course to the ESE and then to the SSE, a distance of 18 miles; having accomplished this, I found the water 17 fathoms deep and very clear. I went for 9 miles with the same depth. Then it was only 12 fathoms as far as the head of the mountain; beyond the head, at a distance of 3 miles, I found the depth to be 9 fathoms and clear, the bottom all fine sand. I followed this route until I entered between the mountain and the small island, where the depth at low tide is 3½ fathoms. It is a very remarkable harbor and I anchored here.

I took the boat to the small island,[1] where I found a fire and signs that fishermen had been here. There I saw many colored rocks, like a rock quarry, very beautiful and formed naturally. They would be suitable for building churches or royal structures, and are like those I found on the island of San Salvador.
    I also found on this small island many mastic tree roots.

Monte Cristi is very beautiful and high and accessible, and has a pretty shape. All this country near the mountain is low, forming a lovely plain, and the mountain is so tall that when one sees it from a distance it looks like an island. Beyond the mountain, 18 miles to the east, I saw a cape that I named *Cabo del Bezerro*.[2] Between Monte Cristi and the cape the reef extends seaward for 6 miles, although it seems to me that there are channels by which one could enter. Nevertheless, it is necessary to try this during the daytime, and a small boat must first make soundings. To the east of Monte Cristi, toward Cabo de Bezerro, the 12 miles is all beach, and the land is very low and beautiful. The rest of the land is very high, with beautiful and well-cultivated mountains. A range of mountains extends inland from the NW to the SE.[3] This is the most beautiful mountain range that I have seen, looking exactly like the mountains of Córdoba. Other very high mountains also may be seen in the distance to the south and SE, as well as very large valleys that are green and beautiful, and many rivers. All of this is so extensive and so delightful that I do not believe I am exaggerating by a thousandth part. To the east of the mountain range I saw another mountain similar to Monte Cristi in size and beauty. To the NE by east the land is not so high and must extend for 75 miles.

---

1. The small island is *Isla Cabra;* Goat Island. The colored rocks are coral and a quarry of this description is found at the eastern end of Samana Cay, where an exposed ridge appears to be man-made.

2. A spelling error in the Log for *Becerro:* Cape of the Calf; now known as *Punta Rucia.*

3. The Log states "NE to SE." The correct orientation is "NW to SE."

Sunday, 6 January 1493

This harbor is sheltered from all winds except those from the north and NW. These prevail very rarely in this country, and behind the small island refuge may be had even from these. The water is from 3 to 4 fathoms deep. After sunrise I made sail to go along the coast to the east, but it is necessary to watch out for many reefs and sandbars on this coast, although it is true that inside them there are good harbors, as well as good approaches through their channels. After midday the wind blew strongly from the east, and I ordered a sailor to climb to the top of the mast to look out for shoals. He saw the *Pinta* approaching from the east,[1] and she came up to me. Because the water was so shallow, I was afraid to anchor, so I retraced my course 30 miles to Monte Cristi, and the *Pinta* went with me.

Martín Alonso Pinzón came aboard the *Niña* to apologize, saying that he had become separated against his will. He gave many reasons for his departure, but they are all false. Pinzón acted with greed and arrogance that night when he sailed off and left me, and I do not know why he has been so disloyal and untrustworthy toward me on this voyage. Even so, I am going to ignore these actions in order to prevent Satan from hindering this voyage, as he has done up until now.

An Indian, among those I had commended to Pinzón, told Pinzón that on the island of Babeque there was a great quantity of gold; since the *Pinta* was light and swift, he wished to withdraw and go by himself, leaving me. I wished, on the other hand, to take my time and explore the coast of Juana and the Isla Española, since both of these were on a course to the east. After Pinzón went to Babeque, the Indian told me that he found no gold. He then came to the coast of the Isla Española (which the Indians call Bohío) because other Indians told him that there was on this island a great amount of gold and many mines. Because of these circumstances he came within 45 miles of the Villa de la Navidad more than 20 days ago. Judging from this, it seems as though the news given by the Indians (on December 27th) that they had seen the *Pinta* was true. It was on this account that King Guacanagari dispatched a canoe, and I sent a sailor with it, but the *Pinta* must have been gone by the time the canoe arrived.

The *Pinta*'s crew traded for a great deal of gold; for a piece of leather strap they were given good pieces of gold the size of two fingers, and at times as large as the hand. Pinzón took half and divided the other half among his people. So, Lords and Princes, I know that Our Lord miraculously ordered that the *Santa María* should remain here because it is the best place on all the islands to make a settlement, and it is near the gold mines.

I learned that behind the island of Juana to the south there is another large island, on which there is a larger quantity of gold than on this one. There they find nuggets larger than beans; on this Isla Española the bits of gold taken from the mines are no larger than kernels of wheat. That island is called *Yamaye*.[2] I also learned that toward the east there is an island where the only inhabitants are women. I have heard this from many people. Further, I have learned that the Isla Española and Yamaye are distant from the mainland a 10 days' journey in a canoe, which might mean 180 or 210 miles, and that the people there wear clothes.

----

1. Since departing the fleet on 21 November, the *Pinta* had sailed to Babeque (Great Inagua Island) and thence to a location east of Monte Cristi on the island of Española.

2. Jamaica. This is the first mention of the large island south of Cuba. It had the same Taino peoples and culture in 1492, and was first sighted by Columbus on May 4, 1494, during the second voyage.

Monday, 7 January 1493

Today I ordered the *Niña*, which was leaking, to be pumped out and caulked. I sent the sailors to land for wood, and they found a great quantity of mastic and aloe.

Tuesday, 8 January 1493

Because of a strong east and SE wind I did not start today, but I ordered the ships supplied with wood and water and everything necessary for the voyage. Although I wanted to sail this entire coast of the Isla Española, which I could do maintaining my course, my captains on the caravels are brothers, that is to say, Martín Alonso Pinzón and Vincente Yáñez Pinzón, and their followers are greedy and untrustworthy. They do not respect the honor I have shown them, and they have not and do not obey my commands. Rather, they have done and said many unjust things against me, and Martín Alonso left me from 22 November to 6 January, without cause or reason, but from disobedience. All this I have endured in silence, in order to finish my voyage successfully. On account of this, in order to escape such bad company, which I have to ignore, I have

A manatee. (Oviedo, 1547)

decided to return with the greatest possible haste and not to stop longer. Although there are many disobedient people among the crew, there are also many good men. Now is not the time to think about their punishment.

I took the boat and went to the river near here, a long 3 miles from Monte Cristi toward the SSW,[1] where the sailors were going to get water for the ship. At the mouth of the river, which is very wide and deep, I found that the sand was full of gold, in such quantity that it is wonderful, although it is in very small grains. I believe it crumbled into small pieces as it came down the river; although in a short space I found many grains the size of lentil seeds, more of them were very small. Since the sea was calm and the salt water mixed with the fresh, I ordered the boat to go up the river a stone's throw. The men filled the barrels, and on the way to the ship they found little pieces of gold caught in the hoops of the barrels, and the same in the hoops of the casks. I named this *El Río del Oro*.[2] It is very deep inside the entrance, although the entrance itself is shallow, and the mouth is very wide. It is 21 miles[3] from this river to the Villa de la Navidad. There are many other large rivers between here and the Villa de la Navidad, and three especially, which are larger than this one, must have more gold, although this river is almost as large as the Guadalquivir at Córdoba. From these rivers to the gold mines it is not 60 miles. I am not taking this sand which contains so much gold because Your Highnesses have it in your possession and at the door of your Villa de la Navidad. Besides, I want to return as soon as possible to bring the news and to rid myself of the bad companions I have. I have always said that they were a disobedient people.[4]

----

1. *SSE* in the Log, an obvious error.

2. River of Gold; now known as *Río Yaque del Norte*.

3. The Log gives 17 leagues, an obvious error for 7 leagues (21 NM).

4. The "disobedient people" were mainly the "Pinzón clique," mostly aboard the *Pinta*. The northern Spaniards on the *Santa María* were generally loyal, but Columbus felt that those from Palos-Moguer-Huelva could not be trusted.

Wednesday, 9 January 1493

At midnight I raised sails with the wind SE and sailed to the ENE. I reached a point I named *Punta Roja*,[1] which is exactly east of Monte Cristi some 45 miles. In the shelter of this point I anchored at 3 o'clock in the afternoon. I dared not depart from there at night because of the many reefs. After these reefs are investigated, they will be advantageous, since they all must have openings. The water inside is very deep and forms a secure anchorage against all winds. The land from Monte Cristi to which I am anchored is high and smooth, with attractive fields, behind which are very beautiful mountains extending from east to west. All these mountains are green and cultivated, and it is a wonderful thing to see their beauty. There are also many rivers.

In this country there are many tortoises; the sailors captured some of them that had come ashore to lay their eggs at Monte Cristi. They are very large, like great wooden shields. Yesterday, when I was going to the Río del Oro, I saw three sirens[2] that came up very high out of the sea. They are not as beautiful as they are painted, since in some ways they have a face like a man. I have seen them on other occasions in Guinea on the coast of Manegueta.[3] Tonight, in the name of Our Lord, I will start on my journey without further delay for any reason, since I have found what I have sought. Also, I do not wish to have more trouble with this Martín Alonso until Your Highnesses learn the news of this voyage and what he has done. Then I will not suffer from the evil actions of persons without virtue, who, with little regard, presume to follow their own wills in opposition to those who did them honor.

----

1. Red Point; now known as *Punta Cabo Isabela*.

2. The common manatee, known in Spanish as *sirena* until the Taino word *manatí* came into use after Columbus, thence into English.

3. Malagueta Coast of Liberia and Sierra Leone.

Thursday, 10 January 1493

I departed the place where I was anchored and at sunset reached a river that I named *Río de Gracia*,[1] 9 miles to the SE. I found a good anchorage at its mouth, on the eastern side. The entrance is very narrow, and I discovered a bank where the water is only 2 fathoms deep. Within there is a good sheltered harbor, but there are a great many shipworms. The *Pinta* had remained here 16 days trading for gold, since that is what Martín Alonso desired, and had suffered severely from the worms. It was here that Martín Alonso learned from the Indians that I was on the coast of the Isla Española and that he could not avoid me, so he came to me. He wanted all the people on his ship to swear that he had only been there six days, but his wickedness is so well known that he cannot hide what happened. Martín Alonso had made a rule that he was to get half the gold that was traded for or obtained. And when he had to leave this river, he took four Indian men and two young girls by force. I ordered them clothed and returned to land so that they might go to their own houses. This is for the service of Your Highnesses because all the men and women on this island belong to you, as do those on the other islands. But here, where Your Highnesses already have a settlement, honor and favor must be shown to the people, since there is so much gold on this island and such good lands and so much spice.

----

1. River of Grace (or Attractiveness); now known as *Puerto Blanco*.

Friday, 11 January 1493

At midnight I departed the Río de Gracia with a land breeze and sailed to the east as far as a cape that I named *Bel Prado,* a distance of 12 miles. To the SE from here is a mountain I named *Monte de Plata,*[1] 24 miles away. About 14 miles[2] from the *Cabo de Bel Prado*[3] to the east by south is a cape I call *Cabo del Ángel.*[4] Extending from this cape to the Monte de Plata is a gulf and the best and most lovely lands in the world, all high with beautiful fields. These extend a long distance inland; beyond is a very high and beautiful mountain range, stretching from east to west. At the foot of the mountain there is a very good harbor, 14 fathoms deep at one entrance. Looming above it, the mountain is very high and beautiful. This area is well populated and must contain good rivers and much gold. Twelve miles from the Cabo del Ángel to the east by south there is a point, which I named *Cabo del Hierro.*[5] Twelve miles farther in the same direction is a point I named *Punta Seca;*[6]

18 miles from there, still in the same direction, is *Cabo Redondo.*[7] East of that is *Cabo Francés,*[8] on the east side of which is a large bay that does not appear to me to have an anchorage. Three miles from there is the *Cabo del Buen Tiempo,*[9] and a long three miles from there to the south by east there is a cape I have named *Cabo de Tajado.*[10] South of this cape I saw another at a distance of about 45 miles. I made a great distance today because the winds and currents were favorable. I did not dare anchor for fear of the shoals so I beat about all night.

----

1. Silver Mountain; now known as *Pico Isabel de Torres.*

2. Another league/mile transposition. The Log entry of 18 leagues (54 NM) is too great; 18 Columbian miles (about 14 NM) is close to the correct value.

3. Beautiful Meadow Cape; now known as *Punta Patilla.*

4. Angel Cape; now known as *Cabo Macorís.*

5. Iron Cape; now known as *Punta Cabarete.*

6. Dry Point; now known as *Cabo de La Roca.*

7. Round Cape; possibly *Cabo Tutinfierno.*

8. French Cape; now known as *Cabo Frances Viejo.*

9. Cape of the Good Weather; now known as *Cabo Tres Amarras.*

Saturday, 12 January 1493

Before dawn I sailed to the east with a fresh breeze, making 15 miles by sunrise, and in the next two hours I went another 18 miles. From there I saw land to the south, at a distance of about 36 miles, and made for it. I remained a safe distance from land and steered SSE[1] this night for 21 miles.

----

1. The Log states that the direction was NNE, but Columbus was following the coast to the SSE.

Sunday, 13 January 1493
(Included in the Log under the entry for 12 January)

At dawn I saw the land: a cape that I named *Cabo de Padre é Hijo*[1] because at the eastern end it has two small rocky points, one larger than the other. Six miles to the east I came to a large and very beautiful inlet between two great mountains and saw that it was a spacious harbor, well protected, with a very nice entrance. But it was quite early in the morning, and in order not to lose time (because most of the time the wind here blows from the east and one is carried NNW), I could not delay any longer. I continued on to the east as far as a very high and beautiful cape of jagged rock, which I named *Cabo del Enamorado*.[2] This cape is 24 miles east of the harbor mentioned above, which I named *Puerto Sacro*.[3] Upon arriving at this cape I discovered yet another, even more beautiful and

higher and rounded,[4] all rock, like the Cabo de San Vincente in Portugal. It is 9 miles east of Cabo del Enamorado. Between these two capes there is a large bay,[5] 9 miles wide, in the middle of which there is a very tiny island. The water of the bay is quite deep right up to the land. I anchored here in 12 fathoms of water and sent the boat ashore for water and to see if my men could speak with the people, but they all fled. Another reason I anchored was to see if this land is part of the Isla Española, or if the two are separated by this bay. I am amazed to find that the Isla Española is so large.

I did not leave this anchorage because there was no land breeze. I would like to have left to get to a better harbor because this place is somewhat exposed. Also, I wanted to observe the conjunction of the moon[6] with the sun, which is expected to occur on the 17th of this month, as well as the conjunction of the moon with Mercury, and the opposition of both the moon and the sun to Jupiter, which is the cause of great winds.

I sent the men ashore to a beautiful beach to get some ajes to eat, and they found some men with bows and arrows. They traded for two bows and many arrows and begged one of the Indians to come to the ship to speak to me. He came, and he is much uglier in the face than any of the other Indians I have seen; it was all smeared with charcoal, although everywhere the Indians are accustomed to painting themselves different colors. He wears his hair very long, drawn back, and tied in a

Caribs eating Spaniards, ca. 1497–1504. (Winsor, 1886)

pony tail, then gathered in a net of parrot feathers. He was naked like all the others. I assume that he is one of the Caribes[7] who eat men, and that the bay I saw yesterday separates the land and makes this an island by itself. When I asked him about the Caribes, he made signs to the east, nearby, which I saw yesterday before I entered this bay. The Indian told me that there is a great deal of gold in that land; he pointed to the poop of the caravel, which is very large, and indicated that there are pieces as large as that. He called gold *tuob* and did not understand it as *caoma,* as it is called in the first part of the Isla Española, nor as *nozay*[8] as it is called in San Salvador and the other islands. On the Isla Española they call copper or a poor quality of gold tuob. This Indian told me of the island of *Matinino,*[9] farther to the east of Caribe, and said that it is

inhabited only by women, and that on it is a great deal of tuob, which is gold or copper. He also told me about the island of *Goanin,*[10] where there is a lot of tuob. I have already been told about these islands by many persons in the past several days. In the islands I have passed the inhabitants greatly fear the Caribes, which in some places they call the Canibas, but in the Isla Española they are called Caribes. They must be very daring people since they go to all the islands and eat the people they are able to capture. I understood a few words, and in this way I learned other things; the Indians with me understood more, although the languages are different because of the great distances of these lands from each other. I ordered that the Indian be given something to eat, and I gave him pieces of green and red cloth and some small glass beads, which they like very much. I sent him ashore and told him to bring gold if he had it, which I think he had, based on some of the jewelery he wore.

When the boat reached land there were at least 55 men behind the trees, all naked and wearing their hair long, as the women wear it in Castile. On the back of their heads they wore head-dresses of parrot feathers and other feathers, and each one carried a bow. The Indian in the boat went ashore and made the others lay down their bows and arrows, and the heavy, club-like sticks that they carry in place of a sword. These Indians came to the boat, and my men landed and began to trade for the bows and arrows and other arms because I had ordered them to do so. But after trading two bows, these Indians did not wish to give up any more; rather, they prepared to attack the sailors and capture them. They ran to get their bows and arrows where they had laid them and returned with cords in their hands to bind the men. The sailors were ready, since I always advised my men to be on guard; when the Indians approached, the sailors attacked. They gave one Indian a great cut on the buttocks and wounded another in the breast with an arrow. When the Indians saw that they could gain little, although there were only seven Spaniards and more than 50 of them, they took flight until not one remained. One left his arrows here; another, his bow there. The men would have killed many of them if the pilot who went ashore as captain had not prevented it. The men then returned to the caravel and told me of the affair. In one way it troubled me and in another it did not, i.e., in that now they might be afraid of us. Without doubt, the people here are evil, and I believe they are from the island of Caribe, and that they eat men. If the boat I left with 39 men in the fortress and Villa de la Navidad comes here, these people may be afraid to do them any harm. If these people are not Caribes, they must at least be inhabitants of lands fronting them and have the same customs and the same fearlessness, not like the others on the other islands who are without arms and cowardly beyond reason. These people also build many fires according to the custom on this Isla Española, and I would like to take some of them with me.

----

1. Father and Son Cape; now known as *Punta Pescadores*.

2. Lover's (Leap) Cape; now known as *Cabo Cabrón*.

3. Sacred Port; now known as *Puerto Escondido*.

4. The name is not formally mentioned until 16 January, but Columbus is referring to *Cabo de San Théramo* (Cape of Saint Theramo); now known as *Cabo Samaná*.

5. The large bay, between Cabo del Enamorado (*Cabrón*) and San Théramo (*Samaná*) is *Puerto Rincón*. On 16 January Columbus tells us that he has named it the *Golfo de las Flechas*. To my knowledge, *every* student of Columbus has mislocated this last bay visited. *Bahía de Samaná,* the very large bay south of Cabo Samaná, has been the unanimous choice. But the description of Puerto Rincón, and its entrance-guarding capes in thoroughly convincing. Cabo Cabrón is a mountainous cape that projects NE. It terminates in a white, perpendicular cliff, prompting Columbus to name it for the Lover's Leap near Granada. Cabo Samaná consists of bold, double cliffs, red in color and steep-to. Columbus compares it to Cabo de San Vincente (São Vicente) in Portugal. Even Morison, who misplaces the Golfo de las Flechas and both capes, says, "Cape Samana is about 500 feet in elevation and looks more like Cape St. Vincent than does any other headland in that region." (*Journal,* p. 151.) Puerto Rincón is not only the correct width for the Golfo, but it has a small island in its entrance right where Columbus said there was one. It was on the shores of this bay that Columbus and his men had their first skirmish with the Indians, hence the name Gulf of the Arrows.

6. The astronomy is correct, except that Mars is omitted; it is Mars that is in conjunction with Mercury. Columbus obviously carried an astronomical table with him on the voyage.

7. Columbus has encountered the *Ciguayos,* according to Las Casas, further evidence that he is on the cultural frontier.

8. On 1 November Columbus used the word *nuzay* (*nuçay*). This appears to be the same word for gold as *nozay*. *Caoma* was the most common word for gold, according to Las Casas.

9. The island of Martinique. The Island of Women was a myth, but it certainly fired up a lot of explorers, rivaling the legend of the Seven Cities and *El Dorado*.

10. *Goanin* was not an island, but a gold/copper alloy, mostly the latter. Today the word is *guanín*.

Monday, 14 January 1493

I could not go ashore last night and search for the houses of the people I believe to be Caribes because the wind blew strongly from the east and NE and the sea was very rough. At daylight we saw many Indians on the shore. I ordered the boat to go to the land with well-armed men, and the Indians all came to the stern of the boat, including the Indian who had come to the caravel yesterday and to whom I had given various articles of trade. Along with this Indian came a king who had given this Indian some beads for the people in the boat, as a sign of security and peace. This king, with three of his people, got into the boat and came to the caravel. I ordered that they be given honey and biscuits to eat, and I gave the king a red cap and beads and a piece of red cloth; to the others I also gave pieces of red cloth. The king promised that tomorrow he would bring a gold mask and said that there was a great deal of gold in Caribe and Matinino. I then sent them ashore well pleased.

The caravels are leaking badly at the keel, largely because they were caulked very badly in Palos. Before we departed Spain, when I saw the poor work of the caulkers and tried to compel them to do the job right, they fled. Despite the considerable amount of water that the caravels are taking in, I have faith in Our Lord that He who brought me here will lead me back in His pity and mercy, for His Divine Majesty well knows how much controversy I had before starting from Castile, and no one else was supportive of me except God, because He knew my heart; and, after God, Your Highnesses supported me, but everyone else opposed me without any reason whatsoever. And they have been the reason why the Royal Crown of Your Highnesses does not have a hundred million more in revenue that it has, because I came to serve you seven years ago, on the 20th of January, this very month. In addition, there would have been the natural increase from that time on. But Almighty God will take care of everything.

Tuesday, 15 January 1493

I wish to depart because nothing is gained by staying here. Too many disagreements have taken place. I have also learned today that the bulk of the gold is in the vicinity of Your Highnesses' Villa de la Navidad. There is a great deal of copper on the island of Caribe and on Matinino, but it would be difficult to obtain it in Caribe because the people eat human flesh. I can see the island of Caribe[1] and have determined to go there, since it is on the course to the island of Matinino, which is inhabited only by women. I want to see both of these islands and take some of the inhabitants with me.

I sent the boat ashore; although the king of that country did not come because his village is a long way off, he did send the crown of gold that he promised, and many other men came with cotton, bread, and ajes, all carrying their bows and arrows. After we had traded everything with the Indians, four young men came to the caravel and gave such a good account of these islands lying to the east on my intended course that I have decided to take them with me to Castile. These Indians have no iron or other metal here that can be seen, although in a few days you cannot learn much about a country because of the difficulty with the language. I can understand it only by intuition, nor did the Indians learn what I was asking in a few days.

The bows of these people are as large as those in France and England. The arrows are just like the spears of the other people I have seen before, made from cane stalks that have gone to seed. They are very straight and one-and-a-half or two yards long, and they place a sharpened stick in the end, a palm-and-a-half long. At the end of this little stick some of them insert a fish tooth, and most of them put poison on the tip.

They do not shoot as in other places, but in a peculiar way that cannot do much harm. The bows seem to be made of yew.

There is a great deal of cotton here, very fine and long, as well as a lot of mastic, and gold and copper. There is also much *ají*,[2] which is their pepper and is worth more than our pepper; no one eats without it because it is very healthy. Fifty caravels can be loaded each year with it on this Isla Española. There is a lot of seaweed in this bay of the same kind that we found in the ocean when we came to make the discovery. Because of this, I believe there are islands lying in a straight line to the east from where I began to find them. I am certain that this seaweed grows in shallow water near the land; if this is so, then these Indies are very close to the Canary Islands. For this reason I believe that the Canaries are less than 1,200 miles from the Indies.

---

1. Columbus can see the eastern half of the *Cordillera Oriental*, across Samana Bay and thinks it is a separate island.

2. Chili pepper; the word is still commonly used. Not to be confused with *aje* (yuca or sweet potatoes) or *ajo* (garlic).

"The wind and sea increased greatly, and seeing the great danger, I began to run before the wind."

THE LOG OF CHRISTOPHER COLUMBUS

THE HOMEWARD VOYAGE
16 January to 15 March 1493

Wednesday, 16 January 1493

hree hours before dawn I departed the gulf, which I have named the *Golfo de las Flechas,*[1] first with a land breeze and then with a west wind. I turned the prow to the east by north, in order to go to the Isla de Caribe, where the people are whom the inhabitants of all these islands and countries fear so greatly. This is because the Caribes cross all these seas in their countless canoes and eat the men they are able to capture. One of the four Indians I took yesterday in the Puerto de las Flechas[2] has shown me the course. After we had gone about 48 miles, the Indians indicated to me that the island lay to the SE. I wanted to follow that course and ordered the sails trimmed, but after we had gone 6 miles the wind again blew very favorably for going to Spain. I noted that the crew were becoming dismayed because we had departed from a direct course for home; and as both ships were taking in a great deal of water, they had no help save that of God. I was compelled to abandon the course that I believe was taking me to the island; I returned to the direct course for Spain, NE by east, and held it until sunset, 36 miles. The Indians told me that on this course I would find the island of Matinino, which is inhabited only by women. I would like to carry five or six of them to the Sovereigns, but I doubt if the Indians know the course well, and I am not able to delay because of the danger with the leaking caravels. I am certain that there is such an island, and that at a certain time of year men come to these women from the Isla de Caribe, which is 30 or 36 miles from us; if the women give birth to a boy they send him to the island of the men, and if a girl they keep her

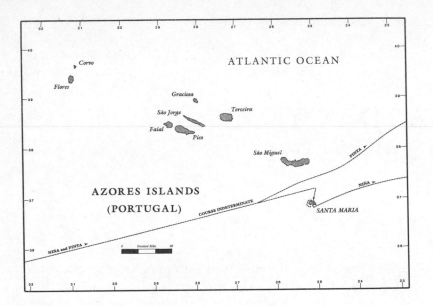

ATLANTIC OCEAN

Corvo

Flores

Graciosa

São Jorge *Terceira*

Faial *Pico*

São Miguel

AZORES ISLANDS
(PORTUGAL)

COURSE INDETERMINATE

SANTA MARIA

NIÑA and PINTA

0 Nautical Miles 60

3. San Théramo is a variant spelling for San Erasmo (better known today as St. Elmo), the patron saint of sailors. Manuscripts of the period record many variant spellings: Sant Théramo, Sant Éramo, Sant Ermo, San Thermo, Sant 'Ermo (in Portuguese), and San Elmo.

Thursday, 17 January 1493

Yesterday at sunset the wind died down a little. I went for seven hours[1] until the passing of the first quarter, at the speed of 3 knots, which is 21 miles. Then the wind picked up, and I went all the second quarter and 6 more half-hour glasses till sunrise at a speed of 6 knots. All told, I made 63 miles to the NE by east. From sunrise to sunset I went to the east 33 miles. First one tern came to the caravel and then another, and I saw a great deal of seaweed.

----

1. For a more extensive discussion of timetelling, see Prologue. The first quarter watch was 7 p.m. to 11 p.m., second quarter, 11 p.m. to 3 a.m., third quarter (or dawn) watch, 3 a.m. to 7 a.m.

Friday, 18 January 1493

I sailed with little wind last night, to the east by south for 30 miles, then to the SE by east for 22½ miles, until sunrise. After the sun came up, I sailed all day with little wind to the ENE, NE, and east, more or less, turning the prow sometimes to the north and sometimes to the north by east, and at times to the NNE. Altogether I estimate that I made about 45 miles. There has been little seaweed, but yesterday and today the sea seemed to be clogged with tuna. I think they must go from

with them. These two islands could not have been more than 45 or 60 miles from where we started, and I believe they are to the southeast and the Indians do not know how to point out the course. After I lost sight of Cabo de San Théramo[3] on the Isla Española, 48 miles to the west, I went 36 miles to the east by north. The weather is very good.

----

1. Gulf of the Arrows; now known as *Puerto Rincón*. See note for Sunday, 13 January.

2. Port of the Arrows; an unspecified anchorage, probably on the north shore of the Gulf.

here to the tuna fisheries of the Duke at Conil and Cádiz. A frigate bird flew around the caravel and headed SSE, making me believe that there are some islands in that direction. The island of Caribe and the island of Matinino, and many other islands, lie to the ESE of the Isla Española.

Saturday, 19 January 1493

Last night I went 42 miles to the north by east and 48 miles to the NE by north. After sunrise I sailed to the NE with a strong wind ESE and then sailed to the NE by north; I made about 63 miles. I saw the sea choked with tuna. There were also terns, ringtails, and frigate birds.

Sunday, 20 January 1493

The wind calmed last night, but at intervals there were gusts. All in all, I went about 15 miles to the NE. After sunrise I went about 8 or 9 miles to the SE, then 27 miles to the NNE. I saw an infinite number of small tuna. The breeze is as mild and sweet as in Sevilla in April or May, and the sea, God be given many thanks, is very calm all the time. Frigate birds, petrels, and many other birds were seen.

Monday, 21 January 1493

Yesterday after sunset I sailed to the north by east, with the wind east and NE. I made about 6 knots until midnight, which would be 42 miles. Then I went to the NNE at the rate of 6 knots—a total for the night of 78 miles to the NE by north. After sunrise I sailed to the NNE with the same east wind, and at times to the NE by north, making about 63 miles

in 11 hours, which is the duration of daylight. I have reduced the distance by 3 miles because I fell off to the leeward toward the *Pinta* to speak to her. The wind is cooler, and I expect to find it more so each day as I proceed to the north, and also because the nights are longer as the sphere narrows. Many ringtails and petrels are to be seen, along with other birds, but not as many fish because the water is colder. There is a great deal of seaweed.

Tuesday, 22 January 1493

Yesterday after sunset I sailed to the NNE with the wind east and veering to the SE. I made 6 knots during five half-hour glasses and for three before the watch began. I thus made 24 miles. Then I went to the north by east for six glasses, which would be another 18 miles. I then went for four glasses of the second watch to the NE at 4½ knots, which is 9 miles to the NE. From then until sunrise I went to the ENE during 11 glasses at 4½ knots, or 24¾ miles. I then went ENE until 11 o'clock in the morning, 24 miles. The wind became dead calm and I went no further today. The Indians went swimming, and we saw ringtails and a great deal of seaweed.

Wednesday, 23 January 1493

Last night there were many changes in the wind, and having been on the alert for everything and having taken the precautions good sailors are accustomed to take and must take, I went last night to the NE by north about 63 miles. I waited many times for the *Pinta*, which had a lot of difficulty sailing close to the wind because the mast was not sound and the

Fish in the ocean. America. *Theodor De Bry, 1594. (Courtesy Rare Book Division, New York Public Library, Astor, Lenox, and Tilden Foundations)*

mizzen helped her very little. If her captain, Martín Alonso Pinzón, had taken as much trouble to provide himself with a good mast in the Indies, where there are so many good ones, as he did to separate himself from me with the intention of filling his ship with gold, he would have been better off. Many ringtails appeared and much seaweed. The sky is very disturbed these days, but it has not rained and the sea is very calm all the time, as in a river, many thanks be given to God. After sunrise I made about 22½ miles for part of the day straight to the NE. The remainder of the day I went to the ENE another 22½ miles.

Thursday, 24 January 1493

Last night I made about 33 miles to the NE, considering the many changes which the wind made. From sunrise until sunset I went to the ENE about 42 miles.

Friday, 25 January 1493

I sailed last night to the ENE for 13 half-hour glasses, 28½ miles; then I went to the NNE another 4½ miles. After the sun came up and the wind died down, I went to the ENE about 21 miles. The sailors killed a porpoise and a very large shark. These were very necessary because we had nothing to eat except bread, wine, and ajes from the Indies.

Saturday, 26 January 1493

Last night I went to the east by south for 42 miles. After sunrise I sailed at times to the ESE and at times to the SE, going about 30 miles up until 11 o'clock in the morning. Then I made another tack and went close to the wind, and by night I had gone 18 miles to the north.

Sunday, 27 January 1493

Yesterday after sunset I went to the NE and to the north by east, making 3¾ knots for 13 hours, which is 48¾ miles. From sunrise until noon I went to the NE 18 miles, and from that time until sunset I went about 9 miles to the ENE.

Monday, 28 January 1493

All night I sailed to the ENE, making about 27 miles. From sunrise until sunset I went to the ENE, 15 miles. The winds are temperate and gentle. I saw ringtails, petrels, and a lot of seaweed.

Tuesday, 29 January 1493

I sailed to the ENE, and went last night with the wind, which was south and SW, about 29¼ miles. Between sunrise and sunset I sailed about 24 miles. The winds are very temperate, as they are in Castile in the month of April, and the sea is very calm. Dorados came alongside the ship.

Wednesday, 30 January 1493

Last night I went 21 miles to the ENE. During the day I ran to the south by east for 40½ miles. I saw ringtails, a lot of seaweed, and many porpoises.

Thursday, 31 January 1493

I sailed this night to the north by east for 22½ miles, then to the NE for 26¼ miles. From sunrise until night I went to the ENE 40½ miles. I saw ringtails and petrels.

Friday, 1 February 1493

Last night I went ENE for 49½ miles. During the day I ran on the same course a distance of 87¾ miles. The sea is very calm, thanks be to God.

Saturday, 2 February 1493

I went last night to the ENE for 30 miles. Today, with the same wind in the stern, I made 5¼ knots, so that in 11 hours I went 57¾ miles. The sea is very calm, thanks be to God, and the winds very gentle. The sea is so thickly covered with seaweed that if we had not seen that it was weed, we would have thought it was shoals. We saw petrels.

Sunday, 3 February 1493

Last night, with a calm sea and the wind astern, thanks be to God, I went about 87 miles. The North Star seemed to be very high, the same as at Cabo de San Vincente. I could not take its altitude with the astrolabe or quadrant[1] because the waves would not permit it. During the day I continued on my course to the ENE, making about 7½ knots; thus in 11 hours I went 82½ miles.

----

1. Columbus did carry both an astrolabe and a quadrant, but heavy seas made it impossible to use either. His visual fix on the North Star was incredibly accurate: Santa Maria in the Azores is at 37 degrees 09 minutes north; Cape St. Vincent, Portugal, is 37 degrees 07 minutes north. Even so, Columbus

placed greater faith in his dead-reckoning skills and thought he was about 225 NM south of that parallel.

Monday, 4 February 1493

Last night I sailed to the east by north, some of the time at 9 knots and some at 7½ knots, and thus went 97½ miles. The sky is very overcast and rainy, and it is somewhat cold. Because of this I knew that I have not reached the Azores. After sunrise I changed course and sailed east, for 57¾ miles during the day.

Tuesday, 5 February 1493

Last night I sailed to the east and went 40½ miles. After sunrise I ran at a speed of 7½ knots, and in 11 hours I went 82½ miles. I saw petrels and some little sticks, which are signs that we are near land.

Wednesday, 6 February 1493

I sailed last night to the east and went about 8¼ knots. In 13 hours of the night I made about 107¼ miles. I saw many birds and petrels. During the day I ran at a speed of 10½ knots, therefore going 115½ miles. All told, between night and day I went 222¾ miles,[1] more or less. Vincente Yáñez Pinzón told me this morning that the island of Flores[2] lies to the north and the island of Madeira to the east. Bartolomé Roldán, a pilot of the *Niña*, said that the island of Fayal,[3] or San Gregorio, lies to the NNE, and Porto Santo[4] to the east. Much seaweed appeared.

----

1. Best run of the entire trip for one day.

2. Westernmost island of the Azores.

3. Now known as Faial, Azores.

4. In the Madeira Islands.

- -

Thursday, 7 February 1493

I sailed to the east last night, making about 7½ knots, and so in 13 hours I went 97½ miles. During the day I made 6 knots for 11 hours, or 66 miles. This morning I am 225 miles south of the island of Flores. The pilot Pedro Alonso Niño reckoned that if we went north, we would pass between Terceira and Santa María;[1] by going east we would pass to the windward of the island of Madeira, 36 miles to the north of it. The sailors saw a different kind of seaweed from what they had passed earlier, of which there is a great deal in the vicinity of the Azores Islands. Later we saw the same kind of seaweed as before.

- -

1. Both are in the Azores.

- -

Friday, 8 February 1493

I went to the east last night at 2¼ knots for a short time, then I changed course to the east by south. During the night I made 36 miles. From sunrise until noon I ran 20¼ miles, and from then until sunset I ran as many more, that is, 39 miles to the SSE.

Saturday, 9 February 1493

For a short time last night I went about 9 miles to the SSE,

and then to the south by east. Later I went to the NE until 10 o'clock in the morning for another 15 miles; and by sunset I added another 27 miles to the east.

Sunday, 10 February 1493

Last night after sunset I sailed all night to the east, a distance of 97½ miles. Between sunrise and night I made 6¾ knots, and thus in 11 hours I went 74¼ miles. Aboard the *Niña*, Vincente Yáñez Pinzón and his two pilots, Pedro Alonso Niño and Bartolomé Roldán, charted our course, and my pilot from the *Santa María*, Sancho Ruíz de Gama, did the same; all four had us passing much beyond the Azores to the east. Plotting a course due north, they all missed the island of Santa María, which is the last island in the Azores, by 15 miles to the east, in the vicinity of the island of Madeira or of Porto Santo. I calculate that we are way off course and place us far west of the position reckoned by the others because tonight the island of Fayal lies to the north, and we are heading east toward Nafe,[1] in Africa, and will pass windward of the island of Madeira to the north by (30?)[2] miles. According to the reckoning of the pilots, we are 450 miles[3] closer to Castile than I think we are. When, God willing, we sight land, we will see whose calculations are the closest. On the voyage west we went 789 miles from the island of Hierro before we saw the first seaweed.

- -

1. The present Casablanca.

2. There is a blank in the Log; 30 NM is my guess.

3. 450 miles. Columbus still relied on his compass and charts for dead-reckoning, placing the ship too far south. His longitude correction (450 NM behind the pilots' position) appears to be based on two things: (1) in going over his notes and charts, he apparently realized that he had not allowed for the strong westerly current along the north coast of Española. This meant that he had not gone as far east as he thought he had, and it explains the excessive distances logged at Española; (2) he may have noted where he picked up the main weed of the Sargasso Sea on the outward leg of the voyage and corrected his longitude on the homeward leg so that it would conform to the first course.

Monday, 11 February 1493

I maintained my course last night at 9 knots and made 117 miles by sunrise. From then until sunset I ran another 49½ miles. I saw many birds; because of this, I think we are near land.

Tuesday, 12 February 1493

I sailed to the east at 4½ knots during the night, and by sunrise had made a distance of 54¾ miles. At this time I began to experience heavy seas and stormy weather. If the caravel had not been very sound and well equipped, I fear we would have been lost. During the day I made about 33 or 36 miles with great difficulty and in constant danger.

Wednesday, 13 February 1493

From sunset yesterday until sunrise this morning I experienced great difficulty with the wind, high waves, and a stormy sea. There has been lightning three times toward the NNE, which is a sure sign that a great storm is coming from that direction or from the direction contrary to my course. I went with bare masts most of the night, then raised a little sail and went about 39 miles. The wind abated a little today; then it increased and the sea became terrible, with the waves crossing each other and pounding the ships. I made about 41¼ miles to sunset.

Thursday, 14 February 1493

The wind increased last night, and the waves were frightful, coming in opposite directions. They crossed each other and trapped the ship, which could not go forward nor get out from between them, and they broke over us. I carried the mainsail very low, simply to escape somewhat from the waves. I went this way for three hours and made about 15 miles. The wind and the sea increased greatly, and seeing the great danger I began to run before the wind, letting it carry me wherever it wanted, for there was no other remedy. Then the caravel *Pinta*, on which was Martín Alonso, began to run also and eventually disappeared from sight, although all night long I showed lights and the *Pinta* responded until it was not able to do so any longer because of the force of the storm, and because she was far off from my course. I went this night to the NE by east for 40½ miles. After sunrise the wind became stronger and the crossing waves more terrible. I carried only a low mainsail, so that the ship might escape some of the waves breaking over her and not sink. I went on a course to the ENE and then NE by east. I went like this for 6 hours and made 22½ miles.

I ordered that a pilgrimage to Santa María de Guadalupe be pledged, during which a wax candle weighing five pounds should be carried, and that each man should swear that whoever is chosen by lot will fulfill this promise. For this reason I ordered that a chick-pea be brought for every man on board; one was marked by a knife with the sign of the cross, and they were shaken up in a cap. I was the first person to draw, and it was I who took out the pea marked with the sign of the cross. Thus I was elected by chance, and from that time I considered myself obliged to fulfill the vow and make the pilgrimage. Lots were again drawn to make a pilgrimage to Santa María de Loreto, which is in the province of Ancona, the land of the Pope. This is the house where Our Lady has performed and performs many great miracles, and chance selected a sailor named Pedro de Villa, from the port of Santa María. I promised to pay his expenses for this pilgrimage. I also decided that another pilgrim should be sent to keep a vigil for one night at Santa Clara de Moguer[1] and cause a mass to be said, and for this purpose lots were again drawn with the peas marked with a cross. Once again I drew the marked pea. Then I and all the men made a vow that on the first land we reached we would all go in our shirts in a procession to pray in a church dedicated to Our Lady.

Besides the general vows made in common, each man made his own personal vow, for none of them expected to escape, and all were resigned to being lost due to the terrible storm we were experiencing. The danger was further increased by the fact that the ship was short of ballast, since the load had been lightened by the consumption of the provisions, water, and wine. I had not provided these in sufficient quantity, having hoped for favorable weather like I found in the islands, and having planned to take on ballast at the Island of Women. The solution I found for this problem, when I was able to do it, was to fill the empty water and wine casks with sea water; by this means I corrected the problem.

It seems to me that the great desire I have to bring this wonderful news to Your Highnesses, and to show that I have been proven truthful in what I have said and volunteered to discover, causes me to fear greatly that I will not succeed in doing so. It seems to me that even a gnat can disturb and impede it. I attribute this to my little faith and lack of confidence in the Divine Providence. On the other hand, I am comforted by the favors that God has bestowed upon me by giving me such a victory, in discovering what I have discovered. And after so many adversities and contradictions in Castile, God has fulfilled all my desires. And as before, I have committed myself to God and have conducted my enterprise for Him, and He has heard me and given me all that I have asked, and I believe that God will fulfill what was begun and that He will deliver me safely. This is especially so since He delivered me from the difficulties I had at the outset of the voyage, when I had greater reason to fear than now, on account of the trouble with the sailors and people who were with me, who all with one voice determined to return and rebel against me, making protestations; and the eternal God gave me strength and courage against them all. And there are many other wonderful things that God has manifested in me and by me on this journey, besides those which Your Highnesses know from persons of your household. Therefore, I ought not to fear this storm. But my weakness and anxiety will not allow my mind to be reassured.

I also feel great anxiety because of the two sons I have in Córdoba at school, if I leave them orphaned[2] of father and mother in a foreign land. And I am concerned because the Sovereigns do not know the service I have rendered on this voyage and the very important news I am carrying to them, which would move them to help my sons. For this reason, and so that Your Highnesses might know how Our Lord has given me victory in everything I desired about the Indies, and so that they might know that there are no storms in those regions (which may be known by the fact that the grass and trees spring up and grow almost into the sea), and so that if I am lost in this storm the Sovereigns might have information about my voyage, I have written on a parchment everything I can concerning what I have found, earnestly beseeching whomsoever might find it to carry it to Your Highnesses. I sealed the parchment in a waxed cloth, tied it very securely, took a large wooden barrel, and placed the parchment in the barrel,[3] without anyone knowing what it was (they all thought it was some act of devotion), and had it thrown into the sea.

Afterwards, with showers and squalls, the wind shifted to the west, and I sailed before the wind with only the foresail for about five hours. The sea was very rough and I went about

7½ miles to the NE. I have taken down the mainsail for fear that some wave will carry it all away.

----

1. A church in Moguer, hometown of the Pinzóns and many of the crew.

2. It is odd that Columbus should speak of leaving both his sons without a mother. Although Diego's mother was deceased, Fernando's mother, Beatriz Enríquez de Arana, did not die until ca. 1521.

3. Morison writes (*Journals*, p. 166): "In 1891 an enterprising London firm brought out a 'limited edition' printed in Germany of the 'Journal found in a barrel,' entitled *My Secrete Log Boke*, printed in imitation handwriting in English (!) on antique paper, the cover liberally encrusted with barnacles and seaweed. It was accompanied by an illiterate letter from a fisherman, who claimed to have picked it up (after four centuries' floating about) off the coast of Wales. Nevertheless, this transparent fake found ready sale, and copies are still circulating."

Friday, 15 February 1493

Last night, after sunset, the skies commenced to clear toward the west, indicating that the wind was about to blow from that direction. I had the bonnet placed on the mainsail. The sea was still very high, although it was subsiding a little. I sailed to the ENE at a speed of 3 knots, and in 13 hours of the night I went 39 miles. After sunrise we saw land, off the prow to the ENE. Some said it was the island of Madeira; others, the Rock of Sintra in Portugal, near Lisbon. The wind changed and blew ahead from the ENE, and the sea came very high from the west. The caravel must have been 15 miles from land. According to my navigation I think we are off the Azores and believe the land ahead is one of those islands. The pilots and sailors believe that we are already off Castile.

Saturday, 16 February 1493

All last night I beat against the wind in order to fetch land, which I already saw was an island. At times I went to the NE and at others to the NNE, until sunrise. Then I changed course to the south in order to reach the island we no longer saw because of the murky conditions, and I saw at the stern another island about 24 miles[1] away. From sunrise until sunset I tacked about trying to reach land, in spite of the strong wind and the high sea it caused.

----

1. The Log says "8 leagues" (24 NM), but 8 Columbian miles (6 NM) would seem more logical.

Sunday, 17 February 1493
(Included in the Log under the entry for 16 February.)

At the time when the *Salve Regina* is said, that is, at the beginning of night, some of the men saw a light to the leeward, and it seemed to be the island we first saw yesterday. All night I continued to beat about, drawing as near as possible in order to see if I could make out any of the islands at sunrise. I rested a little last night because I have not slept since Wednesday, and my legs have become cramped from exposure to the cold and water and from having so little food. At sunrise I sailed to the SSW and at sunset reached the island, but because it was so dark and cloudy I could not recognize what island it was.

Monday, 18 February 1493

Yesterday after dark I went around the island to see where I could anchor and in order to hail someone. I managed to anchor with one anchor, but lost it, and set sail again and beat about all night. After sunrise this morning I again approached the northern part of the island, cast anchor where it seemed best, and sent the boat ashore. The men learned that this is the island of Santa María, one of the Azores. The inhabitants indicated to them a harbor we could enter with the caravel; they also said that they had never seen such a storm as that which has prevailed for the past 15 days, and they wondered how we had escaped. The people offered many thanks to God and rejoiced greatly when they heard the news that we had discovered the Indies.

My navigation has been very accurate, and I have steered well, for which many thanks should be given to Our Lord. Although I had fixed our position a little beyond its true location, I was sure that we were in the vicinity of the Azores, and this island was one of them. I pretended to have gone a longer distance to confound the pilots and sailors who steered, and to remain master of the route to the Indies, because none of them is at all certain of my course and none can be sure of my route to the Indies.

Tuesday, 19 February 1493

Last night after sunset three men came down to the shore and hailed us. I sent the boat for them and they came out to the ship, bringing fowls and fresh bread. It was Carnival Day.[1] They brought other things as well, which the captain of the island, Juan de Castañeda,[2] had sent, along with a message from him saying that he knew me very well and had not come to see me because it was night. He promised that he would come at dawn with more refreshments and bring with him the three men from the ship, who had remained on the island. He said that he had not sent them back because of the great pleasure he was having hearing about the voyage.

I ordered that the messengers should be properly honored and that they be given beds in which to sleep because it was late and the village was distant.

Because last Thursday, when we were in the midst of the anxiety occasioned by the storm, we made several vows, one of which was to go in shirts to a shrine of Our Lady when we came to the first land, I decided that half my people would go to fulfill the vow at a small house near the sea, a place like a hermitage. After this group completed their vow, I would go with the other half. Feeling that the country was safe, and having confidence in the offers of the captain and in the peace existing between Portugal and Castile, I asked the three messengers to go to the village and send a priest to say a mass for us.

The first half of the crew went in their shirts to fulfill their vow, and while praying they were attacked and seized by all the villagers, on horseback and on foot, and by the captain as well. At the time I did not know this and remained, unsuspectingly, until 11 o'clock in the morning, expecting the boat to return so that I might go myself with the other people to fulfill our vow. When I saw that our people did not return, I suspected that they were detained or that the boat had wrecked, since the entire island is surrounded by very high cliffs. I was not able to see what was going on because the hermitage is behind a point. I raised anchor and set sail directly toward the hermitage. It was then that I saw many horsemen, well armed, who dismounted, got into the boat, and came to the ship to take me.

The captain stood up in the boat and asked for safe conduct from me, and I granted it. But I wondered why none of my people was in the boat. I told the captain that if he came aboard, I would do what he wished. I tried to cajole him into coming aboard, so that I could take him in order to get my people back. I do not think that I was violating any oath in giving him a false promise of security because he had broken his own promise after offering us peace and safety. Since the captain knew his intentions were evil, he did not dare come aboard. When I saw that the captain was not going to get too close, I asked him to explain why he was detaining my people. I told him that this action would surely annoy the King of Portugal, and that in the land of the Sovereigns of Castile the Portuguese are well treated and they can come and go and are as safe as they are in Lisbon. I also told him that the Sovereigns had given us letters of recommendation for all the Princes and Lords and men in the world, which I would show him if he would approach. I informed the captain that I was Your Highnesses' Admiral of the Ocean-Sea and Viceroy of the Indies, which now belong to Your Highnesses, the provisions for which, signed with your signatures and sealed with your seals, I would show him, and which I did show him from a distance. I said that the Sovereigns felt much love and friendship for the King of Portugal and had ordered me to pay all due respect to the ships of Portugal I might encounter. I also told the captain that even if he would not surrender my people, I was not going to give up going to Castile, since I had sufficient people to navigate to Sevilla. And I promised him that he and his people would be severely punished for insulting us in this manner.

The captain and the others replied that they did not recognize the King and Queen of Castile here, nor their letters, nor were they afraid; rather, they would have us to understand that this is Portugal, and they said this in a threatening way.

When I heard this, I felt great resentment and assumed that some problems had arisen between the Kingdoms since my departure. I could not refrain from answering the Portuguese in kind, which was proper. Then that captain stood up again in the boat, at a distance, and told me to take the ship to the

"The first half of the crew went in shirts to fulfill their vow, and while praying they were attacked."

harbor, that everything he was doing and had done had been ordered by the King, his Lord. I called on those who were on the caravel to witness what I was about to say, and again I called to the captain and his men and gave them my pledge, promising, by right of my authority, not to descend from or leave the caravel until I had taken a hundred Portuguese to Castile and had depopulated the entire island.

And so I anchored again in the harbor where I had first come, since the weather and wind were very unfavorable for doing anything else.

----

1. Shrove Tuesday, the day before Ash Wednesday and Lent.

2. The correct Portuguese name is João de Castanheira.

Wednesday, 20 February 1493
(Part of this entry is under the Log entry for 21 February.)

I ordered the ship repaired and the casks filled with sea water for ballast because I am in a very bad harbor and am afraid the anchor lines might be cut—and so it happened. Because of this I set sail toward the island of San Miguel, although there is not a good harbor in any of the Azores Islands for the weather we are experiencing now. Really my only recourse was to put to sea. There was a great deal of wind and a high sea, and I went until dark without being able to see land in any direction on account of the extreme darkness and thick clouds caused by the wind and sea. There was no pleasure in this because I only have three sailors with me who know the sea; most of those with me know nothing of it.

Thursday, 21 February 1493
(Part of this entry is under the Log entry of 22 February.)

I beat about all last night in a very great storm, in constant danger and difficulty. The Lord showed His mercy for me in that the waves came only from one direction. If there had been a cross-sea, as in the past, I would have suffered very serious injury. After sunrise, when I found that I could not see the island of San Miguel, I decided to return to Santa María, to see if I could recover my people, the boat, and the anchors and lines that I left there.

I am astonished at such bad weather as there is in these islands and their vicinity. In the Indies I sailed all winter without anchoring because of the weather, and the weather was good all the time; not for a single hour was I unable to see the sea so that I could not navigate well. In these islands I have experienced a terrible storm, and the same thing happened to me on my departure, between Spain and the Canary Islands. But once I was past the Canaries I always found the winds and sea very temperate.

The sacred theologians and learned philosophers were quite correct when they said that the earthly Paradise is at the end of the Orient, because it is a most temperate place. Those lands which I have now discovered are at the end of the Orient.

I anchored at the island of Santa María, in the harbor where I had first anchored. A man came and hailed us from atop some rocks that we were facing, telling us not to leave. Then the boat came with five sailors, two priests, and a notary. They asked for a guarantee of security, which I granted, and they came aboard. Since it was night they slept on the ship, and I paid them what honors I was able to.

Friday, 22 February 1493

This morning they requested me to show them the commission I have from Your Highnesses, in order to prove to them that I had made this voyage by the authority of the Sovereigns. I felt that they did this so as to make it appear that they had done no wrong before, when they came in the armed boat with every intention of seizing me. But when that game did not turn out favorably for them—since they could not get their hands on me, and because they feared what I had said and threatened, and which I intended to do and believe I could have carried out successfully—they changed their tune. Finally, in order to get my people back, I was obliged to show them the general letter from the Sovereigns to all the Princes and Lords, and the other provisions. I showed them what I had, and they went ashore satisfied and let all the people go, along with my boat. My men later told me that if they had captured me, they would never have let me go free because the captain said that the King, his Lord, had commanded him to do what he did.

The weather began to improve, and I raised anchors and went around the island in search of a good anchorage where I could take on wood and stone ballast. I did not find an anchorage until the hour of complines, that is, about 9 o'clock in the night.

Saturday, 23 February 1493
(Part of this entry is under the Log entry of 24 February.)

Last night, after we anchored, the wind began to blow west and SW. I ordered the sails raised on account of the great danger one finds here in these islands if he remains at anchor with a south wind, and a SW wind easily shifts until it blows south. Since it was good weather for going to Castile, I gave up the idea of taking wood and stone and ordered the course to the east. I went until sunrise, which would be 6½ hours, at a speed of 5¼ knots, which is about 34⅛ miles.

Sunday, 24 February 1493

From sunrise today until sunset I made 4½ knots, which in 11 hours is 49½ miles.

Monday, 25 February 1493

Last night I sailed east at 3¾ knots. In 13 hours of the night I made about 48¾ miles. From sunrise till sunset I made another 49½ miles with the sea calm, thanks be to God. A very large bird, which appeared to be an eagle, came to the ship.

Tuesday, 26 February 1493

Last night I sailed to the east, on course, the sea calm, thanks be to God. Most of the night I made about 6 knots, for a total of 75 miles. After sunrise there was little wind. There were showers, and I went some 24 miles to the ENE.

Wednesday, 27 February 1493

Last night and today I had to get off my course because of contrary winds, great waves, and a high sea. I fix my position at 375 miles from Cabo de San Vincente, 240 miles from the island of Madeira, and 318 miles from the island of Santa María. I am very much concerned with these storms, now that I am so near the end of my journey.

Thursday, 28 February 1493

I maintained my course last night with shifting winds, to the south and SE, one side and then the other, and to the NE and ENE. I went in this manner all day.

Friday, 1 March 1493

Last night I went to the east by north 36 miles. During the day I ran to the east by north for 70½ miles.

Saturday, 2 March 1493

I continued last night on my course to the east by north for 84 miles. During the day I made 60 miles.

Sunday, 3 March 1493

After sunset last night I sailed on my course to the east. A squall came upon me that split all the sails and I found myself in great danger, but God willed that I be delivered from it. We drew lots to send a pilgrim to Santa María de la Cinta in Huelva, who was to go in his shirt, and the lot fell to me. We also all made a vow to fast on bread and water the first Saturday after our return. I went about 45 miles before the sails split. We then went with bare masts on account of the fury of the wind and sea, which rolled over us in two directions. We saw indications of being near land and found ourselves quite near to Lisbon.

Monday, 4 March 1493

Last night we experienced a terrible storm and thought we would be lost because the waves came from two directions, and the wind appeared to raise the ship in the air, with the water from the sky and the lightning in every direction. It pleased Our Lord to sustain us, and we continued in this fashion until the first watch, when Our Lord showed us land. In order not to approach the land until we knew more about it and until we could find a harbor or place to save ourselves, I raised the mainsail, since there was no other remedy, and we sailed some distance with great danger, putting to sea. Thus God protected us until daylight, but it was with infinite labor and fright.

When the sun came up I recognized the land, which was the Rock of Sintra, near the river at Lisbon. I decided to enter because I could not do anything else. One cannot imagine how terrible the storm was at the village of Cascaes, which is at the entrance to the river. The people of the village offered prayers for us all that morning after they sighted us inside the river, wondering how we had managed to escape. At 9 o'clock

The return to Lisbon. America. *Theodor De Bry, 1590. (Courtesy Rare Book Division, New York Public Library, Astor, Lenox, and Tilden Foundations)*

PART FIVE THE HOMEWARD VOYAGE *16 January to 15 March 1493*

in the morning I stopped at Rastelo, inside the river at Lisbon, where I learned from the seafaring people that there never has been a winter with so many storms; 25 ships had been lost in Flanders, and there were others here that had not been able to depart for four months.

I wrote to the King of Portugal, who was 27 miles from here, that Your Highnesses had ordered me not to fail to enter the harbors of His Highness and ask for whatever I might need in return for my money. I requested that the King permit me to take the ship to the city of Lisbon, for here in this sparsely populated place some dishonest persons who thought that I might be carrying a great deal of gold might undertake to commit some crime against me; also, His Highness should know that I did not come from Guinea but from the Indies.

Tuesday, 5 March 1493

This morning, Bartolomé Diaz[1] of Lisbon, master of the large ship of the King of Portugal, which was also anchored in Rastelo and which was better equipped with canons and arms than any ship I have ever seen, came to the caravel with a small, armed vessel. He told me to get aboard the small vessel in order to go and give an account of myself to the Factors of the King and to the Captain of the great ship. I replied that I am the Admiral of the Sovereigns of Castile, and that I did not render such accounts to such persons, nor would I leave my ship unless compelled to do so by force of arms. The master replied that I might send the master of the caravel, and I replied that I would send neither the master nor any other

person unless it was by force because I consider it the same to allow another person to go as to go myself, and it was the custom of the Admirals of the Sovereigns of Castile to die rather than surrender their people. The master moderated his demands and said that since I had made that determination, it should be as I wished, but he requested to see the letters from the Sovereigns of Castile, if I had them. It pleased me to show them to him; then the master returned to his ship and related the matter to his Captain, who was named Alvaro Dama. The Captain came to the caravel with great ceremony, complete with drums, trumpets, and pipes, making a great display. He spoke with me and offered to do everything that I ordered him to do.

----
1. Bartolomeu Dias in Portuguese, one of the greatest of the 15th century navigators and explorers. Dias discovered the Cape of Good Hope in Africa in 1488, opening Portugal's route to India. Columbus met him in Lisbon that year upon the latter's return. In 1497 he was with the fleet that discovered Brazil; he was later lost at sea near the cape he had discovered in South Africa.

Wednesday, 6 March 1493

When word spread that I had come from the Indies, many people came from the city of Lisbon to see me and the Indians. It was wonderful to see the way they marveled at us. They gave thanks to the Lord, saying that because of the great faith the Sovereigns of Castile possess and their desire to serve God, the Divine Majesty has given them all of this.

Thursday, 7 March 1493

Today an exceedingly large number of people came to the ship, along with many men of distinction, among them the agents of the King. They all offered infinite thanks to Our Lord for such a wonderful expansion of Christendom, which they attribute to the fact the Your Highnesses have labored and applied themselves to spreading the Christian religion.

Friday, 8 March 1493

Today I received a letter from the King of Portugal, delivered by Don Martín de Noroña,[1] which invited me to come to see him. Since the weather was not suitable for departure with the ship, I went in order to avoid suspicion, although I did not want to go. I went as far as Sacavem to spend the night. The King has ordered his agents to give me and my people everything we need for the ship, without charge, and to make sure that everything is done that I wish.

----

1. Noronha in Portuguese, a nobleman in a distinguished family that descended from a bastard son of King Enrique II of Castile.

Saturday, 9 March 1493

I left Sacavem this morning to go to the King, who was at the Valle del Paraíso, 27 miles from Lisbon. Since it rained, I was not able to get there until night. The King ordered that I should be received with great honor by the principal personages of his household, and he himself received me with great honor and showed me much respect, asking me to sit down and talking very freely with me. He told me that he would order everything done which would be of use to Your Highnesses and to your service, even more fully than if it were for his service. He indicated that he was greatly pleased that the voyage had been accomplished successfully, although he understood that in the capitulation between the Sovereigns and himself the conquest belonged to him. I told him that I had not seen the capitulation and did not know anything other than that the Sovereigns had commanded me not to go to La Mina nor to any part of Guinea, and that this had been proclaimed in all of the ports of Andalucía before I started on the voyage. The King graciously responded that he was certain that there would be no need for mediators in this matter. He made me the guest of the Prior of Clato, who was the most important person there, and from whom I received many honors and favors.

Sunday, 10 March 1493

Today, after mass, the King told me again that if I needed anything he would give it to me at once. And he talked with me a great deal more about the voyage, always asking me to be seated and paying me great honor.

Monday, 11 March 1493

Today I took leave of the King, who gave me some messages for the Sovereigns on his part and showed me great kindness all the time. I left after eating, and the King sent Don Martín de Noroña with me. All his cavaliers came to accompany me, and they paid me honors for quite a period of time. I then went to the monastery of San Antonio, which is near a place called Villafranca, where the Queen was staying. I went to pay homage to her and to kiss her hands, for she had sent me a message saying that I was not to leave until she saw me. With her was the Duke and the Marquis, and there I received great honor. I took leave of her at night and went to Alhandra to sleep.

Tuesday, 12 March 1493

Today, as I was about to start from Alhandra for the ship, a squire from the King arrived and offered me, on the part of the King, land transportation to Castile, if I desired to take that route, including lodgings, beasts for travel, and everything I might need. When I left the squire, he gave me a mule, and another to my pilot who was with me, and he gave my pilot 20 gold coins. It is said that this was done so Your Highnesses might know of it. I reached the ship at night.

Wednesday, 13 March 1493

This morning, at 8 o'clock in a rough sea with the wind NNW, I raised anchors and set sail for Sevilla.

Thursday, 14 March 1493

Yesterday after sunset I followed my course to the south and before sunrise I found myself off Cabo de San Vincente, which is in Portugal. Then I sailed east to go to Saltes, and I went all day with a light wind until now, when I find myself off Faro.

Friday, 15 March 1493

Yesterday after sunset I continued on my course until dawn, with a light wind; by sunrise I was off Saltes. At noon, with the tide rising, I entered the bar of Saltes until I was inside the harbor from which I had departed on August 3 of the past year. Thus, the writing is now completed, except that I intend to go by sea to Barcelona, where, I have been informed, Your Highnesses are staying. This is in order to give them a full account of my voyage, which Our Lord has permitted me to make, and for which He inspired me. His Divine Majesty does all good things, and everything is good except sin, and nothing can be imagined or planned without His consent. This voyage has miraculously proven this to be so, as can be learned from this writing, by the remarkable miracles which have occurred during the voyage and for me, who has been in the court of Your Highnesses for such a long time, with opposition and against the advice of so many of the principal persons of your household, who were all against me and treated this undertaking as a folly. I hope to Our Lord that it will be the greatest honor for Christianity, although it has been accomplished with such ease.

EPILOGUE

APPENDIX A

THE LANDFALL THEORIES

No chart made during the first voyage to America has survived, and Columbus was never to return to the Bahamas after the brief initial contact. For all practical purposes, the islands were ignored by successive waves of Spanish explorers and settlers, with a single exception. Raids were periodically made on the islands to capture Indians for work in the mines and fields of Española after 1500. Within 30 years or so, every member of that gentle race encountered by Columbus had vanished. Those not taken into virtual slavery died of European-introduced diseases, mostly smallpox and measles.

With no population, and no commodity worthy of immediate exploitation, the Bahamas became geographically extinct. After the Juan de la Cosa chart of 1500 (and even this date is questioned by a few scholars), *there was not a single Spanish attempt to map the islands until 1523* (the Turin Map). And the state of cartographic knowledge at this time, 31 years after Columbus made his first landfall and 10 years after Ponce de León discovered Florida, depicted the latter as an island.

The Bahamas occupy about 37,000 square miles of the Atlantic Ocean, of which 5,380 square miles is above water. Of this land area, which extends from NW to SE for some 750 miles, there are 36 islands, 687 cays, and 2,414 rocks. We can discount the rocks in our search for the landfall, but that still leaves 723 islands of one size or another that we must choose from to find the one and only San Salvador. The Log of Columbus, as abstracted by Las Casas, is our only good source, and it provides no dimensions nor coordinates.

The Log does provide us with a general description, but many of the islands meet the requirements set forth. Inasmuch

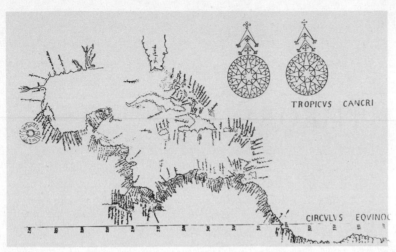

TROPICVS CANCRI

CIRCVLVS EQVINOC

Turin map, 1523. The first Spanish map of the West Indies since 1500, and the first to show Florida by name. (Harrisse, 1892)

as there is a physical sameness about the area—geological, botanical, climatological, hydrological, and zoological—and they were occupied by a uniform Indian cultural group, a general description of the first island gives us very little to go on.

Another way to say this is, they all look pretty much alike, especially from the sea. Even "experts" often confuse the islands from the air and have trouble identifying them from a modern chart before their eyes.

San Salvador, called *Guanahaní* by its native inhabitants, and according to the Log, must be low with no mountains,

level and green, and surrounded by a reef. There must be a peninsula that is attached to the island by a very narrow neck, one that may be cut through in two days of digging (using 15th century tools, of course). The reef enclosed a harbor "large enough for all of the ships of Christendom," but we do not know how many ships that meant, nor do we know if this were any more than an expression of enthusiasm after 33 days at sea. Besides, this was a favorite phrase of Columbus, used a number of times during the voyage for vastly different places. The island was also inhabited.

Many Bahamian islands (including some in the politically separate Turks and Caicos Islands) fit this description. But there are three other facts given by Columbus that help to narrow the field a bit. First, there must be a number of ponds or lakes in the interior of the island. (Columbus says "*muchas aguas*," "many waters"; rivers may be eliminated from consideration because the geology of the islands does not allow for them, except possibly for one on Andros Island, the largest in the archipelago.) The number of candidates is diminished by this requirement, even though the possibility remains that some islands with no permanent lakes or ponds could still be considered to have "*muchas aguas*" in the form of standing water after a period of heavy rains.

Second, San Salvador must have some sort of natural rock formation that looks like an abandoned quarry. Exposed limestone is common throughout the area, but a quarry-like formation is somewhat unusual. This eliminates a number of islands, unless any cliff or exposed beach rock is meant. Since Columbus made this reference quite late in the voyage (on 5

January), after visiting and seeing a number of islands and after coasting much of Cuba, Haiti, and the Dominican Republic, it must have struck him as unique.

Last, there is the statement about a large lagoon in the middle of the island. Although *laguna* may sometimes be translated as *lake*, Columbus usually made the distinction. In his entry for 24 November he made specific reference to *laguna* as oceanic, not terrestrial in nature. On another occasion he gave the name "Cape of the Lagoon" to a feature with a lake behind it and a lagoon—a saltwater marsh joining the ocean—in front. Though the reference could be considered ambiguous, it seems more likely that the cape was named for the oceanic feature in that case. There is no proof positive, but it would seem that if San Salvador had a large *lake* in its center, that is what Columbus would have called it.

To be sure, many seekers of the first landfall have translated *laguna* as *lake,* if an interior lake supported their argument. But what if Columbus actually meant to say *lagoon* the way he used the term on at least two other occasions, and the way it is used today? What if he meant that there was a quiet, sheltered, saltwater body, *on the coast,* about halfway along the island's length? A "lagoon in the middle of the island" could mean "a small embayment in the middle of the island." It does not have to mean "a lake in the interior center."

This is an important reference point, for San Salvador may have a large lake in the center, a lagoon midway on one of its coasts, or both. If an island has neither, it must be eliminated.

With the clues provided, then, the many islands of the region may be sifted and sorted in the quest for the true San Salvador. Between 1625 and 1987, nine different islands have emerged as San Salvador nominees. In historical sequence the islands so nominated are: Cat, Watlings, Grand Turk, Mayaguana, Samana, Conception, Caicos (with South/East/Middle/North Caicos considered as one island), Plana Cays, and Egg/Royal.

It is beyond the scope of the effort at hand to discuss these in detail, for weighty tomes have been written about some (viz., Cat and Watlings), and all the others are treated in lengthy articles. An excellent summary of the many theories may be found in *Terrae Incognitae,* Volume 15 (1983), published by the *Society for the History of Discoveries,* and also in *In the Wake of Columbus* (Wayne State University Press, 1985).

Historical list of landfall sites and their advocates. The list is by no means inclusive and takes into account only *published* expressions of opinion. A question mark means that the individual is or was "leaning" toward the site listed, but without a firm commitment. The dates given are only for the first time a landfall theory was advanced; many of the advocates have published numerous articles and books after the date cited.

Date	Site	Advocate
1625	Cat	de Laet
1731	Cat	Catesby
1767	Cat	Knox
1768	Cat	Drake
1793	Watlings	Muñoz

1825	Grand Turk	Fernández de Navarrete	1959	Watlings	Roukema
1827	Grand Turk	Kettell	1960	Watlings	Vigneras
1828	Cat	Irving & Mackenzie	1961	East Caicos	Fuson
1828	Cat	de La Roquette	1961	Watlings	Doran
1828	Cat	Montlezun	1964	Watlings	Durlacher-Wolper
1837	Cat	von Humboldt	1972	Watlings	Taviani
1846	Grand Turk	Gibbs	1974	Plana Cays	Didiez Burgos
1847	Grand Turk	Major	1981	Grand Turk	Sadler
1856	Watlings	Becher	1981	Egg/Royal	Molander
1858	Watlings	Peschel	1982	Grand Turk	Fuson
1864	Mayaguana	Varnhagen	1983	Watlings (?)	Dunn
1870	Watlings	Major	1983	Watlings (?)	Kelley
1882	Samana	Fox	1983	Grand Turk	Power
1884	Watlings	Murdock	1986	Samana	Judge
1891	Watlings	*Chicago Herald*	1986	Samana	Marden
1892	Watlings	Cronau	1986	Conception	Custín
1892	Samana	Fiske	1987	Samana	Fuson
1892	Samana (?)	Harrisse			
1893	Watlings	Markham			
1894	Samana	Redway			
1902	Watlings	Thacher			
1924	Cat (?)	Nunn			
1927	Watlings	Gould			
1930	Watlings	Jane			
1941	Watlings	McElroy			
1942	Watlings	Morison			
1943	Conception	Gould			
1947	East Caicos	Verhoog			
1958	East Caicos	Link			

Recent research has cut the number of serious candidates to two: Watlings and Samana. Grand Turk was considered a viable possibility for some time, but is now out of the running, with no support among academicians.

The ultimate test is to take one of the above (or any of the 723 islands and cays, for that matter) and follow the guidelines laid down by the Admiral. All one needs is the Log presented here, a good hydrographic chart, and a ruler. Lay out the distances and bearings provided by Columbus. Even if the results do not astound you, they should convince you. Of all the islands and cays in the Bahamas, *only by starting at Samana Cay will you be able to follow the Admiral to Cuba.*

If you commence with Watlings (erroneously called San Salvador, albeit the legal name since 1926) you will encounter an immediate problem: the second island, Rum Cay in this theory, is too far away. Also, Columbus said he saw many islands after departing San Salvador. On this track you see only one. If you extend the distance given by Columbus, and ignore the blank spaces where he said there were islands, you arrive at Rum Cay. Try to follow its north coast for 30 nautical miles; the coast only extends a third of that distance! And so it goes; the whole theory collapses at the outset, and gets even worse as it progresses.

Juan Bautista Muñoz, who was commissioned by King Carlos III of Spain to write a history of the New World, was the first to name Watlings Island as the San Salvador of Columbus. In his *Historia del Nuevo Mundo,* Madrid, 1793, Muñoz identified Watlings as the landfall island, which was soon to win favor over Cat. Though the latter was first introduced on a map as early as 1625, and in print in 1731, it was eventually to lose the debate. Even Cat's support by the likes of Washington Irving and Alexander von Humboldt was to no avail. Nor was the challenge of Grand Turk, first presented by Martín Fernández de Navarrete, the man who discovered in 1790 and published in 1825 the Las Casas abstract of the Log.

Though other landfall islands made their debuts, or older ones found new support, Watlings was the one that consistently attracted the most powerful champions. Beginning with the 19th century, there was Captain A.B. Becher of the Royal

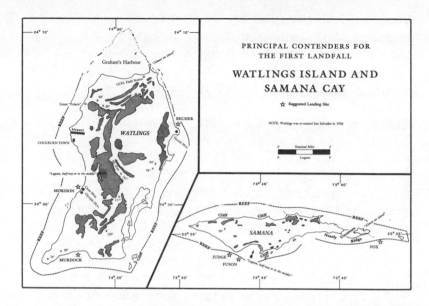

PRINCIPAL CONTENDERS FOR
THE FIRST LANDFALL

WATLINGS ISLAND AND
SAMANA CAY

☆ Suggested Landing Site

NOTE: Watlings was re-named San Salvador in 1926

Navy; Oskar Peschel, the great German geographer; R.H. Major, who switched from his earlier position and deserted Grand Turk; Admiral J.B. Murdock, who disposed of the many problems connected with the route and laid down the modern Watlings-school track; J.B. Thacher, the truly overpowering Columbus scholar at the turn of this century; and in recent decades, Samuel Eliot Morison.

Morison, both an admiral and a Ph.D. in history, collected a large group of followers, many of them active today. With his Harvard and Navy connections, Morison successfully held off all challengers. Though the debate raged, particularly after 1947 when Pieter Verhoog made a very convincing argument for Caicos, Morison lost few supporters among mapmakers, encyclopaedia editors, and the educated public. All through the Watlings era, there was hardly a notice given when a new island theory was interjected. Only a handful of scholars ever heard of Varnhagen and Mayaguana Island (1864), Fox and Samana Cay (1882), Gould and Conception (1943), or Didiez Burgos and the Plana Cays (1974). Edwin and Marion Link attracted some attention in 1958 with their interesting (but impossible) route from Caicos to Cuba, via Samana and Long, bypassing several large islands in the process. But this was mainly because Link was the well-known inventor of the Link Trainer and also had the maritime credentials to back up his claims. Few ever accepted his ideas on Columbus.

But Verhoog would not give up the fight. He restated his Caicos theory in 1954, again in 1980, and once more in 1985 (in a paper published posthumously). This rekindled the fires, and several scholars began to revise their notes. At this juncture, largely encouraged by the Society for the History of Discoveries, who had held a special annual meeting devoted to Columbus and had devoted a special issue of its journal to the topic, the National Geographic Society became interested.

It was not National Geographic's first plunge into Columbus matters. In October 1894, the Society had published an article by Jacques W. Redway, a Fellow of the Royal Geographical Society in London, supporting the little-known work of Captain Gustavus V. Fox, Assistant Secretary of the Navy under President Abraham Lincoln, which claimed the landfall island to be obscure Samana Cay. But nothing was to come of this, and by 1975, the lead article in the November

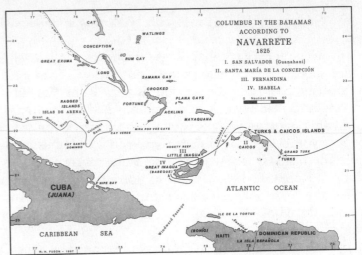

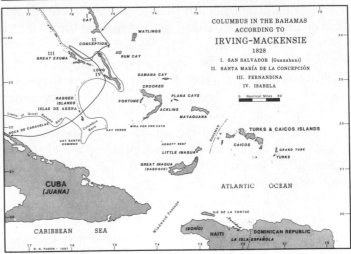

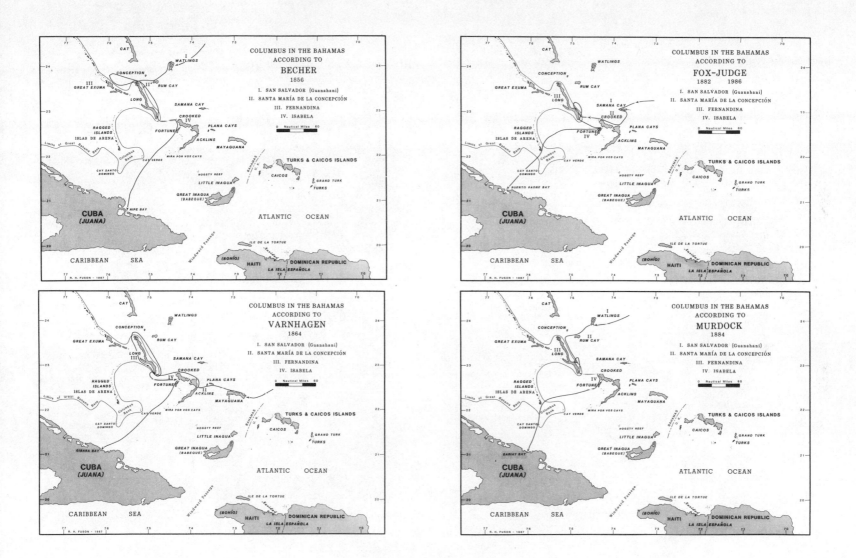

COLUMBUS IN THE BAHAMAS ACCORDING TO BECHER
1856

I. SAN SALVADOR (Guanahani)
II. SANTA MARÍA DE LA CONCEPCIÓN
III. FERNANDINA
IV. ISABELA

COLUMBUS IN THE BAHAMAS ACCORDING TO FOX-JUDGE
1882   1986

I. SAN SALVADOR (Guanahani)
II. SANTA MARÍA DE LA CONCEPCIÓN
III. FERNANDINA
IV. ISABELA

COLUMBUS IN THE BAHAMAS ACCORDING TO VARNHAGEN
1864

I. SAN SALVADOR (Guanahani)
II. SANTA MARÍA DE LA CONCEPCIÓN
III. FERNANDINA
IV. ISABELA

COLUMBUS IN THE BAHAMAS ACCORDING TO MURDOCK
1884

I. SAN SALVADOR (Guanahani)
II. SANTA MARÍA DE LA CONCEPCIÓN
III. FERNANDINA
IV. ISABELA

APPENDIX A THE LANDFALL THEORIES

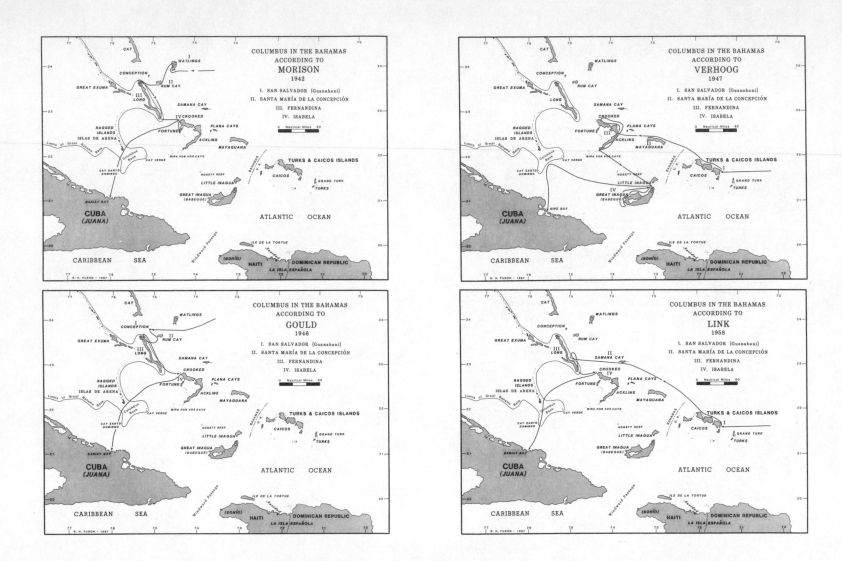

THE LOG OF CHRISTOPHER COLUMBUS

COLUMBUS IN THE BAHAMAS
ACCORDING TO
DIDIEZ-BURGOS
1974

I. SAN SALVADOR (Guanahani)
II. SANTA MARÍA DE LA CONCEPCIÓN
III. FERNANDINA
IV. ISABELA

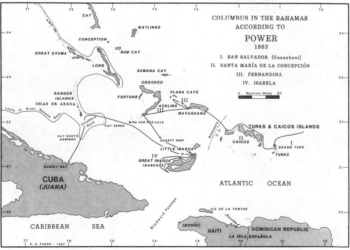

COLUMBUS IN THE BAHAMAS
ACCORDING TO
POWER
1983

I. SAN SALVADOR (Guanahani)
II. SANTA MARÍA DE LA CONCEPCIÓN
III. FERNANDINA
IV. ISABELA

issue of *National Geographic* fell back into lockstep with Morison and Watlings.

There is no doubt that all the activity of the early 1980s had its origin with a small group of Columbus buffs within the Society for the History of Discoveries. Old ideas were dusted off; new ones were tried. The computer was brought into play for the first time by James E. Kelley, Jr., while Oliver Dunn began to transcribe and translate the Las Casas abstract the old way—one word at a time. Eventually, the two men were to join forces. Columbus would have understood this coming together of two worlds.

Field trips were made to the Bahamas; symposia were organized. And many began to catch the excitement of the coming Quincentennial of the Discovery. Solving the landfall question seemed an appropriate celebration.

Joseph Judge, Senior Associate Editor of *National Geographic,* put together a team of computer specialists, archaeologists, mathematicians, cartographers, transcribers-translators, navigators, artists, photographers, camera people, a talented boat captain, an excellent pilot, a few scholarly consultants, and several Bahamian islanders. The result of this massive team effort was a stunning vindication of Gustavus V. Fox and his pioneering study done in 1882, supported by the Redway research of 1894. In November 1986 *National Geographic* announced its findings in a blockbuster article, "Where Columbus Found the New World," accompanied by extensive maps, photography, and illustrations. It also made available to its membership Eugene Lyon's new translation of the landfall portion of the Log, based on his own direct transcription of Las Casas (see Prologue).

Although a great deal of high technology was brought into play—from navigational computers to a special computer program developed by Control Data Corporation—the 1986 study varied from the one Fox did 104 years earlier in only two minor instances. First, the Fox landfall on Samana Cay is about six or seven miles east of the one offered by Judge (but on the same side of the island). Second, Fox places "the harbor with two mouths" (on Island III) about eight miles north of the Judge position. Other than that, the two theories are almost identical.

National Geographic's main contribution to the landfall debate is to present Fox's obscure study to more than 12,000,000 members of the Society and, therefore, to the world. And it elevates Fox to the place he deserves as the man who solved the riddle of San Salvador. It will help cleanse our maps, encyclopaedias, and textbooks of a longstanding historico-geographical mistake.

Inasmuch as the *National Geographic* study is well known and widely available, there is no need to summarize it here. Portions of the Fox article are reproduced, however, for it is still difficult to find except in the large research libraries.

GUSTAVUS VASA FOX AND THE SAMANA CAY LANDFALL THEORY

Gustavus Vasa Fox was born "within a lombard shot" of the Atlantic Ocean, just a few miles north of Boston, in Saugus, Massachusetts, on June 13, 1821. He attended high school in nearby Lowell and the Phillips Academy in Andover. By the age of 17 he had already charted his life's course. When he entered the U.S. Navy as a midshipman on January 12, 1838, he was never to leave the sea for more than a few short periods the rest of his life. Of all of the people associated with the Columbus saga, including more than a few admirals, none was as close to the sea and sailing as Fox.

At the age of 20, Fox was in the Mediterranean, stationed aboard the USS *Cyane*. In 1842 he served on the USS *Boston,* and in 1843 found himself off the coast of Africa on the sloop, USS *Saratoga*. After three years overseas, Fox drew a Stateside tour, in 1844, at the Naval School in Philadelphia. Then, after

a year, he was back to sea, to serve aboard the USS *Preble*. In 1847 he was assigned to the U.S. Coast Survey, forerunner of the U.S. Coast & Geodetic Survey.

Between 1848 and 1851, Fox was stationed in the East Indies, first aboard the sloop USS *Plymouth* and later on the USS *Dolphin*. From 1853 until 1855 he commanded the U.S. mail ships *Ohio* and *George Law.* Then, after a brief fling with civilian life, he was named chief clerk of the Navy Department on May 9, 1861. Less than three months later, President Lincoln appointed him Assistant Secretary of the Navy, an office he held until November 1866.

Gustavus Fox served Secretary of the Navy Gideon Wells with efficiency and brilliance. For all practical purposes, Fox was chief of naval operations during the Civil War. He planned the capture of New Orleans and the reopening of the Mississippi River, as well as perfecting the ironclad ships of his day and making many improvements in the personnel of the Navy Department.

On June 1, 1866, Fox was reappointed Assistant Secretary of the Navy and, four days later, was sent by Congress to Russia. This was a goodwill tour aboard the USS *Miantonomoh,* the first ironclad ship to make such a voyage. Fox, with the naval rank of captain, was in command. The voyage was much more than a mere gesture of goodwill toward Czar Alexander II, who had abolished serfdom in his country. Fox, during his stay in Russia, took an active part—some say the leading part—in negotiating the purchase of Alaska from Russia. He returned to the United States on December 13, 1866, and again resumed his civilian life, first as manager of the Middlesex Mills in Lowell, and later as an executive with E.R. Mudge, Sawyer & Co., Boston.

But the salt water still flowed in Fox's veins. During the winter of 1879–80, he returned to the Bahamas, an area to which he was no stranger. The first landfall of Columbus had always intrigued Fox, and he is said to have whiled away many long hours at sea with a well-worn copy of Fernández de Navarrete's transcription of the Log as his companion.

Fox also had many well-placed friends in the Navy, Coast & Geodetic Survey, the State Department, and in major universities. Drawing on all of his experience at sea, and making full use of the resources at his disposal, Fox made his landmark study for the U.S. Coast & Geodetic Survey, some of which is reproduced here. On October 29, 1883, one year after the pub-

lication of his findings, Captain Gustavus V. Fox passed away in New York City.

*   *   *

(APPENDIX NO. 18, COAST AND GEODETIC SURVEY REPORT FOR 1880.)

AN ATTEMPT TO SOLVE THE PROBLEM OF THE FIRST LANDING PLACE OF COLUMBUS IN THE NEW WORLD.

By Capt. G. V. FOX, Assistant Secretary of the Navy from May, 1861, to November, 1866, Member of the Massachusetts Historical Society, etc.

INTRODUCTION

The discovery of America by Christopher Columbus is, perhaps, the most important event recorded in secular history. Ancient philosophers had suggested the sphericity of the earth, the zone of water, and the theoretical possibility of reaching the Indies by sailing west; and Columbus recalled these suggestions before the great councils that ridiculed and rejected his proposal.

It takes not a jot from the glory of his discovery that he underestimated the size of the earth; or that he died in ignorance of the transcendent importance of his deed; or that the Northmen had preceded him. The fulfilment of his design, to steer west until he reached the Indies or found intervening land, was the triumph of human reasoning; it was the soul's work, into which neither chance nor the fickle winds intruded.

The aim of this monograph is to try to solve the problem of the first landing-place of Columbus in the New World. It is founded, as all others are, upon Las Casas' (abridged) copy of the "log-book," or journal, of Columbus. Nothing has been raked from the arcana of the past to impeach this; and it will continue to be used until the original journal is produced or this copy is shown to be spurious.

It is manifest that no landfall, or track, can stand which is supported by assertions that are in opposition to Las Casas' narrative. Knowing this to be true I have tested in the following pages every track, by placing paragraphs from each author and from the journal in juxtaposition so that any one, with the help of the correct appendix chart, shall discern the contradictions.

The selection of a new landfall and track through the Bahamas, different from all hitherto ascribed to Columbus, is the natural result of this sifting. The track which I have laid down was chosen because it appears to be the only one that can be made to fit the courses, distances, and descriptions in the log-book.

NARRATIVE AND DISCUSSION

. . . The method of applying Columbus's words in detail to refute each of the alleged tracks, and the study that I gave to the subject in the winter of 1878–'79 in the Bahamas, which had been familiar cruising ground to me, have resulted in the selection of Samana or Atwood Cay for the first landing-place. It is a little island 8.8 miles east and west; 1.6 extreme breadth, and averaging 1.2 north and south. It has 8.6 square miles. The east end is in latitude 23° 05′ N.; longitude 73° 37′ west of Greenwich. The reef on which it lies is 15 by 2½ miles. On the southeast this reef stretches half a mile from the land, on the east four miles, on the west two, along the north shore one-quarter to one-half of a mile, and on the southwest scarcely one-quarter. Turk is smaller than Samana, and Cat very much larger. The selection of two so unlike in size shows that dimension has not been considered essential in choosing an island for the first landfall.

When Columbus discovered Guanahani, the journal called it "little island." After landing he speaks of it as "bien grande," "very large," which some translate, *tolerably,* or *pretty large.* November 20, 1492, Navarrete, first edition, the journal refers to Isabela, a larger island than Guanahani, as "little island," and the 5th of January following, San Salvador is again called "little island."

. . . Columbus said that Guanahani had abundance of water and a very large lagoon in the middle of it. He used the word *laguna*—lagoon, not *lago*—lake. His arrival in the Bahamas was at the height of the rainy season. Governor Rawson's *Report on the Bahamas,* 1864, p. 92, Appendix 4, gives the annual rainfall at Nassau for ten years, 1855–'64, as 64 inches. From May 1 to November 1 is the wet season, during which 44.7 inches fall; the other six months 19.3 only. The most is in October, 8.5 inches. Andros, the largest island, 1,600 square miles, is the only one that has a stream of water. The subdivision of the land into so many islands and cays, the absence of mountains, the showery characteristic of the rainfall, the porosity of the rock, and the great heat reflected from the white coral, are the chief causes for the want of running water. During the rainy season

Samana Cay, showing "laguna" and "muchas aguas." This is the location favored by the author and the National Geographic Society as the first Bahamian landfall of Columbus. (Photo: author)

the "abundance of water" collects in the low places, making ponds and lagoons that afterward are soaked up by the rock and evaporated by the sun. Turk and Watling have lagoons of a more permanent condition, because they are maintained from the ocean by permeation. The lagoon which Columbus found at Guanahani had certainly undrinkable water, or he would have gotten some for his vessels, instead of putting it off until he reached the third island. There is nothing in the journal to indicate that the lagoon at Guanahani was aught but the flooding of the low grounds by excessive rains; and even if it was one communicating with the ocean, its absence now

may be referred to the effect of those agencies which are working incessantly to reshape the soft structure of the Bahamas.

Samana has a range of hills on the southwest side about 100 feet high, and on the northeast another, lower. Between them, and also along the north shore, the land is low, and during the season of rains there is a row of ponds parallel to the shore. On the south side a conspicuous white bluff looks to the southward and eastward. The two cays, lying respectively half a mile and 3 miles east of the island, and possibly the outer breaker, which is four miles, all might have been connected with each other, and with the island, four hundred years ago. In that event the most convenient place for Columbus to anchor in the strong N. E. trade-wind, was where I have put an anchor on the sub-sketch of Samana.

He did not note the direction of the wind while running for, nor when at Guanahani. I feel confident that it was the N. E. trade, since he gives the speed of the vessels from sunset (5^h 41^m) until 2 a.m. the next morning—October 11–12—as 22½ leagues—79½ nautical miles—which is at the rate of 9½ miles per hour, an unusual speed, and plainly indicating that he was running with a strong quartering wind under all sail, with fine weather. The "trades" generally freshen near the islands, but they are always in the eastern quarter. In the Bahamas they break up and are very light at east and southeast, but frequently blow strong when they get to the southward and westward, and the circuit ends with heavy squalls from the northward and westward; afterward north and northeast winds and fine weather prevail.

Columbus had none of the strong winds from a western quarter, because he was steering west. If the weather had not been fine he could not have seen the light at 10 p.m.—"like a small wax candle."

Neither could he have discovered the land at 2 a.m., 2 leagues—6.4 miles distant. Varnhagen (note I, p. 16) says the "moon shown bright, and a sailor saw by its light a white point; fired his lombard; called out land." I am greatly indebted to Professor William Harkness, United States Navy, of the Naval Observatory at Washington, for the moon's place. It was full October 5, O. S., 1492, at 10h 58m p.m., Greenwich mean time. It rose the 11th of October at 11 p.m., and at 2 a.m., when the land was sighted, it was 39° high, latitude 5° S., longitude 106° 03'. Those who were admonished by the admiral to keep a sharp lookout from the forecastle were, of course, looking ahead—west—and the moon, then nearly at the third quarter, was partly behind them and shone directly upon the white bluff. This was most favorable for seeing the land at night, and it is a memorable fact that Columbus first saw the New World through the light of the moon.

In the journal of the 14th of October the Admiral wrote that he "went along the island, in a north-northeasterly direction, to see the other side, which was on the other side of the east." The same date he said that in going along in the boats he "found a piece of land, like an island, although it was not one, with six houses on it, which in two days could easily be cut off and converted into an island." The first quotation is the language of a seaman who had anchored under a jutting point of land which stretched to the eastward and was in sight; he could see one side as far as the east end, but he desired to see the *other side of the east end*. Columbus was at anchor on an open coast; each vessel had but one boat, and he took all the boats for his exploration of the 14th. For this reason, according to the usage of the sea, he ought not to withdraw far from his ships. The second quotation confirms the first, as to his being in the neighborhood of a peninsula. Both agree well with the east end of Samana. The point of land that Columbus said could easily be cut off has already been separated by the erosion of the waves.

. . . After he had left Guanahani he saw so many islands that he was undecided which to sail for first, but he determined to make for the largest. A vessel that leaves the east part of Samana and steers to the southward with some westing comes into view of the hills of Plana Cays, Acklin, and Crooked, on bearings from south-southeast to west by south, and to a stranger these hills would appear like so many islands. After Columbus anchored at the second island he wrote that it was five leagues, rather seven—15.9 or 22.3 nautical miles—from the first. The northeast end of Acklin bears S. W. by S. ¼ S., 23 nautical miles from the east part of Samana. For this discussion I consider Acklin and Crooked to be one island, under the name of Crooked. The channel which separates them is of modern origin, no doubt. It has the appearance of having been made by erosion; it is so shallow that it can be waded across, even at high water, and it is invisible to a passing vessel.

Columbus wrote that the second island had a north-and-south side 15.9, and one east and west over 31.8 miles long. Crooked has a north-and-south side 13, and another which runs west by north and east by south 29 miles. A navigator of to-day could not come nearer to the truth, in describing the island in like circumstances; but Columbus kept his time with a sand-glass, and reckoned his speed by the eye. I wish the reader to take heed that it is the *second island, and no other,* of which the journal records the length and trend of two separate sides; and that *Crooked is the only one in the Bahamas* which conforms to this description.

A seeming objection to Crooked arises from the language in the journal of the 15th of October, that the side of the second island toward San Salvador ran north and south, whereas the side of Crooked which is in the direction of Samana runs east and west. Columbus could not note this fact *at* the first island, because Crooked is not visible from his anchorage there. After leaving Guanahani he saw many islands, and made for the largest. As he stood off and on all night, and the tide detained him on the 15th till about noon, he might have noted the side he then came to. This is the understanding of R. H. Major, who, in the *Journal of the Royal Geographical Society,* vol. xli, p. 198, translates the passage thus: "I found that the face of it, on the side toward San Salvador [or rather, I would suggest, on the side approached by the ships in coming from San Salvador], ran north and south five leagues, and the other side which I coasted ran east and west ten leagues."

From the data kindly supplied by the officers of the Naval Observatory in Washington, I learn that the moon crossed the meridian of Crooked Island on the 14th of October, 1492, at 6^h 36^m a.m., Civil time. The British Admiralty Tide Tables for 1881 give VII o'clock for the "Establishment of the Port" at Crooked. Therefore it was high water there on the 14th of October at 1^h 36^m p.m.; low at 7^h 48^m, high at 2 a.m. on the 15th; low at 8^h 12^m and high at 2^h 24^m p.m. The sun set at 5^h 40^m and twilight lasted about 1^h 19^m. The journal does not give the wind *at* Guanahani, nor until the 16th, at the second island, when it is entered as S. E. I believe I have proved [already] that Columbus made the land on the 12th of October with a strong N. E. trade; and the invariable circuit of winds would give light easterly ones, sometime from the 12th to the 16th. During the regular "trades" the current between Samana and Crooked flows W. N. W. a knot an hour; but at other times the set and drift are uncertain. On the north side of Crooked the flood *tide* runs always to the eastward and the ebb contrarily. When Columbus neared the second island he estimated it to be 15.9 miles from the first; but the next day he called it 22.3. In the mean time he was detained by the *tide* so that he did not reach it again until about noon. Captain Becher (pp. 111–345) said that this detention was "set of the current"; but Columbus used the word *maréa,* not *corriénte;* the former signifies *tide,* flux and reflux; the latter *current,* progressive motion of the water; a distinction held in both languages and especially among seamen, and one of importance here.

These facts, in connection with the journal, enable me to offer a reasonable theory as to the movements of his vessels on the 14th and 15th of October. He left the south side of the east part of Samana on the 14th, undoubtedly after noon; and steered to the southward and westward, with light easterly winds, for Crooked. Midway he found the usual westerly current, and on the other side he ran into a stronger one setting in the same direction; but this was the *ebb tide* which flowed west, along the north shore of Crooked, from 1^h 36^m to 7^h 48^m p.m. He did not reach the land in time to see his anchoring-ground before dark, and the night was moonless. In consequence, he began, about sunset (5^h 40^m), to stand off and on; that is, he beat to the eastward to overcome this westerly set and keep his place until morning, when he intended to run in and anchor. At 7^h 48^m p.m. the tide turned and flowed east until 2 a.m. on the 15th. So that in the darkness of the night he had, unknowingly, six hours and twelve minutes of current, *contrary* to that for which he was allowing. In this way he got so far to the eastward that it was noon before he reached the island again; when he coasted the north shore and near sunset anchored at the west end. On the following day, the 16th, he wrote his journal of the 15th, by which time he had observed the distinction between the currents and tides in the neighborhood of Crooked, and he noted the one which caused his detention.

The second island of Columbus has been such a stumbling-block to investigators that many of them assert that he sighted it, but passed on without stopping. See translation from Muñoz, *ante,* p. 36, and discussion with Captain Becher, *ante,* p. 37. Major (p. 198) wrote: "Here I beg to call your attention to the fact that Columbus neither lands upon nor gives any name to the first island which he reaches after leaving Guanahani, a fact which argues its unimportance and sanctions our assuming it to be Rum Cay." The weight of these authorities makes it necessary for me to try to answer them before I go on. The following paragraph from the Spanish text of the journal is the authority upon which Major and Captain Becher found their assertion that Columbus did not land upon the second island (*Navarrete*, 1st edition, p. 25, October 15, and *ante*, p. 35): "*Y como desta isla vide otra mayor al Oueste, cargué las velas por andar todo aquel dia fasta la noche, porque aun no pudiera haber andado al cabo del Oueste.*" Major's translation (p. 198) is: "And as from this island I saw another larger one to the west, I started for the purpose of sailing the whole of that day until night, for otherwise I could not have reached the westernmost cape." Captain Becher (p. 109) renders it: "And as from this island I saw another larger one to the westward, I made sail, continuing on until night; for as yet I had not arrived at the western cape." Mr. Thomas's translation, which I have adopted, is: "And as from this island I saw another larger one to the west, *I clewed up the sails,* for I had gone all that day until night, because I could not yet have gone to the western cape." The essential difference is with, *cargué las velas*. Major makes it, "I started"; Captain

Becher, "I made sail"; and Thomas, "I clewed up the sails." In *Diccionario Maritimo Español,* etc., *por D. José de Lorenzo, D. Gonzalo de Murga y D. Martin Ferreiro, Empleados en la Direccion de Hidrografiá,* Madrid, 1864, the definition agrees with that given by Mr. Thomas. So of all other Spanish dictionaries which I can find. I have also submitted the phrase to Spanish officers with like result. The signification is, to clew up, or brail up; that is, take in sail. A similar expression occurs in the first part of the journal of October 15: "I had been standing off and on this night fearing to approach the shore for anchorage before morning not knowing whether the coast would be clear of shoals, and intending to clew up—*cargar velas*—at dawn." If he had been hove to all night he might have written "I will make sail in the morning"; but as he was standing off and on, the two clauses—"Fearing to approach the shore for anchorage before morning," and "Intending to clew up at dawn", are connected, and the meaning of *cargar velas* in the latter is obviously to take in, not to make sail.

. . . Remembering, then, that all the things done on the 15th were recorded [in the journal] on the 16th—after he had left the second island—they might be put into a concise and truthful statement as follows: Columbus explored Guanahani in the boats before noon of the 14th, and sailed after noon to the southward and westward, the direction of the gold. Many islands coming shortly into sight, he made for the largest, but did not reach it in time to see the anchoring-ground before dark. The wind being light from the eastward, and a strong current running west, he decided to stand off and on, or beat to the eastward, to hold his position during the night, that he might anchor in the morning *at that part of the island which he had seen before dark*. The next forenoon, the 15th, he found himself so far to the eastward that it was noon before he got back. He observed two sides of the island, one north and south, five leagues; the other, east and west, over ten. He approached the first, but as it was a lee-shore he followed the other all the afternoon, arriving at the western cape about sunset, whence he saw another large island to the west. Not wishing to be under weigh again at night, among the tides and currents, and the wind having canted to the southward and eastward, which gave him a weather shore to anchor under, he clewed up his sails and came to. On the morning of the next day, the 16th, he went on shore to explore the island, but, as the wind increased from the S. E., and his ships were riding to a weather tide, they were liable to be set across it and foul their anchors. The Admiral observing this from the shore, returned and weighed anchor before or at noon, for the island in the west . . . My interpretation is that he did not go beyond this second island on the 15th, but that he anchored about sunset at the west cape of the side he had followed. This would make his run 10 leagues—31.8 nautical miles—in 5^h 40^m, equal to 5.6 miles each hour. Major and Captain Becher say that, in addition to coasting this side, he kept on eight leagues—25.5 nautical miles—farther, where he came to anchor at sunset, making a sum of 18 leagues—57.3 nautical miles—in 5^h 40^m, which gives a speed of 10.1 nautical, or 12.7 Italian, miles for every hour—greater than is recorded anywhere for his vessels. He must have had a gale of wind all the afternoon of the 15th to have been driven at such extraordinary speed; but there is no mention of it in the journal. His log across the Atlantic was 105½ nautical miles a day, equal to 4.4 miles every hour. The best day's run was October 4, 200.5 nautical miles, an average of 8.4 each hour.

Columbus wrote on the 14th of October, in respect to the second island: "I looked for the largest one and determined to make for it, and I am so doing." On the 15th—written on the 16th and relating solely to past events—he said: "It was about noon when I reached the said island . . ."

Columbus anchored at the northwest cape of Crooked (Santa Maria), at sunset, October 15, and waited there until the following forenoon. He wrote: "And as from this island I saw another larger one to the west, I clewed up the sails." It would appear from this paragraph that the island referred to came into view when he reached the west cape, near sunset. Writing of what took place the next day, he said: "I set sail for the other large island that appeared at the west." He begins the 16th with, "About noon I left the *islands of Santa Maria de la Concepcion* for the *island of Fernandina,* which appears to be very large to the west." Long Island lies 25 miles west of Crooked, and the range of hills upon it, marked 150 feet high, are two miles farther. The distance of visibility for 150 feet is 14 miles, and for Columbus's lookout, of 60 feet, it is 8.8 miles; total, 22.8 miles. In consequence Long Island cannot be seen from Crooked.

I have alluded [already] to probable physical changes among the Bahamas in the past, but I shall not appeal to these here. Seamen understand very well that, in favorable circumstances, the appearance of land is very striking over coral islands which are below the range of visibility from the observer. This is especially noticeable in the Bahamas, because all the necessary conditions are there: low islands of white coral; not enough trees or undergrowth to hinder radiation; a high degree of heat, and the air loaded with moisture. When a fall of temperature happens this is precipitated into a cloud cap which often covers the island like a blanket, and outlines it. It is this and the blending of cloud and land that makes the latter appear, frequently, to be above the horizon when truly below it.

Columbus sailed from the northwest end of Crooked, October 16, either at 10 a.m. or noon, for he gives both times, toward the island which appeared in the west. Calm weather retarded him until daylight of the 17th, when he anchored at a cape of an island, which he named Fernandina. Here, he said, the coast ran north-northwest and south-southeast. On the way over he estimated the distance from the second to the third island at nine leagues. After he had arrived he called it eight leagues—25.5 nautical miles. A course from Crooked W. ¼ N. 25 miles strikes a cape of Long Island where the coast line runs as given by Columbus. The appearance of Long Island (Fernandina) from Crooked (Santa Maria), the course and distance between them, the southeast cape and the trend of the coast of Long Island (Fernandina), all conform accurately to the facts; and we need not linger upon them.

At noon of the 17th of October, Columbus sailed from this southeast cape, steering along the shore to the N. N. W., "the wind being S. W. and S." When he was near the end of the island "two leagues off" he found a marvellous port with two entrances formed by a rocky islet in the middle. Both were narrow, but within was ample room for 100 ships, if there had been sufficient depth free from obstructions, with a deep entrance. He was so much impressed with this marvellous port that he anchored outside of it and went in with all the boats and sounded it and saw that it was too shoal. This was the first opening into the land that he had met with and he thought it betokened a fresh-water river, therefore he took in the water casks.

His former visit to a tropical country was to Guinea (Africa) where all the openings into the shore are made by fresh-water streams.

The wind was off the land, and he remained in this harbor with the boats, getting water, for two hours, when he returned to the vessels and sailed. Columbus wrote that the entrance of this marvellous port was two leagues from the end of the island. The reader will observe how often the journal uses leagues and miles in such a way that an interchange of them was possible on the Admiral's part and very probable with the copyist. If the two leagues of the journal were a clerical error for two Italian miles, it corresponds with the chart. He wrote that he sailed on this course until he discovered that part of the island which ran east and west; and afterward the Indians persuaded him to go back, and because the wind ceased and then sprang up from the W. N. W., which was contrary to his course, he turned around. This and the subsequent courses point out that he was following this east-and-west shore on a likely course of W. N. W. when the wind came out ahead. After turning around he sailed all night, E. S. E., sometimes E. and also S. E. to clear the land. He wrote that the atmosphere was very misty and the weather threatening, but that the wind was *light* and it did not permit him to reach the land to anchor, and that it rained hard after midnight until almost day. He adds, "We [are] at the southeast cape of the island where I hope to anchor until it gets clear." He closes the journal of the 17th with general remarks, which was his frequent habit. It is evident that he wrote this paragraph, and the last observations of the 17th, on the morning of the 18th, at the southeast cape of the island, where, as he was exposed to rainy weather and light winds, he desired to anchor.

These words imply that he was at the cape from which he had sailed the day before. In other words, that he had retraced his steps as he was advised to do, and getting back to a familiar anchorage, with unfavorable conditions for coasting such shores, he wished to anchor and wait for clear weather.

. . . We find recorded in the journal certain physical characteristics concerning the second island which belong to Crooked only; and in like manner is the third island established. This is so important that I briefly recapitulate. Columbus anchored at a cape of the third where the coast line was north-northwest and south-southeast. He followed it N. N. W. until he came to a marvellous port, two leagues [miles?] from the end. He sounded it in the boats and found it capacious, but shallow. He sailed N. W. until he opened that part of the shore which ran east and west; he steered along it W. N. W. till the approach of night and the advice of the Indians caused him to turn about.

. . . There is an element of time here which is important as it limits the ground passed over on the afternoon of the 17th. The Admiral left the southeast cape at noon and turned around while heading W. N. W., and then he steered an opposite course during the night, to clear the land. It is fair to select sunset, 5^h 40^m, as the time of his turning. As long as he could see the land and reefs he might keep on, but *not after dark*. He would choose the day only to explore new shores. In the night he might retrace his steps steering well off, or anchor, or heave to, or stand off and on, nothing else. The distance from the southeast cape past the shallow port and around to the end of the east-and-west side is 22 nautical miles. As he stopped at the above port two hours, he was under way only 3^h 40^m. This gives a speed of 6 miles an hour, which is fully as much as his vessels were

likely to do. Any track which is longer, or which requires more speed than this, must be very liable to error.

If Columbus turned at sunset on the 17th and returned to the southeast cape at "almost day" of the 18th he sailed in a night which had ten hours of darkness, the distance he went over in 3^h 40^m of day. This is not strange. In addition to the various courses steered to clear the land, he says, of this night, that the atmosphere was misty and the weather threatening, but *the wind light*. The fact that he followed this shore at all during such a moonless night is proof that he had gone along it the day previous and learned the direction of the shores, so that he retraced his steps without much hazard *provided he steered well off*. This he could do; for in coasting the island the afternoon before he must have observed that there was no land on the other side to pick him up.

Columbus is now at anchor on the southwest side of the south end of the third, or Long Island (Fernandina). He sailed from here at dawn on the 19th. Sunrise was at 6^h 21^m, twilight 1^h 19^m, dawn at 5^h 2^m. The flag-ship steered S. E., the Pinta E. and S. E., and the Nina S. S. E. Three hours had not elapsed when they saw an island to the east for which all the vessels headed, and before mid-day they arrived at the northern extremity, where there is a rocky islet. I take this to be the north end of Fortune Island. The Admiral gives no distances in sailing across. If he was fairly under way at 5^h 30^m and anchored at 11^h 30^m, the time was 6 hours, half of which he steered S. E. and half E., making E. S. E. if each three hours was equal speed. From the south end of Long Island to the north end of Fortune the course and distance are E. by S. ¾ S. 32 nautical miles. This gives a little more than 5.3 miles an hour, which is fair sailing for his vessels. Columbus wrote on the evening of the 19th that this rocky islet "lay from the island of Fernandina, whence I had come east [and] west, and the coast afterwards ran from the rocky islet to the westward, and there was in it twelve leagues." If the last clause is an error for 12 Italian miles, it agrees with the chart, as the coast inclines from here two points to the west and measures 10.5 nautical miles, or 13.2 Italian miles.

Long Island is invisible from the rocky islet, and the line between them is not east and west. In steering from Fernandina Columbus spread his vessels from an E. to a S. S. E. course, to get hold of the land; then he drew them together on one course and afterward anchored. A bearing entered at this time with reference to an island no longer in sight, and from which they had arrived by steering several courses, might easily be 1¾ points in error.

Fortune is the fourth island of Columbus's visitation, the one he named after that manful and lovable queen, *Isabela,* who sent him on his way when kings and councils rejected him. It will be noticed that the journal makes the third island lie west of the second, and the fourth east of the third. This brings the second and fourth adjacent to each other, as they are found upon the chart. If a landsman thinks that the Admiral ought to have known that the land now north of him was the same which lay south on the evening of the 15th, it can be answered truly, that one of the most perplexing things in the vocation of the sea is the recognition of lands or islands that have no conspicuous marks. Light-houses, beacons, and pilotage grew out of this difficulty.

. . . At the beginning of October 24 Columbus sailed from the rocky islet, at the north end of Fortune, on a predetermined W. S. W. course. The day was characterized by rain, calms, little wind, and then a "lovely" breeze. The night of the 24th–25th he had strong winds with rain, and being on unknown ground he first reduced, then took in all sail. He said he had made much headway, of which he was doubtful, but he estimated that he did not go this night two leagues. The direction of the wind is not noted. He says that it grew strong suddenly, with mist and rain. At sunrise on the 25th he made sail at W. S. W., but at 9 a. m. he steered west—no doubt to make the former course good, which he had lost somewhat in the night, by drifting under bare poles. At 3 p. m. the Admiral saw land. "There were seven or eight islands, all extending from north to south; distant from them five leagues," 15.9 nautical miles. He anchored on the 26th of October in the shallow water south of these, which he called Sand Islands.

About 60 miles N. N. E. of the northeast coast of Cuba, a line of cays and islands extend N. N. W. ½ W. and S. S. E. ½ E. for 21 miles. The principal ones are eight: Nurse, Bonavista, Racoon, Double Breasted, Maycock, Hog, Great Ragged, and Little Ragged. From the southernmost a coral bank stretches 28 miles south, and 30 east, having from 4 to 11 fathoms of water, interspersed with rocky heads and shoal spots. This is known as the "Columbus Bank"; it terminates the Great Bahama Bank on the southeast. Here, then, is the fifth island, or islands, visited by Columbus; and it should be noted that such a string of islands, and bank of shallow water stretching from them, described so correctly in the journal, *cannot be found anywhere else in the Bahamas.*

He left this anchorage Saturday, October 27th at sunrise ($6^h 23^m$) and steered S. S. W. for Cuba. By sunset ($5^h 37^m$) he had made 17 leagues—54.1 nautical miles—about 4.8 knots an hour. He saw the land before dark, but kept off "on the look-out during the night with much rain." Sunday he resumed his course S. S. W., striving to reach the nearest land. Arriving there he entered a beautiful river which had 12 fathoms at the mouth. The courses "logged" from the Sand Islands are S. S. W., and the distance 54.1 miles, which was made by sunset Saturday.

. . . Columbus designated this beautiful river and port with his favorite title, *San Salvador*. This name has not been preserved, and each investigator points out his own choice. I select Port Padre. Port Naranjo answers the description of the journal as well as Padre, but it is S. ¾ W. 62 miles from South Ragged, and a vessel could not, of course, get to it steering S. S. W. with a westerly current. I choose Padre because it is the only port west of Naranjo that has depth of water enough at the mouth to satisfy the journal, and in other respects is free of objections.

As a matter of interest, I have laid down a track for the vessels of Columbus from Padre west, as far as Boca de Guajaba, where he probably turned. He then coasted the northeast shore of Cuba, crossed to Haiti, and followed the north side to the present bay of Samana, where his first voyage in the New World ended. This track coincides, sometimes, with the track of Navarrete, but both are liable to be inaccurate, owing to the imperfection of the charts of the north coast line of Cuba and Haiti.

SUMMARY

. . . First. There is no objection to Samana in respect to size, position, or shape. That it is a little island, lying east and west, is in its favor. The erosion at the east end by which islets have been formed, recalls the assertion of Columbus that there it could be cut off in two days and made into an island. The Nassau vessels still find a snug anchorage here during the N. E. trades. These blew half a gale of wind at the time of the land-fall; yet Navarrete, Varnhagen, and Captain Becher anchored the squadron on the windward sides of the coral reefs of their respective islands, a "*lee shore*." The absence of permanent lagoons at Samana I have tried to explain.

Second. The course from Samana to Crooked is to the southwest, which is the direction that the Admiral said he should steer "tomorrow evening." The distance given by him corresponds with the chart.

Third. The second island, Santa Maria, is described as having two sides which made a right angle, and the length of each is given. This points directly to Crooked and Acklin. Both form one island, so fitted to the words of the journal as cannot be done with any other land of the Bahamas.

Fourth. The course and distance from Crooked to Long Island is that which the Admiral gives from Santa Maria to Fernandina.

Fifth. Long Island, the third, is accurately described. The trend of the shores "north-northwest and south-southeast"; the "marvellous port" and "the coast which runs east [and] west," can nowhere be found except at the southeast part of Long Island.

Sixth. The journal is obscure in regard to the fourth island. The best way to find it, is to "plot" the courses *forward* from the third island, and the courses and distances *backward* from the fifth. These lead to Fortune for the fourth.

Seventh. The Ragged Islands are the fifth. These he named *las islas de Arena*—Sand Islands. They lie W. S. W. from the fourth, and this is the course the Admiral adhered to. He did not "log" all the run made between these islands; in consequence the "log" falls short of the true distance, as it ought to. These "seven or eight islands, all extending from north to south," and having shoal water "six leagues to the south" of them are seen on the chart at a glance.

Eighth. The course and distance from these to Port Padre, in Cuba, is reasonable. The westerly current, the depth of water at the entrance of Padre, and the general description, are free of difficulties. The true distance is greater than the "logged" because Columbus again omits part of his run.

. . . From end to end of the Samana track there are but three discrepancies. At the third island two leagues ought to be two miles. At the fourth island twelve leagues ought to be twelve miles. The bearing between the third and fourth islands is not quite as the chart has it, nor does it agree with the courses he steered. These three are fairly explained, and I think that no others can be mustered to disturb the concord between this track and the journal.

THE CREWS OF THE NIÑA, PINTA, AND SANTA MARÍA, AND THE COST OF THE EXPEDITION

There is a general agreement that the total crew number of the three ships was between 87 and 90 men. A number of historiographers (Oviedo, Martyr, and Giustiniani, to mention three) placed the number at 120. But Las Casas and Fernando both give 90, and certain details given in the Log about the ships support the lower figures. Alice Gould and J.B. Thacher say 87; Samuel Eliot Morison accepted 90. The apparent discrepancy seems to center around whether there were 39 or 42 men left at Navidad in January 1493. Two different numbers are given by Columbus. On January 2 he specifically said that he was leaving 39 men and three officers. On January 13 he made reference to the 39 men he had left behind, and it is inconceivable that he would have excluded his lieutenants from that count.

It is reasonable that the number of men left at Navidad would approximate the total crew complement of the lost *Santa María*, though not all the men left behind came over on the *Santa María*. The *Santa María*, therefore, carried a crew of about 40 men. The two smaller caravels together were manned by the other 50. Inasmuch as the *Pinta* was slightly larger than the *Niña*, it is likely that the former had about 26 men; the latter, 24. When the *Niña* put in at the Azores on the return voyage, half the crew was able to go ashore in the caravel's small boat.

Though some of the names are well known, and a number of crewmembers are mentioned by Columbus in the Log, many of the ordinary seamen and ships' boys get little or no notice.

There were 19 seamen with no specified duties, and 16 cabin boys. Twenty-two seamen had specific tasks and were more likely to be named in one place or another. If the crew rosters totaled 90, the subtraction of that list of seamen and cabin boys leaves 33 of some rank above deckhand. Take away the Captain-General (Columbus; he was not an Admiral at the beginning), and we have 32 (or 29, if the lowest count is accurate). In addition to being cited in the Log, some of these names appear in the court proceedings that followed years later. One problem that every researcher has faced is that a number of men claimed to have been on the historic voyage and may not have been. And there is some confusion and double-counting with the names. Custom required no more than a given name and place of birth (or residency)—Juan de Sevilla or Pedro de Palos, for example.

Not only is the total count uncertain, but the roster for each ship within that count is indefinite. Some men who are listed on one ship actually sailed on another. The crews from the *Santa María* and *Niña* were mingled, both in the group left at Navidad and in the crew returning in the *Niña*. Also, some Indians made the voyage back—probably about 10—and their number might have affected the number of Spaniards remaining in the New World. Since the *Pinta* deserted the fleet before the *Santa María* was lost and Navidad was established, its crew over and back remained stable, though some Indians did return on the caravel.

The rosters below undoubtedly contain names that are double-counted; not only are spellings inconsistent in the historical records, but formal usage (proper given names) and casual usage ("Pedro the Archer" or "Juan from Sevilla") are difficult to discern. Many formal names evolved from casual names (from place of origin or occupation). Thacher's lists were built upon those before him (such as those of Muñoz and Harrisse); Gould's lists added to those of Thacher. One word of caution in using the Gould rosters (which most scholars hail as the most complete and accurate): she directly contradicts the Log in one or two major instances. She seemed to make the roster fit the crew complement for each ship, as earlier determined by others.

The first section of each roster lists the crew that meets with the general approval of most scholars. To this are added those names that are not generally agreed upon, or where there is disagreement concerning the ship on which they sailed.

ROSTER OF THE *PINTA*

Martín Alonso Pinzón, from Palos, captain

Francisco Martín Pinzón, from Palos, master (captain's cousin)

Cristóbal García Xalmiento (Jalmiento, Sarmiento), pilot

Cristóbal Quintero, from Palos, owner of the caravel

Francisco García Vallejo, from Moguer

García Hernández (Fernández), from Palos, steward

Gómez Rascón, from Palos

Juan Bermúdez, from Palos

Juan Quintero, from Palos

Juan Rodríquez Bermejo, from Molinas (first to sight land, says Gould)

Pedro de Arcos, from Palos

Thacher adds:

Bartolomé García, from Palos, boatswain
Diego Bermúdez, from Palos
Francisco García Gallego, from Moguer
García Alonso, from Palos
Juan de Sevilla
Juan de Jérez (Xéres), from Palos
Juan Pérez Viscaino, from Palos, caulker
Rodrigo de Triana, from Lepe (first to sight land, says Log)

Gould adds:

Alonso de Palos
Alvaro Pérez
Antón (Antonio) Calabrés, from Calabria, Italy
Bernal, servant
Diego Martín Pinzón, from Palos (oldest brother of captain)
Fernando Méndes (Méndez, Mendel), from Huelva
Francisco Méndes (Méndez, Mendel), from Huelva
Gil (Gutiérrez ?) Pérez
Juan Quadrado
Juan Reynal
Juan Verde de Triana
Juan Veçano (Vezano), from Venice
Maestre Diego, surgeon
Pedro Tegero (Tejero, Terreros ?)
Sancho de Rama

ROSTER OF THE *NIÑA*

Vincente Yáñez Pinzón, from Palos, captain
Juan Niño, from Moguer, owner of the caravel and master
Francisco Niño, from Moguer
Bartolomé Roldán, from Palos, apprentice pilot

Thacher adds:

Alonso Gutiérrez Querido, from Palos
Pero (Pedro) Alonso (Peralonso) Niño, from Moguer, pilot
Gutiérrez Pérez, from Palos
Juan Ortíz, from Palos
  (Note: Thacher includes some of the *Niña's* crew among those listed with that of the *Santa María* remaining behind at Navidad. He does not separate the two.)

Gould adds:

Alonso de Morales, carpenter
Andrés de Huelva
Bartolomé García, from Palos, boatswain
Diego Lorenzo
Fernando de Triana
García Alonso, from Palos
Juan Arias, from Tavira, Portugal, cabin boy
Juan Arraes
Juan Romero
Maestre Alonso, from Moguer, physician
Miguel de Soria, servant

Pedro de Soria
Pero (Pedro) Arraes
Pero (Pedro) Sánches (Sánchez), from Montilla
Rodrigo Monge (Monte)
Sancho Ruíz (de Gama ?), pilot

ROSTER OF THE *SANTA MARÍA*
(Note: an asterisk (*) denotes person remaining
at Navidad.
RON indicates crew member that returned on *Niña*.)

Cristóbal Colón (Christopher Columbus), captain-general,
RON
Juan de la Cosa, from Santoña, owner of the ship and master,
RON
*Diego de Arana, master-at-arms of the fleet, captain at
Navidad
*Pedro Gutiérrez, representative of the royal household, lieu-
tenant at Navidad
*Rodrigo de Escobedo, secretary of the fleet, lieutenant at
Navidad
Rodrigo (Pedro ?) Sánchez, from Segovia, comptroller of the
fleet, *RON*
Diego de Salcedo, servant of Columbus, *RON*
Luis de Torres, interpreter, *RON*
Rodrigo de Jérez (Xéres), from Ayamonte, *RON*

Thacher adds (including some of the *Niña* crew left at
Navidad):
*Alonso Vélez de Mendoza, from Sevilla

*Alvar Pérez Osorio, from Castrojeriz
*Antonio de Jaén, from Jaén
*Bernardino de Tapia, from Ledesma, lawyer
*Cristóbal del Alamo, from Condado de Niebla
*Castillo, from Sevilla, silversmith
*Diego García, from Jérez
*Diego de Tordoya, from Cabeza de Vaca
*Diego de Capilla, from Almadén
*Diego de Torpa
*Diego de Mambles, from Mambles
*Diego de Mendoza, from Guadalajara
*Diego de Montalban, from Jaén
*Domingo de Bermeo (Bermejo), cooper
Francisco de Huelva, from Huelva, *RON*
*Francisco Fernández
*Francisco de Godoy, from Sevilla
*Francisco de Henao, from Ávila
*Francisco de Vergara, from Sevilla
*Francisco de Aranda, from Aranda
*Francisco Jiménez, from Sevilla
*Gabriél Baraona, from Belmonte
*Gonzalo Fernández de Segovia, from Leon
*Gonzalo Fernández, from Segovia
*Guillermo Ires (William Harris or William Penrise), from
Galway, Ireland
*Hernando de Porcuna
*Jorge González, from Trigueros
*Juan de Urniga
*Juan Morcillo, from Villanueva de la Serena

*Juan de Cueva, from Castuera
*Juan Patiño, from Villanueva de la Serena
*Juan del Barco, from Barco de Avila
*Juan de Villar, from Villar
*Juan de Mendoza
*Martín de Lograsan, from near Guadalupe
Master Alonso, from Moguer, physician, *RON*
Master Diego, boatswain, *RON*
*Pedro Cabacho, from Cáceres
Pedro de Acevedo, cabin boy, *RON*
Pedro de Terreros (Tejero), steward, *RON*
Pedro de Bilbao (or de Larrabezua), a Basque, *RON*
Pedro de Villa, from Santoña, *RON*
*Pedro de Talavera
*Pedro de Foronda
Rodrigo de Escobar, *RON*
Ruíz (Ruy) Fernández, from Huelva, *RON*
Ruíz (Ruy) García, from Santoña, *RON*
Sancho Ruíz (de Gama ?), pilot, *RON*
*Sebastián de Mayorga, from Mayorga
*Tallarte de Lajes (Arthur Laws or Arthur Larkins, from England)
*Tristán de San Jorge

Gould adds:
Alonso Chocero
Alonso Clavijo, from Vejer (criminal granted amnesty)
Andrés de Yrüenes (Yebénes ?)

Antonio de Cuellar, carpenter
Bartolomé Biues (Vives ?), from Palos
Bartolomé de Torres, from Palos (criminal granted amnesty)
Bartolomé García, boatswain
Chachú, boatswain
Cristóbal Caro, goldsmith
Diego Bermúdez, from Palos
Diego Leál
Diego Pérez, painter
Domingo de Lequeitio
Domingo Vizcaino, cooper
Gonzalo Franco
Jacomél Rico, from Genoa
Juan, servant
Juan de Jérez, from Palos
Juan de la Plaça (Plaza), from Palos
Juan Martínes (Martínez) de Açoque, from Denia
Juan de Medina, tailor
Juan de Moguer, from Palos (criminal granted amnesty)
Juan Ruíz de la Peña, Biscayan
Juan Sánchez, from Cordoba, physician
Lope (López), joiner
Maestre Juan
Martín de Urtubía
Pedro de Terreros, cabin boy
Pero (Pedro) Niño, pilot
Pedro Yzquierdo, from Lepe (criminal granted amnesty)
Pedro de Lepe
Rodrigo Gallego, servant

TOTALS:	Thacher	Gould
Niña	8[1]	20
Pinta	19	26
Santa María	60[2]	41
	87	87

[1]Does not include men remaining at Navidad; only those that made the round-trip in the Niña

[2]Includes Niña's crew remaining at Navidad

Total Cost of the Expedition
(adapted from John Boyd Thacher)

Salary list (officers)	268,000 m.
Wages	252,000 m.
Maintenance	319,680 m.
Rent *Santa María*	172,800 m.
Furniture, arms, powder, trading supplies	155,062 m.
Actual total cash expense	1,167,542 m.
The Crown of Castile contributed	1,000,000 m.
Christopher Columbus "	167,542 m.
Total cash contributions	1,167,542 m.

Cash equipment of the fleet	1,167,542 m.
Palos furnished the *Pinta,* 80 tons, estimated at 120 maravedíes per month, per ton	115,200 m.
Palos furnished the *Niña,* 40 tons, estimated at 120 maravedíes per month, per ton	57,600 m.
Total commercial interest represented in fleet	1,340,342 m.

(Note: The wages are given in *maravedíes,* small copper coins worth approximately $.05 in 1985. Direct comparisons between 1492 and today are risky, however, because purchasing power is difficult if not impossible to measure.

In terms of the value of gold in 1985, the total cost of the expedition was approximately $63,000 in 1492. The same cost today would be approximately $700,000, a good investment by anybody's standards. It has been estimated that during the 16th century, Spain received 1,733,000 *maravedíes* for *each maravedí* invested in the enterprise. Regardless of the value of the *maravedí,* this return would certainly attract attention on Wall Street today.)

APPENDIX D

COLUMBUS' VOYAGES BEFORE 1492

Taking Columbus at his word, rather than the word or speculation of others, we know these facts about his travels before the Discovery Voyage. On 21 December Columbus tells us in the Log: "I have seen all the East and the West, and I have traveled through Guinea." Las Casas made a parenthetical insertion in the midst of this sentence to explain that "the West" meant "to the north, i.e., England." This is a reasonable assumption, for it is an expression from the Portuguese point-of-view and did not mean simply the western Mediterranean, which Portugal does not even bound.

From this statement we learn that Columbus had sailed the entire breadth of the Mediterranean Sea, the Atlantic as far south as the Portuguese fort at La Mina (now Elmina, Ghana), and northward (probably) to England. And if the English voyage were made, it was undoubtedly to Bristol.

These voyages alone would give Columbus an intimate knowledge of such places he mentions in the Log as Chios, Sicily, Guinea, the Cape Verde Islands, Madeira Islands, and Canary Islands. He was well acquainted with the mastic trade of Chios; had obviously seen Mt. Etna, Sicily, in eruption; knew of the African yams, manatees, rivers, and linguistic complexity of Guinea; accurately described the frigate birds of Cape Verde; had lived in the Madeira Islands (where Diego was born); and could not have sailed the African coast without knowledge of the Canaries.

The voyages with the Portuguese—to England, perhaps, and to the Portuguese holdings to the south (Madeira, Cape Verde, Guinea) occurred between 1476 and 1485. Columbus married Doña Felipa in 1479 and took up residency in Madeira and Porto Santo about that time. He probably made several voyages before departing Lisbon for Madeira and several more while living in Madeira. There is substantial evidence that he went to Madeira in 1478 to bring back a load of sugar to Lisbon.

If Columbus voyaged to England, it would have been before the Madeira residency, i.e., between 1476 and 1479. It is during this three-year period that a number of real and/or imagined adventures took place. Many believe Columbus visited Galway, Ireland, at the time he was supposedly in England. Some (Martínez-Hidalgo, for instance) believe the same voyage included stops in Flanders and Germany. Some of the most respected students of Columbus, such as Taviani, are positive that Columbus went to Iceland in February (of all months!) 1477. At least one person places Columbus in Nova Scotia, Canada.

The Iceland sojourn is supported by a statement of Fernando, who says that his father sailed to Thule and 100 leagues beyond. Fernando tells us that the "sea was not frozen." Inasmuch as the Portuguese reopened the Viking route to Iceland, Greenland, and even Labrador (which they named), and were fishing the Newfoundland Banks before 1492, such a trip is possible. But it is difficult to believe that Columbus forgot about it when he was waxing about his former sailing jaunts "to the East and West and as far south as Guinea."

There is no evidence to prove a voyage to the Azores. The information obtained from such a journey would have come in very handy during the stopover there on the return from America. In all probability, Columbus' knowledge of the Azores came from Portuguese sailors who had been there.

APPENDIX E

LA VILLA DE LA NAVIDAD

The Log documents the founding of the first European settlement in the western hemisphere, *La Villa de la Navidad*. Founded on Christmas Day, 1492 (3 January 1493 by the reckoning of our Gregorian Calendar), the settlement was accidental, due to the loss nearby of the *Santa María*. Navidad was located in the heart of the Taino Indian village of the great cacique Guacanagari. Some 39 Spaniards (possibly 42) were left to erect proper fortifications and await the Admiral's return. Also, they were left with a specific set of instructions. The apparent disregard of these led to the total destruction of the Spanish town and the deaths of all of its inhabitants.

The precise location of Navidad has been sought ever since the first voyage became a matter of interest to scholars. Because the Indians in the area were soon destroyed by the ravages of smallpox, measles, and slave-labor, the native settlement vanished. In 1503 Spain established *Puerto Real* within a mile of Navidad, and the depopulated original settlement was either overgrown by indigenous vegetation or farmed over by imported Africans.

In 1958 Dr. William H. Hodges, a medical missionary, came to Limbé, Haiti, a few miles west of the area. The search for Navidad became Dr. Hodges' hobby, and his acquired skills as an archaeologist have won the praise of every professional archaeologist who ever visited the area. It was this dedicated medical missionary who unearthed the first clues to the true identity of Columbus' settlement.

In 1983 the University of Florida began serious excavations at En Bas Saline, the site located by Dr. Hodges. Fieldwork has been ongoing at the site since that time. To date, nothing

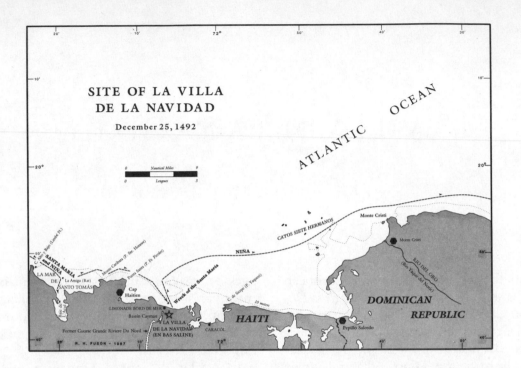

SITE OF LA VILLA
DE LA NAVIDAD

December 25, 1492

dramatic has been found. None of the *Santa María's* cannons or anchors has been unearthed, but Edwin Link may have found one of the anchors nearby in 1956. A Spanish well may have been discovered, but opinion is divided, and such known artifacts as European ceramics and glass may have come from Puerto Real ca. 1503. Pigs' teeth from Sevilla (proven by Strontium isotope analysis) were recovered, along with several bones from the Old World rat (*Rattus rattus*). It is a little ironic that the first European animal brought to America may

have jumped ship!

En Bas Saline is, in the opinion of archaeologists from the University of Florida, the site of Navidad. But Dr. Hodges is now suggesting a site a few thousand feet to the north, nearer the coast. It is almost certain that cacique Guacanagari's village and Navidad are one and the same, and it is just as certain that the site lies within the bounds of the current archaeological zone or within a 4,000-foot radius of it.

APPENDIX F

ROOTS AND TUBERS

On 4 November, soon after reaching Cuba, Columbus made a reference to Indian farming. He said that the land is "full of *niames,*[1] which are like carrots and taste like chestnuts." They are mentioned again on 7 November and 13 December. On 16 December they are called *ajes,* and we are provided with a detailed (and correct) description of their planting and preparation. Columbus tells us on 21 December that *niames* are called *ajes* by the Taino. By 26 December he has learned that the bread made from the *aje* is called *caçabi,* and that there are "two or three kinds of *ajes.*"

These are the first historical notices of two plants, previously unknown to Europeans: *Manihot esculenta* and *Ipomoea batatas.* To both of these species and their varieties he applied the only word he knew for a large, edible root, *niame.* This is a term from the Guinea coast (probably *nyami*), carried to Europe by the Portuguese as *inhame.* The name is retained by modern Portuguese, but in Spanish it had become *ñame* by 1535. A few years later the English corruption *yam* appeared. The African yam (*Dioscorea* species), Columbus' *niame,* was compared with the Taino *aje* on 16 December, when he said that the ones from Guinea (*yams*) are "as thick as your leg, but the ones in *Española* (*ajes*) taste better."

Columbus lumped all the Taino roots and tubers into the general group he called *ajes,* but he was really confronted with several varieties of two different species. Today we know each of these by different and somewhat confusing names. *Manihot esculenta* is known variously in English as manioc, yuca,[2] cassava, and tapioca. *Manioc* is from the Tupí Brazilian word, *mandioca; yuca* is a Taino word for one of the varieties; *cassava* (*cazabe* in Spanish) is the Taino word for the bread (*caçabi*)

Indians planting sweet potatoes in mounds. (Oviedo, Historia, *1547)*

made from the plant; *tapioca* is a Tupí Brazilian name for the food of the same name made from the plant, and widely used as a general name in India.

Manihot esculenta is represented by no less than 98 species, all indigenous to tropical America. None are known in the wild state. At one time the genus was thought to include two species, "bitter" manioc (poisonous) and "sweet" manioc (nonpoisonous). This has been proven to be invalid, for all species contain hydrogen cyanide (HCN; prussic acid) to a greater or lesser degree. The HCN content will vary within plants of the same garden, even from root to root of the same plant. It is necessary, therefore, to remove the juice by grating, squeezing, and drying before eating. This is what Columbus described on 16 December.

Ipomoea batatas is one of more than 400 species in the Morning Glory family, known to us as the sweet potato. Native to tropical America, the species has many varieties, with a wide range of internal and external colors. In Española, the plant produces the telltale blue flower so characteristic of the family. *Batata* was the named used for the sweet potato in the region of Santo Domingo. Later the Spanish applied a corruption of *batata* (*patata*) to the white potato (found in the Andes) and eventually the English corrupted this to *potato*. To further confuse things, the English then borrowed the Afro-Hispanic word *ñame,* changed it to *yam,* and applied it to the sweet potato!

Columbus undoubtedly called all sweet potatoes and manioc *ajes,* after learning the new word. The *ñames* that he compared these American roots with were not to enter the New World until a few years later when they came over on the first African slave ships. All the edible *Dioscorea* species are of African origin.

The bread of the *aje* (cassava) was of critical importance to Columbus and his men on the return trip. On 13 January he sent men ashore to collect *ajes,* and on 25 January (the day the crew killed a porpoise and a shark) the Admiral stated that this "was very necessary because we had nothing to eat except bread, wine, and ajes from the Indies."

Manioc is the "staff of life" for millions of people in the tropics today. Where this is true, manioc is the leading starch by far. In America, where manioc was the primary vegetable, corn (maize) was of minor importance. The latter barely caught Columbus' eye during the first voyage, and then he thought it was millet.

----

1. Mistranscribed as *mames* (the handwritten "ni" becoming "m") on 4 and 7 November, and misspelled (*niamas*) on 13 December. Some have rendered *mames* as *mameys* (*Mammea americana*), a tasty tropical fruit that is unrelated to any of the plants Columbus was describing.

2. Not to be confused with *yucca* (*Yucca* spp.) an arid-region plant commonly called Spanish bayonet and a member of the family *Liliaceae*.

Casa de Colón, Valladolid, the house in which the Admiral passed away, 20 May 1506. (Thacher)

THE DEATH AND BURIAL OF COLUMBUS

Christopher Columbus died in Valladolid, Spain, on May 20, 1506. The house in which he died has been preserved, located on a street that runs from La Magdalena church. The street bears the name *Calle de Cristóbal Colón*.

As John Boyd Thacher has pointed out, "It is a strange commentary on man's forgetfulness of his fellow that Christopher Columbus, who had filled so large a place in the world at the close of the fifteenth century, should die and be buried without any unusual expression of public sorrow and no mention of his end by historian or chronologer."

Even Peter Martyr, a friend of Columbus and one of the most important of the 15th-and 16th-century historiographers, did not mention the Admiral's passing for 10 years. The first public notice of Columbus' death was in Martyr's *Second Decade*, published in 1516. In the second paragraph of this work we read, "Columbus, already having departed out of this life . . ."

Fernando says that his father died from afflictions caused by "the gout and by grief at seeing himself fallen from his high estate, as well as by other ills." During the Fourth Voyage (1502–04) Fernando accompanied his father. The latter's illness on this trip was so serious that 13-year-old Fernando maintained most of that journal himself. Columbus seems to have been in a coma for part of the Second Voyage and incapacitated for five months. This illness has been attributed to diabetes by some; others say he was suffering from syphilis. Either could have killed him in the end.

Columbus left no instructions for his interment. He did request that a church, to be called Santa María de la Concepción, be built in Española, in which masses could be said for the repose of his soul, the souls of his ancestors, and those of his successors. But disposition of his remains was left to the family.

Upon the death of Columbus, Fernando and Diego buried their father in the church of San Francisco de la Santa María de la Antigua, in Valladolid. Three years later (1509), the remains were moved to Sevilla and deposited in the monastery of Nuestra Señora Santa María de las Cuevas, immediately across the Guadalquivir River from Fernando's home.

After the death of Diego in 1526, he, too, was buried at Las Cuevas. In 1537 Diego's widow, María de Toledo, obtained a royal decree for the removal of both bodies from Las Cuevas to Santo Domingo, for reburial in the Cathedral of that city. Another decree was issued in 1539 for such action, but the Santo Domingo church resisted, largely because the royal order made virtually a private Columbus-family chapel of the cathedral. A third order, in 1540, was firm and uncompromising, and sometime between 1541 and 1547 the remains of the first two Admirals of the Indies were returned to the New World. Fernando, who died in 1539, was buried according to his request in the Cathedral of Sevilla. Bartolomé, Christopher's brother, who died in 1514, was buried in the monastery of San Francisco in Santo Domingo, probably never to be removed. Luis, Columbus' grandson and Third Admiral of the Indies, was interred with his father (the Second Admiral) and grandfather (the First Admiral) in the cathedral.

In 1783, during a period when the cathedral was under repair, a broken lead box was discovered inside a stone vault.

Coffer containing bones of Columbus, Cathedral of Santa Domingo. (Winsor, 1886)

The box contained human bones and was said to be similar to some remains found "years earlier" on the *other* side of the altar. These earlier remains were said to be on the left side of the High Altar. The 1783 find was at the right side of the High Altar, near the door to the Chapter room.

On July 22, 1795, Spain was forced to cede all of Española to the French, who had occupied the western portion of the island since 1697. In preparation for the French occupation, the Spanish removed what was thought to be the remains of the Discoverer from the cathedral in Santo Domingo, on December 20, 1795. They were carried to Havana, Cuba, where, on the morning of January 19, 1796, burial was by entombment in the wall of the High Altar of the Cathedral of Havana.

Another century later, and after losing yet another island of the First Discovery, Spain was forced once again to remove the coffin. On December 12, 1898, the coffin was placed aboard a Spanish cruiser for the transatlantic journey, arriving in Cádiz on January 17, 1899. From here it was carried by boat to Sevilla, arriving January 19, 1899. This coffin, the one that now rests in the great Cathedral of Sevilla, is the same one that was taken from Santo Domingo in 1795. It was the one from the right side of the High Altar.

In 1877 the Santo Domingo cathedral was again repaired. During the course of this work, in May of that year, a lead coffin was discovered on the left side of the wall. The box was already ravaged by time; almost as a final insult, it was further damaged by a piece of falling timber. The inscription on the box identified the remains as those of Don Luis Colón, grandson of the First Admiral.

In September 1877 the empty vault, from which the coffin had been removed for shipment to Havana in 1795, was rediscovered. Next to this vault, was discovered another, containing a metal box encrusted with lime. This box was inscribed, identifying the remains as those of "The illustrious and excellent man, Don Cristoval Colon."

Some of the ashes that fell to the floor during the examination of the remains have found their way to Genoa, Pavia, Rome, New York, and to at least four individuals who may have disposed of their portions in one way or another.

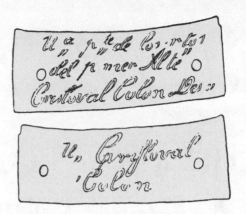

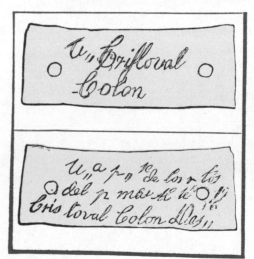

Inscription on silver plate found inside lead box. (Thacher and Winsor, 1886)

D. de la A. P.^{eλ} A.^{te}

Ill.^{tre} y Es.^{do} Daron

D.ⁿ Cristoval Colon

Inscription found in lead box, Cathedral of Santa Domingo. (Thacher and Winsor, 1886)

Under the dust and ashes at the bottom of the lead box was found a small silver plate, about 1½ inches × 3½ inches. It is engraved, "The last part of the remains of the First Admiral, Don Cristóbal Colón, the Discoverer." With it were found the two screws that had fallen loose. Further examinations, in 1878 and 1879, merely substantiated the earlier investigations.

One more time an enigma surrounded the Admiral: a lead pellet was found within the box. During the Fourth Voyage, in a letter to the Sovereigns, Columbus wrote, "My wound has opened again." Could this have been the source of the ball in the coffin?

BIBLIOGRAPHY

Albetti, Giorgio. *The History of Astronomy.* New York: Henry Schuman, Inc., 1952.

Alvar, Manuel. *Diario del Descubrimiento,* 2 vols. Gran Canaria: Ediciones del Excmo. Cabildo Insular de Gran Canaria, Comisión Educación y Cultura. 1976.

Anderson, C. L. G. *Old Panama and Castilla del Oro.* New York: North River Press. 1944.

Arce, Joaquin and M. Gil Esteve, eds. *Diario de a bordo de Cristóbal Colón.* Torino: A. Tallone. 1971.

Ballesteros Beretta, Antonio. *Cristóbal Colón y el descubrimiento de América,* 2 vols. Barcelona: Salvat editores, S.A. 1945.

Becher, A. B. *The Landfall of Columbus on His First Voyage to America.* London: J. D. Potter. 1856.

Benzoni, Girolano. *Novae novi orbis historiae.* Genevae: apud Eustathium Vignon. 1581.

Boggs, R. S., et al. *Tentative Dictionary of Medieval Spanish,* 2 vols. Chapel Hill: no publisher given. 1946.

Bowditch, Nathaniel. *American Practical Navigator.* Defense Mapping Agency, Hydrographic/Topographic Center. Washington: Government Printing Office. 1984.

Caddeo, Rinaldo. *Giornale di bordo di Cristoforo Colombo.* Milano: V. Bompiani. 1939.

Campbell, David G. *The Ephemeral Islands: A Natural History of the Bahamas.* London: Macmillan Education, Ltd. 1978.

Columbus Casebook, A. Supplement to Joseph Judge, "Where Columbus Found the New World," *National Geographic* (vol. 170, no. 5, November 1986), pp. 562–599. Supplement of 70 pp.

Columbus, Ferdinand. *The Life of the Admiral Christopher Columbus.* Translated by Benjamin Keen. New Brunswick: Rutgers University Press. 1959.

Corominas, J. *Diccionario Crítico Etimológico de la Lengua Castellana,* 4 vols. Berna: Editorial Francke. 1954.

Cristoforo Colombo e la Scuola Cartografica Genovese, 3 vols. Edited by Paolo Revelli. Consiglio Nazionale delle Ricerche. Genova: Stabilimenti Italiani Arte Grafiche. 1937.

Diccionari Català-Valencià-Balear, 10 vols. Edited by Francesc de B. Moll. Palma de Mallorca: 1964 (vols. 1–2); Barcelona: 1968–69 (vols. 3–10).

Diccionario de la Lengua Española, 20th ed., 2 vols. Madrid: Real Academia Española. 1984.

Didiez Burgos, Ramón J. *Guanahani y Mayaguan.* Santo Domingo: Editoria Cultural Dominicana. 1974.

Dunn, Oliver. "Columbus's First Landing Place: The Evidence of the Journal," *Terrae Incognitae* (vol. 15, 1983), pp. 35–50.

Dunn, Oliver C. and James E. Kelley, Jr. *The Diario of Christopher Columbus' First Voyage to America: 1492–1493.* Norman: University of Oklahoma Press. 1987.

Fiske, John. *The Discovery of America,* 2 vols. Boston & New York: Houghton, Mifflin & Co. 1902.

Fox, Gustavus V. "An Attempt to Solve the Problem of the First Landing Place of Columbus in the New World," *Report of the Superintendent of the U. S. Coast and Geodetic Survey* (Appendix No. 18, June 1880). Washington: Government Printing Office. 1882.

Fuson, Robert H. *A Geography of Geography.* Dubuque: Wm. C. Brown Co. Publishers. 1969.

Fuson, Robert H. "The *Diario de Colón:* A Legacy of Poor Transcription, Translation, and Interpretation," *Terrae Incognitae* (vol. 15, 1983), pp. 51–75.

Fuson, Robert H. "Manioc and Yuca," *The Quipu* (vol 1, no. 3, July 1962), pp. 10–11.

Fuson, Robert H. and Walter H. Treftz. "A Theoretical Reconstruction of the First Atlantic Crossing of Christopher Columbus," *Proceedings of the Association of American Geographers,* (vol 8, 1976), pp. 155–159.

Gómez de Silva, Guido. *Elsevier's Concise Spanish Etymological Dictionary.* Amsterdam: Elsevier Science Publishers. 1985.

Gould, Alice B. "Nueva lista documentada de los tripulantes de Colón en 1492," *Boletín de la Real Academia de la Historia* (vols. 85–88, 90, 92, 110, 111). Madrid, 1922–1938.

Gould, R. T. "The Landfall of Columbus: An Old Problem Restated," *Geographical Journal* (vol. 49, 1927), pp. 403–429.

Gould, R. T. *Enigmas.* New Hyde Park: University Books. 1965. (reprint of 1945 London edition).

Guillén y Tato, Julio F. *El primer viaje de Cristóbal Colón.* Madrid: Instituto Histórico de Marina. 1943.

Guillén y Tato, Julio F. *La parla marinera en el diario del primer viaje de Cristóbal Colón.* Madrid: Instituto Histórico de Marina. 1951.

Haggard, J. Villasana. *Handbook for Translators of Spanish Historical Documents.* Austin: University of Texas. 1941.

Harrison, Lucia C. *Sun, Earth, Time and Man.* Chicago: Rand McNally & Co. 1960.

Harrisse, Henry. *The Discovery of North America.* London & Paris: 1892.

Harrisse, Henry. *The Diplomatic History of America.* London: B. F. Stevens, Publisher. 1897.

Heathcote, N. H. de Vaudrey. "Christopher Columbus and the

Discovery of Magnetic Variation," *Science Progress* (vol. 27, 1932), pp. 82–96.

Herrera y Tordesillas, Antonio de. *Historia general de los hechos de los Castellanos, en las islas, y tierra-firme de el mar occeano,* 5 vols. Asunción: Editorial Guarania. 1945. (a facsimile edition of the 1726–30 publication).

Howe, H. H. and L. Hurwitz. *Magnetic Surveys.* U. S. Coast and Geodetic Survey Serial No. 718. Washington: Government Printing Office. 1964.

In the Wake of Columbus: Islands and Controversy. Edited by Louis De Vorsey, Jr., and John Parker. Detroit: Wayne State University Press. 1985.

Irving, Washington. *A History of the Life and Voyages of Christopher Columbus,* 3 vols. New York: G. & C. Carvill. 1828.

Jane, Cecil. *The Journal of Christopher Columbus.* Revised by L. A. Vigneras. New York: Bramhall House. 1960.

Judge, Joseph. "Where Columbus Found the New World," *National Geographic* (vol. 170, no. 5, November 1986), pp. 562–599. (with Supplement of 70 pp. and a map).

Kelley, Jr., James E. "Non-Mediterranean Influences that shaped the Atlantic in the early Portolan Charts," *Imago Mundi* (vol. 31, 1979), pp. 18–35.

Kelley, Jr., James E. "In the Wake of Columbus on a Portolan Chart," *Terrae Incognitae* (vol. 15, 1983), pp. 77–111.

Kerchove, René de. *International Maritime Dictionary,* 2nd ed. New York: D. Van Nostrand Company, Inc. 1948.

Kettell, Samuel. *Personal Narration of the First Voyage of Columbus.* Boston: T. B. Wait. 1827.

Kline, Harry. *Yachtsman's Guide to the Bahamas.* North Miami Beach: Tropic Isle Publishers, Inc. 1983.

Las Casas, Bartolomé de. *Apologética Historia Sumaria,* 2 vols. México: Universidad Nacional Autónoma de México. 1967.

Las Casas, Bartolomé de. *Historia de las indias,* 3 vols. México: Fondo de Cultura Económica. 1951.

Lewis, David. *We, the Navigators.* Honolulu: The University Press of Hawaii. 1979.

Link, Edwin A. and Marion C. "A New Theory on Columbus's Voyage Through the Bahamas," *Smithsonian Miscellaneous Collections* (vol. 135, January 1958). Washington: Smithsonian Institution.

Lyon, Eugene. "The Diario of Christopher Columbus: October 10–October 27, 1492," *A Columbus Casebook,* pp. 6–45 Supplement to *National Geographic* (vol. 170, no. 5, November 1986).

Machado, José Pedro. *Dicionário Etimológico da Língua Portuguêsa,* 2nd ed., 3 vols. Lisboa: Editorial Confluência. 1967.

Madariaga, Salvador de. *Christopher Columbus.* New York: Unger. 1967.

Major, R. H. *Select Letters of Christopher Columbus, With Other Original Documents, Relating to His First Four Voyages to the New World.* London: Hakluyt Society. 1847.

Major, R. H. *Select Letters of Christopher Columbus, With Other Original Documents, Relating to His First Four Voyages to the New World,* 2nd ed. London: Hakluyt Society. 1870.

Marden, Luis. "The First Landfall of Columbus," in "Where Columbus Found the New World," *National Geographic* (vol. 170, no. 5, November 1986), pp. 572–577 (with separate map).

Marden, Luis. "The Diario of Columbus: September 8–October 11, 1492," *A Columbus Casebook,* pp. 48–55 (Supplement to *Na-*

tional Geographic (vol. 170, no. 5, November 1986).

Markham, Clements R. *The Journal of Christopher Columbus*. London: Hakluyt Society. 1893.

Marlowe, Stephen. *The Memoirs of Christopher Columbus*. New York: Charles Scribner's Sons. 1987.

Martínez-Hidalgo, José María. *Columbus' Ships*. Barre: Barre Publishers. 1966.

Martyr, Peter, "The Firste Booke of the Decades of the Ocean," in Richard Eden, *The First Three Books on America (? 1511)–1555 A.D.* Birmingham: Turnbull and Spears. 1885.

McElroy, John W. "The Ocean Navigation of Columbus on His First Voyage," *American Neptune* (vol. 1, 1941), pp. 209–240.

Medina, Pedro de. "The Libro de Cosmographia of 1538," in Ursula Lamb, *A Navigator's Universe*. Chicago: University of Chicago Press. 1972.

Milani, Virgil. "The Written Language of Christopher Columbus," *Forum Italicum* (Supplement, 1973).

Morison, Samuel E. *Admiral of the Ocean Sea*, 2 vols. Boston: Little, Brown & Co. 1942.

Morison, Samuel E. *Christopher Columbus, Mariner*. New York: Mentor Books. 1956.

Morison, Samuel E. "Columbus and Polaris," *American Neptune* (vol. 1, 1941), pp. 1–35.

Morison, Samuel E. *Journals and Other Documents on the Life and Voyages of Christopher Columbus*. New York: The Heritage Press. 1963.

Morison, Samuel E. and Mauricio Obregón. *The Caribbean as Columbus saw it*. Boston: Little, Brown & Co. 1964.

Navarrete, Martín Fernández de. *Viajes de Cristóbal Colón*. Madrid: Espasa-Calpe, S.A. 1934. (reprint of 1825 edition)

Nueva lista documentada de los tripulantes de Colón en 1492. Edited by J. M. de la Peña y Camara. Madrid: Real Academia de la Historia. 1984.

Nunn, George E. *Geographical Conceptions of Columbus*. New York: American Geographical Society. 1924.

Oviedo y Valdés, Gonzalo Fernández de. *Historia general y natural de las indias*, 14 vols. Asunción: Editorial Guarania. 1944.

Oviedo y Valdés, Gonzalo Fernández de. *Sumario de la natural historia de las indias*. México: Fondo de Cultura Económica. 1950.

Oxford English Dictionary, The. Oxford: Clarendon Press. 1961. (13 vols.)

Parker, John. "The Columbus Landfall Problem: A Historical Perspective," *Terrae Incognitae* (vol. 15, 1983), pp. 1–28.

Parker, John. *Antilia and America*. Minneapolis: James F. Bell Book Trust. 1955.

Pohl, Frederick J. *The New Columbus*. Rochester: Security-Dupont Press. 1986.

Polo, Marco. *The Adventures of Marco Polo*. New York: John Day Co. 1948.

Power, Robert H. "The Discovery of Columbus's Island Passage to Cuba, October 12–27, 1492," *Terrae Incognitae* (vol. 15, 1983), pp. 151–172.

Proceedings of the First San Salvador Conference: Columbus and His World. Compiled by Donald T. Gerace. San Salvador: College Center of the Finger Lakes. 1986.

Raccolta di documenti e studi pubblicati dalla Real Commissione Colombiana pel quarto centenario dalla scoperta dell'America, 14 vols. Edited by Cesare de Lollis. Roma: Ministerio Pubblica Istruzione. 1892–1896.

Redway, Jacques W. "The First Landfall of Columbus," *The National Geographic Magazine* (vol. 6, 1894), pp. 179–238.

Rogers, D. J. and S. G. Appan. *Manihot Manihotoides*. Monograph No. 13, Organization for Flora Neotropica. New York: Hafner Press. 1973.

Roukema, Edzar. "Columbus Landed on Watlings Island," *American Neptune* (vol. 19, 1959), pp. 79–113.

Sailing Directions for the Caribbean Sea. Publication No. 147 (Bermuda, Bahamas, Greater Antilles). Defence Mapping Agency, Hydrographic/Topographic Center. Washington: Government Printing Office. 1980.

Santamaría, Francisco J. *Diccionario General de Americanismos*, 3 vols. Méjico: Editorial Pedro Robredo. 1942.

Sanz, Carlos. *Diario de Colón: Libro de la primera navegación y descubrimiento*, 2 vols. Madrid: Gráficas Yagües. 1962.

Sanz, Carlos. *La Carta de Colón*. Madrid: Gráficas Yagües. 1961.

Scofield, John. "Christopher Columbus and the New World He Found," *National Geographic* (vol. 148, no. 5, November 1975), pp. 584–625.

Streicher, Fritz. "Die Columbus-Originale," *Spanische Forschugen I, Görresgesellschaft*. Münster: Aschendorffsche Verlagsbuchhandlung. 1928.

Taviani, Paolo Emilio. *Christopher Columbus: The Grand Design*. London: Orbis Publications Ltd. 1985.

Thacher, John Boyd. *Christopher Columbus: His Life, His Work, His Remains*, 3 vols. New York: 1903–04.

Varela, Consuelo. *Cristóbal Colón. Textos y documentos completos*. Madrid: 1982.

Varela, Consuelo. "Aproximación a los escritos de Cristóbal Colón," *Jornadas de Estudios, Canarias-América (III, IV, V y VI)*. Santa Cruz de Tenerife, 1984, pp. 69–90.

Varnhagen, Francisco Adolfo de. "La verdadera Guanahani de Colón," *Annales de la Universidad de Chile* (vol. 24, 1864), pp. i–x, 1–20.

Venceslada, Antonio Alcalá. *Vocabulario Andaluz*. Madrid: Real Academia Española. 1951.

Verhoog, Pieter H. G. "Columbus Landed on Caicos," *United States Naval Institute Proceedings* (vol. 80, October 1954), pp. 1101–1111.

Vignaud, Henry. *Toscanelli and Columbus*. New York: E. P. Dutton. 1902.

Wiesenthal, Simon. *The Secret Mission of Christopher Columbus*. New York: Christopher Columbus Publishing. 1979.

Winsor, Justin. *Narrative and Critical History of America*, 8 vols. Boston & New York: Houghton, Mifflin & Co. 1889.

Winsor, Justin. *Christopher Columbus*. Cambridge: Riverside Press. 1892.

Wolper, Ruth G. Durlacher. "A New Theory Identifying the Locale of Columbus's Light, Landfall, and Landing," *Smithsonian Miscellaneous Collections* (vol. 148, no. 1, 1964). Washington: Smithsonian Institution.

Wolper, Ruth G. Durlacher. *A New Theory Clarifying the Identity of Christophoros Columbus*. San Salvador: New World Museum. 1982.

INDEX

All words in italics are either names assigned by
Columbus during the First Voyage or Taino Indian
words learned by Columbus. For consistency, italics
on Nina and Pinta have been retained, although
Columbus did not name those ships.